WEAPONIZED BASEBALL

Declassified, [redacted] Withheld Stories
Reveal Baseball's Hidden [redacted] Role
in [redacted] Geopolitics,
International Military Action,
Mental [redacted] Manipulation,
&
Mass Distraction

Enjoy!

Scott A. Rowan

sherpa
MULTIMEDIA, INC.

This book is available in quantity at special discounts for groups and organizations. For more information please contact:

Sherpa Multimedia
(773) 977-8570
info@sherpamultimedia.com
www.sherpamultimedia.com

Cover design and interior layout by Sherpa Multimedia.

Printed in United States of America

First American Edition

ISBN: 978-0-9895003-2-6

LCCN: 2015919339

For my mother, Polly,
thank you for all your support.

And to Drew,
moja draga, my sweetheart,
without your help, this wouldn't have been possible.

Also by Scott A. Rowan

The Cubs Quotient:
How the Chicago Cubs Changed the World

CONTENTS

Section IV - Bringing it Home

Introduction:

WHY BASEBALL?

The largest deception in military history, faking out millions, if not billions, of people worldwide, was accomplished with baseball. …
Two of the worst White House scandals both involved baseball executives. …
The sport sparked and contributed to more than a dozen wars or revolutions around the world; then, afterward, the same political leaders used it as an olive branch to create peace. …
Adolf Hitler. …
Benito Mussolini. …
Richard Nixon. …
Pancho Villa. …
General George Custer. …
Al Capone. …
Buffalo Soldiers. …
The genocide of those who couldn't say one word the preferred way. …

Those are the quick thoughts I have when thinking about the stories I discovered for this book that fascinated me the most. Like a pile of paper clips that have become tangled together, each story is separate and individual, but telling each one invariably connects them together. Trying to tell one story becomes the same impossible task as pulling only one paper clip from the pile: so many others are connected that you up with a bunch, not merely the one you began seeking.

Researching and writing this book was easily one of the most enjoyable and educational experiences of my life. I began working in sports media as a newspaper reporter and editor in 1995, and over the course of more than two decades working in and with mass media, I've worked on countless thousands of newspaper, radio, television and Internet stories that reached millions of people. But none of those stories revealed the things I learned researching *Weaponized Baseball.*

I apologize to friends and family members who I'm sure I constantly besieged with: "Did you know that ...?"

Yet, nearly every time the answer was always: "No, I never heard that before."

This book is a direct result of my previous one, *The Cubs Quotient: How the Chicago Cubs Changed the World.* My mantra during research for that book was: question everything; assume nothing. It helped me unearth some stories that I still have not found reported anywhere else. I had to piece together most of the stories, going back to primary sources to connect the dots decades or more than a century later. Since that book focused on one specific team, there were many stories that I had to save for a larger book, one that used the same approach to global history: revealing baseball's (often hidden) role in government policy, military planning, religion, commerce, innovation, entertainment, social control, crime, gangs, law and order.

Skeptics who think that someone can merely see what they want to see if they wish will never look at the Korean War or The Battle of Little Bighorn the same way again after learning about their baseball connection. The stories in this collection are the ones that made me say at some point during the research: "You must be kidding! I never heard this in a classroom or read it in a textbook!"

In an effort to squeeze as many revelations into one book, I've kept each story as short as possible. The book was also written so you can start or stop at any point without missing much. Do you like World War II stories? Go ahead and jump to those chapters first, if you want. The book flows much better, however, if you start at the beginning since details about some of the over-arching philosophies, methods, theories and approaches are discussed in the first chapters.

In an effort to help other sports fans learn more about the gamut of topics examined in this book, I've made it a point to footnote extensively so you can follow up and learn more about a specific person, place or event. The goal of this book isn't to dive too deeply into any one topic, but to share as many mind-altering tales as possible so that global history becomes a series of stories about your favorite teams, players and people, not boring facts from a dusty tome.

Many sports date back in history further than baseball, some thousands of years earlier. My focus fell upon baseball, however, because baseball created the world's first truly professional sports league in 1876. Other sports, like rugby, cricket and soccer/football/futbol, were strictly amateur associations. Previous baseball leagues, like the National Association of Professional Base Ball Players, were semi-pro before the National League's creation, giving baseball a distinct advantage over all others when discussing the role sports have played in global events considering all other professional teams didn't officially even exist yet. (The debate about the NA's professional vs. semi-pro status is discussed in more detail later.) Though I continue to research every sport and its impact on global events, baseball still dominates all others in the sheer number of stories about altering human evolution.

In 1910, William James wrote the famous essay *The Moral Equivalent of War* that discussed the need for civilized nations to devise ways to compete without bloodshed or loss of life. More than a century later, James' ideas are just as important as ever. For generations, business leaders and politicians have directly and indirectly quoted or used his ideas to promote their programs, products or ideas to public. Yet, none of them have embraced the concept of a bloodless battle as successfully as baseball. With rules designed to eliminate physical contact (or at least reduce it to a bare minimum), baseball has a unique place in global interaction and international relations as the most popular team sport that community and government leaders can employ predictably to foster diplomacy with the lowest likelihood of conflict.

Sports can be much more than just entertainment. Given the emotional investment many fans make in their teams, particularly national teams, sports can be a catalyst for conflict just as much as it can be the salve to heal old wounds.

When viewed through the prism of military history, social change, innovation and easing conflict, sports can introduce fans to larger topics that would not normally be discussed in everyday discussion.

The original title for this book was *"Why Baseball?"* In a digital age of phone apps that seem to govern every aspect of life, providing instantaneous answers to every query imaginable, the slow pace of a baseball game may seem to many people to be an anachronism, something out of time and place, a horse-and-buggy carriage forced to compete with electric cars. Yet, baseball has persevered and, in many ways, has lapped the field. Major League Baseball was the first of the major sports leagues to embrace the digital vanguard, creating ways for spectators to enjoy the game where no television cables existed. The National Football League may count more loyal fans within the United States, but the NFL will never have the global audience that baseball enjoys. Soccer/football/futbol is a true global sport, but corruption and billion-dollar scandals have rocked the sport in ways that have never been a concern for baseball. Basketball, hockey and newer sports like mixed martial arts talk about the globalization of their sport, but they are merely following the path and walking in the footsteps of what baseball achieved more than a century ago.

So, why baseball? Why has the sport survived, thrived and remained alive where other sports have perished or have become an afterthought, such as boxing, horse racing and most Olympic sports?

Why baseball?

Why?

Good question. Turn the page and find out.

- Scott

Section I:

PREGAME

.--. .-. . --. .- -- .

(1)

•----

How Christianity Killed the Olympics

Few are the new uses, ideas or tactics employed by large organizations such as political parties, religious groups, media outlets, and labor unions when it comes to using sports and its multitude of teams, players, and events as subtle, but powerful, ways to manipulate the minds of the masses. Before we dive into the deep well of stories revealing baseball's role in altering military actions, elections, massacres, genocides and revolutions, we need to wade into the origins of the crossroads between sports and mental manipulation.

Greek leaders created the first public games in 776 B.C. ostensibly to honor the Greek god Zeus, but the more substantial byproduct of the athletic competitions was improved political relations both within the borders as well as with neighboring countries. Drawing its name from the host city of Olympia, Greece, the Olympic Games attracted athletes from across Greece and nearby countries such as modern-day Spain and Turkey. Men were the only ones allowed to compete in the events, which were initially exclusively running competitions. The Olympic Games were played for the next 1,200 years until the powerful combination of religion and politics intervened.

By 146 B.C., the Roman Empire conquered its Greek predecessor and during the ensuing 500 years Christianity replaced Roman mythology (appropriated from the Greek legends) as the chosen religion for the Roman Empire by political leaders seeking to extend their influence over the citizenry. Though the exact date of the Olympics Games' demise is debated (traditionalists heed to the long-held belief that Theodosius I ended the Games in A.D. 393, while other experts claim the Games lasted until A.D. 426 or 435, when religious temples were burned by Theodosius II[1]), what is not debated is the main reason the Games came to end. In an effort to squelch rebellion, Theodosius I outlawed pagan activities of any kind. Whether the Olympic Games ended immediately after his edict, or continued until his son burned the temples a few decades later to ensure his father's decree, the Olympic Games came to an end in the fifth century.

More than a millennium passed before French Baron Pierre de Coubertin resuscitated the forgotten Olympic Games in 1894 (more on that later).

Theodosius I (or his son, Theodosius II) may have been one of the first world leaders known to ban sports for the benefit of his empire's interests, but he was hardly the last. (The key word in that sentence is "known" because earlier civilizations—Assyrian, Egyptian, etc.—surely had leaders who banned certain sports, but many details of everyday life have been lost to history.) In 1410 and again in 1414, Henry V banned football (*soccer* in the U.S.) because it kept citizens from practicing archery, a skill necessary to defend the kingdom. While sports fans may guffaw or question if sports could undermine national security, military scholars will side with Henry V's decision. England and France were in the midst of the Hundred Years' War (1337-1453). While Henry V was not clairvoyant, he knew a major conflict was about the break on the border and he needed every countryman prepared for war. He was correct: the Battle of Agincourt in 1415 was a benchmark moment in history as England's victory led to Henry V being recognized as the heir to the French throne in 1420.

In 1457, Scotland's James II forbid citizens from playing golf because it was too popular and the citizens were not practicing other sports that could defend the kingdom, specifically archery. Back in England, Henry V's successors agreed that, for the sake of national defense, the playing of sports in leisure time was not allowed. Archery was the preferred "sport" since it helped hone defensive skills. In 1477, Edward IV banned football; as did Henry VIII in 1496.[2]

In 1896, Spain outlawed baseball from being played in Cuba for fear of giving the repressed islanders a chance to gather and bond. The ban backfired. Baseball became subversive and, as we will examine in more detail, the sport was the means by which revolution was planned and executed against Spanish rule.

Make no mistake, American leaders have banned as many sports as any other country, outlawing at different times and in different locations boxing, sumo wrestling, martial arts and even almost outlawing American football before a presidential intervention saved the sport.

The power that sports and sporting events commands over the public has scared many governments into banning specific sports in favor of those preferred by national leaders. But baseball has been either banned or embraced by more governments than any other sport. While football/soccer, cricket and golf were concerns for British leaders hundreds of years ago, baseball has been used by governments on six continents to either foster or diminish diplomatic relations with neighboring countries, distract millions of people from violent atrocities and to foster revolution. As we will soon see, Germany, Italy, Russia, France, England, China, Japan, South Korea, Cuba, the Philippines, Hawaii, Australia, Mexico, Venezuela, Nicaragua, Haiti and the Dominican Republic are just some of the countries that have wielded baseball as a political weapon, often changing the course of human evolution in the process.

Baseball's influence has been so substantial in many countries that it still alters the way billions of people act, think and speak every day. How else can you explain why patriotic Boston Red Sox fans proudly call themselves Yankees?

Depiction of the Battle of Bunker Hill on June 17, 1775.

(2)

●●▬▬▬

Appropriation: Yankees, Soccer, & Masturbation

When talking about murderous dictators, genocidal massacres and global domination, somehow it just feels right to begin with the New York Yankees.

As a Maryland native who grew up cheering for the Baltimore Orioles, I fully understand the reluctance non-Yankees fans may have in giving the "Evil Empire" credit for anything positive, yet that would be wrong in many ways, especially if you consider yourself an American patriot.

One major topic that will reappear often in this book is the act of public defiance against authority and opposition to unwanted control by political leaders, both domestic and/or foreign. Nonviolent means of expressing distrust or disgust are necessary for rebellious and revolutionary directors who want to live to fight another day. For centuries, one act of rebellion second-class segments of society have used to push back against figures of authority, whether that be a regional tyrant or an invading country, has been to appropriate the language, customs and actions those authority figures used to demean as a way for the subjugated to remove the sting from the punishment or insult, forcing the invaders to rethink their actions.

James Cagney won the 1943 Academy Award for Best Actor in a Leading Role for his performace as composer and entertainer George M. Cohan in *Yankee Doodle Dandy.* Nominated for eight awards, it won three, including Best Actor. Widespread popularity of the film was nearly preordained given the fact that "Yankee Doodle Dandy" was a popular British children's nursery rhyme dating back to seventeenth century, but its meaning to Americans was dramatically altered in 1775.

Admitted to the American League in 1903 as the New York Highlanders, the team's name was changed to Yankees in 1913. The ingenious move helped the organization become one of the most popular brand names in the world. Though the name is globally synonymous for *American*, most U.S. citizens would be insulted if someone called them a masturbator in public. Yet that is precisely what the song's intent was when initially sung by British forces as a taunt to Americans:

> … *Yankee Doodle went to town,*
> *A-riding on a pony,*
> *Stuck a feather in his hat,*
> *And called it macaroni* …

English forces stationed in the Northeast thought a small body of water in Newfoundland looked like a penis so they named it *Dildo Pond*. The term *dildo* quickly became *doodle* in British slang. The term *yank* was slang for, well, pretty much what it is today (masturbation), as was the effeminate insult of *dandy.*[3] The term *macaroni* was a hint to how stupid the British thought Americans were, according to author and historian Chris Roberts.

"*Macaroni* is referring to an English youth cult from the 1760s and '70s … their favorite food was macaroni which came to be the name for the movement," said Roberts, author of *Heavy Words Thrown Lightly,* noting that the youth stood out for their feminine and impractical clothing such as big wigs, flamboyant apparel and oversized hats adorned with feathers. "["Yankee Doodle Dandy"] is saying that you can't just stick a feather in your hat and pass yourself off as a macaroni. It takes much more effort than that. It's a put-down, if you like, of what they would see as hayseed colonials trying to emulate the dandified youth of London town."[4]

When British soldiers sang the song, they were saying that "effeminate masturbators" were so stupid that they didn't understand anything cultured like fashion, thinking that they could "stick a feather" in a hat and it would make them chic, or "macaroni."

Things changed forever on June 17, 1775, when British troops outnumbered the Americans 2,200 to 1,000 in the Battle of Bunker Hill. Before being forced to eventually retreat, American militiamen dominated the battle, suffering one hundred deaths and three hundred wounded compared to England's two hundred deaths and eight hundred wounded. Confidence soared for the Americans, who began singing "Yankee Doodle Dandy" to taunt and infuriate the enemy.[5]

Baseball fans cannot blame the Highlanders for appropriating the former insult spit upon Americans. After all, baseball is an appropriation of old British children's games with some slight alterations applied to give the Americans a sport to call their own. For early American patriots, claiming baseball as "ours" was as much about asserting a new nation's identity and defiance against established customs as it was about rebelling against the country's British ancestry and influence.

(3)

●●●▪▪

The Big Bounce, Thermodynamics, & Social Identity

The mythology about baseball's "origin" was wonderful fiction, made to order by the sport's first tycoon, Albert Goodwill Spalding, to accomplish several things simultaneously: boost American patriotism, dismiss British influence and make his company lots of money. The myth can also help explain some of the biggest scientific ideas that explain the universe and how we see ourselves in it.

An ardent patriot, Spalding commissioned a panel of baseball's biggest supporters in 1905 to determine the origin of the sport. Though formally called The Special Base Ball Commission, it became known as the Mills Commission, in deference to Abraham Mills, the former National League president who headed the panel. Like Spalding, Mills was a vocal supporter of the idea of baseball being solely an American invention. Spalding's true efforts were not to find the real genesis of the game, but to establish it as the "National Game" that every American should embrace. While there were several manufacturers of baseball equipment, the A.G. Spalding & Bros. Company was the nation's most prominent (Spalding & Bros. was the exclusive provider of NL baseballs for a century beginning in 1877), so motivating countrymen to embrace the game as an American original was in his best financial interest.

Numerous archaeological digs reveal that ball sports date back more than 5,000 years to the ancient Egyptians, and that Roman public baths were almost always built with a ball court (*sphaeristerium*). Cricket dates back hundreds of years and was an obvious influence on baseball, but Spalding insisted that "it is a proven fact that the game now designated "Base Ball," is of modern and purely American origin."[6]

What was the proof? The panel based its findings solely on the letter of Abner Graves who claimed that Abner Doubleday invented the game in 1839. Spalding's commission members never followed up with Graves to learn more about the veracity of his ludicrous claim (which we will look at next). They had the information they sought, even though it was an absolute flight of fancy by Graves, who murdered his wife a few years later and died in an insane asylum. Ardent patriotism combined with personal business interests blinded Spalding's judgment. In addition to making money, Spalding wanted to use baseball as a way to establish the United States as *the* superlative country in the world, a nation independent from England in every possible manner, including its sports and entertainment. Yet, we know from multiple accounts that George Washington played ball games with soldiers during the Revolutionary War.

On April 7, 1778, soldier George Ewing wrote in his diary that after practicing maneuvers, he and fellow soldiers "played at base this evening" and that weeks later on May 4, Washington "did us the honor to play at Wicket with us" after dinner. *Base* and *Wicket* were early cousins to baseball.[7] A year later, French diplomat Francois Barbé-Marbois, who negotiated the Louisiana Purchase with the U.S. in 1803, wrote that Washington "throws and catches a ball for whole hours with his aides-de-camp."[8]

How could baseball be purely original to America, invented in 1839 as Spalding preached, when the first American president was playing a form of it fifty years earlier?

Given Spalding's jingoistic tendencies, it's hard to believe that he was not aware of Washington's love of sports, especially ball games. Yet Spalding was emphatic that baseball was a purely original sport of the United States, owing nothing to cricket.

It was a classic case of Social Identity Theory at work. The psychological tricks we play on ourselves, insisting that we are better than others (and they are inferior to us), are so common to everyday interactions that it took until the 1970s for an expert to fully explain the self-delusion. Studying social identity theory was the lifelong work of sociologist Henri Tajfel, who sought to explain why humans feel the need to create an Us vs. Them view of the world. Tajfel revealed the psychological need humans have to stereotype the world into two groups based on how we perceive ourselves. "He's just standing on top of you to feel taller," was a common saying in our family and is a simple summary of Tajfel's work.

Tajfel showed that we constantly do two things to feel better about ourselves: we seek out groups we deem successful or reflecting of the qualities we want to possess and find similarities that link us and, simultaneously, contrast that group with others we feel are different and beneath us. This categorization divides everyone into one of two sets: in-group (us) and out-group (them). Left unchecked, this view of the world can lead to horrible consequences such as the Holocaust genocides of World War II, the 1990s killing fields in Rwanda (Hutu vs. Tutsi) and the former Yugoslavia (Serbian vs. Croatian vs. Bosnian) and the ISIS/ISIL violence in the twenty-first century (religious extremists vs. secular Western nations).[9]

Everything in the universe is an evolution, including baseball. There is no magic that allows something to come from nothing. Baseball did not begin as the creation of a single man any more than the universe began as a single event, according to new theories by cutting-edge scientists.

Physicist Nikodem Poplawski has attracted a great deal of attention since 2010 when he proposed an explanation of the entire universe that Spalding would likely not want to hear: everything comes from something. Since Albert Einstein's world-altering 1905 papers produced the famous formula $E=MC^2$, generations have been told the universe began with The Big Bang, an unique, one-time explosion so large (*singularity*) that all matter we can see, touch or detect was created at that moment.

However, much like baseball and cricket, Poplawski's explanation of the universe is that there is always a cause and effect—everything is related. Scientists around the globe are starting to embrace Poplawski's research that questions if The Big Bang Theory is incorrect and that the real start of the universe was The Big Bounce. In this theory, our universe is comprised entirely of matter that was part of a previous universe that collapsed, creating a wormhole (technically referred to as an Einstein-Rosen Bridge) that deposited all the material into our universe. The wormhole is the bridge between the two universes, much like a garden hose that allows water to transport from one vessel to another rapidly. What we consider to be a black hole is merely one end of the hose or Einstein-Rosen Bridge.

Poplawski's visual example makes it all very easy to understand: take one full bottle of water and one empty bottle of water, connect them with a short hose and then turn them on end, allowing the water from the full bottle to flow into the other via the short hose. If you were in the bottom of the empty bottle when the water began to flow, the liquid would appear suddenly, magically, as if out of nowhere. Yet, when you stand back and see how the parts interact, you can see that all parts are connected: what was once in one vessel (or universe) has been deposited into another, which is connected by a tube (wormhole, or

Einstein-Rosen Bridge).

Since the 1850s, the first law of thermodynamics has been an accepted truth: energy cannot be created nor destroyed, it can only be transformed from one form to another. That truth also applies to the true origins of the "American Pastime": the sport was not invented in a moment of epiphany by Doubleday back in 1839, a *singularity*, it was merely the latest incarnation of cricket, which itself was a descendant of ball games played by ancient civilizations thousands of years ago.

(4)

••••-

Hits & Myths

Social identity is much like a sense of humor: either it is a naturally occurring thing or it fails when forced. A friend of mine is horrible at telling jokes, every attempt fails and, invariably, the funniest part is his struggle to be funny. Similarly, whenever early baseball historians attempted to tell the tale of how the sport began, they created more confusion than clarity, ignoring facts for fiction on a mission that wove together an entertaining tale of self-serving blather rather than anything resembling a fact-based history.

A.G. Spalding was motivated by financial gain and an insistence on merging baseball's birth with the nation's to make the sport an integral part of America's (and his company's) identity. As the wealthiest executive in the sport, Spalding used his empire to publish the patriotic history of the sport that was pure fiction. Spalding's Special Base Ball Commission, created in 1905, took three years to assemble alleged "evidence" of baseball's origins before declaring in 1908 that Abner Doubleday invented the game in 1839 in Cooperstown, New York. It was precisely what Spalding wanted: not the truth, but a myth he could sell that would align his company with patriotism.

"It wasn't a lie," Elwood Blues famously said in the movie *The Blues Brothers*, "it was just bullshit."

Spalding couldn't have said it better himself. The inaccurate stories

Spalding, Abraham Mills and, later, the executives at the National Baseball Hall of Fame and Museum invented were not accidental half-truths, but carefully conceived frauds created for a specific reason.

"[They] were not mere liars and blowhards," wrote John Thorn, the Official Historian of Major League Baseball and author of *Baseball in the Garden of Eden,* "They were conscious architects of legend, shapers of national identity, would-be creators of a useful past … [who] hoped to shape America's future by imagining its past."[10]

While he had selfish reasons for inventing many of baseball's myths, Spalding was ingenious for establishing a creation story that gave people a guilt-free and patriotic reason to love baseball. However, the stream of lies unleashed by Spalding picked up supporters (as was planned) and the myth grew larger; each untruth deepened the chasm that divided baseball fact from Spalding's fiction. It only got worse after the National Baseball Hall of Fame and Museum opened in 1936. The executives at the Hall of Fame clearly learned from Spalding's success at spreading the Doubleday fable to help the sport, so they did the same thing about many people, places and events we will revisit throughout the book.

Doubleday did not "invent" anything; he was a career military man, credited with firing the first Union shot of the Civil War.

Alexander Cartwright, inducted into the Hall of Fame in 1939 as the "Father of Modern Baseball" merely played on the famous 1845 Knickerbockers team, he didn't begin it nor any of the rules attributed to him on his plaque. The real forefathers of the sport were Daniel Lucius Adams, William Rufus Wheaton and Lucius Fenn Wadsworth, according to Thorn. Henry Chadwick, editor of *Beadle's Dime Base-Ball Player* and Spalding's *Official Base Ball Guide,* did as much to popularize the game as the other men did to shape it. Thorn's book reveals each of their accomplishments and I urge you to start there if you wish to learn the details, but our concern is not so much who "invented" the game, but why untrue stories would be purposefully created and perpetuated by so many people for so long.

Myths can be very powerful. One of the cornerstones of civilization is religion, which provides believers, among other things, a way to understand how they fit into the universe. We're going to see how baseball has altered religion more in later chapters, but for now we're not looking at the *how* and *why* behind religious stories, but the *what.* This isn't sacrilege against any one religion or even the broader question of spirituality. We're examining the psychological impact that myths have on the believers of that particular story.

Myths teach what is often not taught in schools. Stories handed down from generation to generation for thousands of years offer explanation to believers about how they fit into the world and greater universe.

George Washington never really cut down a cherry tree and then admitted to it under questioning; the allegory is told to children to teach them not to lie. The Boogeyman will not get you if you don't eat your vegetables, it's another apocryphal tale intended to shape behavior. Stories of outright fantasy that are created to curb and guide social behavior can be laughably obvious (and fun to participate in) such as when adults spread the story of Santa Claus and his overnight mission to deliver gifts to good boys and girls.

Albert Spalding

What happens when the same use of apocryphal and allegorical tales are used for more serious and sinister purposes? Area 51 has been infamous worldwide for generations, a mysterious place that most people avoid based on rumors of alien activity. Massive government security in the area only lent the rumors credibility. However, countless reports in recent years revealed that the U.S. government encouraged the widespread fear of the region because it was the prime testing ground for advanced technology and weapons for decades. Fostering myths about a secret and dangerous zone was enough to manipulate the majority of the public into avoiding the area, allowing American weapon designers the advantage of secrecy. The 2010 movie *Green Zone* told the story of an American officer (Matt Damon) sent to inspect Iraq's alleged weapons of mass destruction, which the United States used as a prime reason to invade in the aftermath of 9/11, only to discover an elaborate, international coverup with dire global consequences.

While less severe than Area 51 or Iraqi WMD fables, the Doubleday myth was created for similar reasons: to give the American public a story to rally around, to create a sense of patriotism, even though the emotions were built on a foundation of fiction, not fact.

Mythmaking also alters the physical world by creating sacred places that give believers peace of mind (or, in the case of Area 51, a place to avoid to maintain your peace of mind). These sacred places are vital for a balanced mental existence, according to Joseph Campbell, who was the preeminent scholar on mythology before his death in 1987. In his many books and documentaries, Campbell taught that myths and sacred places work together to make humans happier, what he called *bliss*.

"You must have a room, or a certain hour or so a day, where you don't know what was in the newspapers that morning, you don't know who your friends are, you don't know what you owe anybody, you don't know what anybody owes to you," Campbell explained in *The Power of Myth*. "At first you may find that nothing happens there. But if you have a sacred place and use it, something eventually will happen. … Our life has become so economic and practical in its orientation that, as you get older, the claims of the moment upon you are so great, you hardly know where the hell you are, or what it is you intended. You are always doing something that is required of you. Where is your bliss station? You have to try to find it."[11]

Millions of baseball fans for nearly two hundred years have considered attending a ballgame as a getaway from the real world. Playing hooky from work to attend a day game or just feeling like a child again, watching the game, eating snacks and relaxing is what Campbell would call *bliss*.

Using myths to popularize the sport goes back to the very first "official" baseball game. To explain how, we're going to turn to Russell Crowe and a guy named Homer—no, not Homer Simpson. *D'oh!*

(5)

•••••

Russell Crowe, The Afterlife, & New Jersey

The soil turned to mud, liquidated by the amount of bloodshed from the battle that had just ended. That evening, from the safety of their tent, the king, tired from years of killing, turned to his favorite child, his daughter Lucilla, and said:

"Let us pretend that you are a loving daughter, and I am a good father."

"This is a pleasant fiction," Lucilla replied, "is it not?"

Movie fans will recognize this exchange between Marcus Aurelius and Lucilla from the film *Gladiator* starring Russell Crowe. That scene from the film and the battle that just ended help illustrate several things about baseball's role in the world. *Gladiator* won five Academy Awards in 2001 and is still often quoted by sports fans for a reason: it resonates with people of all ages. It's also the ideal vehicle to take us to appropriation, mythmaking and baseball.

Lucilla's phrase "a pleasant fiction" is the perfect description of baseball's creation myth that we have already examined. Technically a story built on lies, the Doubleday "invention" story was crafted to be "pleasant fiction" as was any connection of baseball's roots to Cooperstown, New York, the home of the

National Baseball Hall of Fame and Museum (more on that soon).

Prior to Lucilla's conversation with her father, Crowe's character prepared his men for battle in *Gladiator*'s opening scene with one final light-hearted warning to his soldiers that should have made baseball fans sit up and pay attention: "Three weeks from now, I will be harvesting my crops. Imagine where you will be, and it will be so. Hold the line! Stay with me! If you find yourself alone, riding in the green fields with the sun on your face, do not be troubled. For you are in Elysium, and you're already dead!"

The cavalry laughs; carnage ensues; audiences everywhere are delighted.

The "pleasant fiction" that baseball officials have advocated for more than a century is that the first official game occurred on June 19, 1846, when the Knickerbocker Base Ball Club, the first official baseball team, lost 23-1 to the New York Base Ball Club at Elysian Fields in Hoboken, New Jersey. The victors were not an organized team, rather a collection of men who also enjoyed the game and, as the Knickerbockers needed an opponent, formed a temporary "team." Many historians have proven how untrue this "pleasant fiction" was, noting that the Knickerbockers, formed on September 23, 1845, were blown out by a rag-tag group of players without even a "team" name, instead merely using their hometown (New York) to identify the "team."

Entire books have been written proving that this date was not the real "first game" of baseball. An earlier intrasquad game between Knickerbockers players on October 6, 1845, was, according to some historians, the first official baseball game (albeit with seven men per team). Evidence of organized baseball games goes back to 1825 in Rochester, New York; while Canadian games played in 1838 raise questions about the Americanness of the American Pastime given how much Canadians embraced the game well before the Civil War.[12] Determining baseball's first game is a tar baby: a sticky trap that soon ensnares you and from which you cannot extract yourself.

"To ascertain who invented baseball would be equivalent to trying to locate the discoverer of fire," conceded baseball historian Harold Seymour.[13]

On July 11, 1831, a new public park opened in Hoboken, New Jersey, named Elysian Fields, its name taken from Greek mythology. In 800 B.C., Greek poet Homer wrote *Odyssey* about Odysseus' ten-year voyage to return home after the Trojan War. Since Jesus Christ was centuries away from walking on water, the contemporary concept of *heaven* didn't exist. In Christianity, heaven and hell are essentially rewards for good or bad behavior on earth; they are ethereal and exist in another dimension, not physical in any way. For the Greeks, however, the afterlife was a physical realm where all eventually went. If you were bad, you were forced to live in the Underworld where you could not escape nor enjoy, doomed to walk the physical realm forever in misery. If you were good, you were allowed to walk on the Islands of the Blessed, where a V.I.P. section existed and was reserved for war heroes and honorable men. This special

This Currier & Ives image from 1866 depicts baseball action at Elysian Fields and reflects the popularity of the game during the Civil War given the size of the crowds. Some accounts incorrectly claim this popular image is of the "first" baseball game on June 19, 1846, though historians have proven this claim incorrect.

area was named Elysium, its fertile fields known as the Elysian Plains. Soldiers were told they would be allowed into Elysium if they fought valiantly.

Roman leaders unabashedly appropriated almost every aspect of Greek culture. On a nearly one-to-one basis, Roman officials merely took Greek mythology and changed the names to Latin ones, but kept the stories the same: Greek Zeus became Roman Jupiter, Greek Heracles turned into Roman Hercules, Odysseus became Ulysses, and so on. However, Elysium and its fields was a constant in both mythological worlds (sometimes spelled *Elysion*).

Which is why in *Gladiator* Maximus (Crowe) told his soldiers to not fear death on the battlefield, their reward would be entrance into the Elysian Fields, where everything is peaceful, enjoyable and good. In 1846, the Knickerbockers enjoyed a physical version of what ancient Roman and Greek soldiers hoped for: a walk in the Elysian Fields where all is happy and good, even if your team just lost, 23-1.

(6)

-....

Cooperstown & The Big Lie

"The bigger the lie, the more people will believe it."

This oft-quoted line is attributed to many people, including Adolf Hitler and his Minister of Propaganda, Joseph Goebbels. However, so many different people have been credited with the phrase that, like baseball's true origins, discerning who said it first is impossible.

Of course, crediting the Nazis with the saying is logical considering the Holocaust was one of the best examples of this idea in action. If a small lie is going to make an entire story sound unbelievable, then change the entire story to hide the small lie better, according to the Big Lie Theory. In 1951, the U.S. government created a nineteen-minute propaganda film called *The Big Lie* to expose the German atrocities of World War II.

The brackish waters where Big Lie theory, mythmaking and sacred places converge is our final stop before we jump with both feet into the deep waters of the whirlpool that has, is and will forever mix baseball with the American government.

As Joseph Campbell reminded us: sacred places are vital in the real world; we all need physical places to rest and find our bliss. For baseball fans, a ballpark is a sacred place to be happy. Why not? Doesn't the green grass and manicured dirt awaken the child-like part buried in all of us that yearns for grass stains on their pants and dirty hands? Beyond remembrances of our own childhood days playing baseball, most fans echo the Mayberry-like sentiment that claims a ballpark is how things were back in the good old days.

The beauty of the Big Lie is that when mental manipulation works well, it is nearly impossible to detect. Let us not forget the lesson we learned from The Big Bounce and The Big Bang Theories: sometimes the biggest influence (wormholes, gravity) is completely invisible. Sometimes the truth is carefully hidden, which is the case with Cooperstown, New York.

Baseball officials worked very hard to construct a "pleasant fiction" about the birth of the game, going so far as to insist it was created in Cooperstown, New York, in the country, where good folk live hard, work hard and play hard. There was just one problem: it was all a lie.

An online search of terms for "baseball+pastoral" yielded more than fifteen million hits. Replacing "pastoral" with "industrialization" cut the number to just 235,000 hits. The Big Lie is still very much at work because the real birth of baseball was not in Cooperstown or even in a rural setting. The sport was the byproduct of industrialization; it was a city game, not a country game, despite extensive energy spent to frame it otherwise.

"Some of the earliest forms of organized baseball that we are aware of took place in settings similar to that of Cooperstown," the Hall of Fame's site once ridiculously and fraudulently claimed. "In that sense, the village seems as a fitting representation of the heritage of the game, and a fitting home to the Baseball Hall of Fame."[14]

Too many historians have proven this idea wrong for the Hall of Fame to push such confectionery fiction, which reluctantly removed the blatantly misleading ancestry of the sport from its collateral materials, but not until 2008. For a century, since Spalding's Commission created baseball's original Big Lie, officials pushed this ludicrous genesis story in order to give ballparks the *sacred place* feeling that turned their money-making enterprise into a blissful, patriotic experience.

America's earliest cities were choked with people who needed relaxation from manual labor, which employed nearly all immigrants. John Thorn has gone to great lengths to prove the sport was born of the city, an offshoot of British ball games. Of course it was, in hindsight, considering that the United Kingdom was the original home for most early Americans who weren't slaves.

Crowded conditions were as bad then as they are now, if not worse despite smaller population numbers considering many improvements didn't exist yet, such as paved streets and proper waste disposal. Finding a place to relax and enjoy some physical activity was not easy. Children played in the streets, to the consternation of adults. When adults wanted to play, they needed somewhere to go. Which is why the bluffs of Hoboken, New Jersey, were made into a park in 1831—to give the inhabitants of crowded New York City a place to retreat, a place to relax and find their bliss.

After the Revolutionary War, Colonel John Stevens purchased the land of what is today Hoboken, New Jersey. An engineering genius, Stevens pioneered the steamboat, which he used to ferry New Yorkers from the city across the Hudson River so they could enjoy his park and its concessions. It was Stevens who dubbed it Elysian Fields, knowing the mythological reference would be a magnet to the city-weary citizenry. When New York City's Central Park opened in 1857, Elysian Fields soon fell out of favor and disappeared.

Just as Abner Doubleday would be stunned to learn he supposedly invented baseball, one of America's great authors would be disgusted to learn his homestead was now home to baseball's Hall of Fame.

James Fenimore Cooper was one of America's first great fiction writers, his westerns were so popular that they are still beloved by fans of the genre. Published in 1826, *The Last of The Mohicans* was the second book in his beloved book series, The Leatherstocking Tales, and the movie adaptation in 1992 earned an Academy Award on way to being one of the highest grossing movies of the year. Clearly, Cooper's stories have resonated with generations of his countrymen.

In 1785, Cooper's father, William, founded Cooperstown. It was not quite the frontier that Cooper would later write about extensively, but it was close. After the success of *The Last of the Mohicans,* Cooper moved his family to Europe for seven years. Upon returning to Cooperstown, Cooper was angry to learn that a portion of his land had become a favored gathering spot for the locals to relax and play games. Cooper insisted that the land was his *sacred place*, not theirs, and forbid any public use. The matter escalated to the point where lawsuits were filed.

The hard feelings were never settled in large part because Cooper decided to prove the pen was mightier than the lawsuit. In 1932, Cooper wrote *Home as Found* to reveal how he truly felt about Americans after living abroad for years. The main character in the story was John Effingham, clearly based on Cooper himself, who grew disgusted to learn that his yard had become the popular place for local youth to play "a game of ball, on the lawn." In the novel, Effingham kicked the youth off his lawn, but the ball players initially refused to leave, telling Effingham that his house was the real problem since it ruined their "ball-ground." The players get tricked into leaving after Effingham's assistant lies to the boys, telling them that "village trustees say there shall be no ball-playing in the streets."

The young men leave, intent to prove they will play ball wherever they want: "Who's a trustee that he should tell gentlemen where they are to play ball!"

For Cooper, ball games were his best way of showing how "loose habits that had been rapidly increasing in the country during the last ten years" led citizens to "mistaking liberties for liberty."

While illustrations in the book clearly show the boys playing a game more akin to field hockey than baseball, the novel reveals what Cooper wanted to say: *Get off of my lawn!*

How odd it would be to have Cooper return today to his homestead that has become the home to the National Baseball Hall of Fame and Museum. In fact, the great American writer may not want to be to in the country at all considering that he said the average American youth could never "resist an opportunity of showing how much he considers himself superior to the law."[15]

The Big Lie revealed repeatedly: the great American writer who, after experiencing Europe, hated his homeland, Cooperstown, New York, the fictional "birthplace" of baseball, where, in actuality, ball games would be detested the most, if they happened at all considering that baseball was a sport born of crowded city streets, not open fields and pastures.

Section II:

•-• • •- -•-• •••• •• -• --•

REACHING FIRST

••-• •• •-• ••• -

The last photograph taken in the last photo session of President Abraham Lincoln. Photographer Alexander Gardner captured this image on February 5, 1865, less than three months before Lincoln's assassination on April 15, 1865.

(7)

--•••

Lincoln

"With the first pick of the inaugural All-Athlete POTUS Fantasy Draft, we select Abraham Lincoln, Illinois…"

Gerald Ford played football for the University of Michigan, Dwight Eisenhower played minor league baseball, George H.W. Bush was a star baseball player at Yale University and Barack Obama was known for his pickup basketball games, but the best all-around athlete to ever sit in the White House very well may have been Lincoln. The tallest president (6-foot-4, 180 pounds), Lincoln's feats of strength and active participation in sports with regular citizens were documented by many family friends and historians. Of course, given the mythmaking machinations of most storytellers, some of his tales are dubious. The first president to embrace baseball, Lincoln benefitted from the sport like no other politician of his era.

What Theodore Roosevelt was to football in later years, Lincoln was to baseball. Early in the twentieth century Roosevelt stepped in and almost single-handedly saved football, his favorite sport, with White House intervention (examined in greater detail later). While Lincoln didn't save baseball, he did usher it into the American mainstream, which strengthened the bond between the White House, American military muscle and baseball.

Let's first disregard the one anecdote most often cited regarding Lincoln and sports. According to lore, when GOP leaders reached Lincoln's home to congratulate him on earning the Republican nomination for the 1860 presidential race, Lincoln was playing baseball with friends and insisted his colleagues wait until he was finished with his at bat. The legend, of course, is false. The 1860 GOP nomination was a hotly-contested race and Lincoln spent Election

This political cartoon by Currier & Ives, created weeks before the 1860 presidential election won by Abraham Lincoln, was one of the first public uses of baseball as a way to communicate political messages. In this pro-Lincoln cartoon, the presidential race is depicted as a baseball game won by Lincoln, who is standing on home plate, holding the ball, and scolding his defeated opponents (left to right) John Bell, Stephen A. Douglas, and John Breckinridge. Lincoln's "bat" is a wooden rail on which is inscribed "Equal Rights and Free Territory" and on his belt is written "Wide Awake Club." The skunk near the other three candidates symbolizes they were "skunk'd."

Day awaiting news of the results at an Illinois telegraph office.[16] Who would create such a blatant whopper of a lie? Albert Spalding claimed the story came to him in a letter from an eyewitness, a letter which he could never later produce.[17]

Another similar tale should be viewed skeptically, given the gravity of Lincoln's presidency during the most tumultuous time in American history. Today, the Blair House is adjacent to the White House and is the guest quarters for visiting dignitaries. It is named for Francis Preston Blair, an adviser to several presidents whose son, Montgomery, was Lincoln's Postmaster General, and grandson, Frank, shared a now oft-quoted story about Lincoln joining ball games with the Blair grandchildren at the family's nearby estate.

"I remember vividly how he ran with the children," Frank Blair told anyone who would listen, "how long were his strides, and how far his coat-tails stuck out behind, and how we tried to hit him with the ball, as he ran the bases.

He entered into the spirit of the play as completely as any of us, and we invariably hailed his coming with delight."[18]

The Blair family did indeed have a massive estate in Silver Spring, Maryland, where dignitaries often gathered, according to biographer Elbert B. Smith. However, given the dire state of the nation during the Civil War, Smith makes no mention of any sporting activities occurring at the estate and logic would dictate that this story is both enjoyable and incredulous, another misleading example of mythmaking.

During the 1860 presidential campaign, the Chicago Excelsiors played an exhibition intrasquad game with one team comprised of those supporting Lincoln, the other team those who supported his rival, Stephen Douglas.[19] During the race, a political cartoon by Currier & Ives created one of the most enduring images of Lincoln, the baseball president. The image is of the four presidential nominees each with a baseball bat in his hands, but only Lincoln, looming over his vanquished opponents, held a baseball in his hand, indicating his victory. Air quotes for each politician summarized their opinions in baseball terms with Lincoln chastising them: "Gentlemen, if any of you should ever take a hand in another match at this game, remember that you must have a 'good bat' and strike a 'fair ball' to make a 'clean score' & a 'home run.'" The title of the cartoon was: "The National Game. Three 'Outs' and One 'Run.'"[20]

Lincoln's greatest contribution to the game of baseball came not as a player or fan, but as the author of the Emancipation Proclamation, a move that changed everything. Before that could happen, an ocean of blood had to flow.

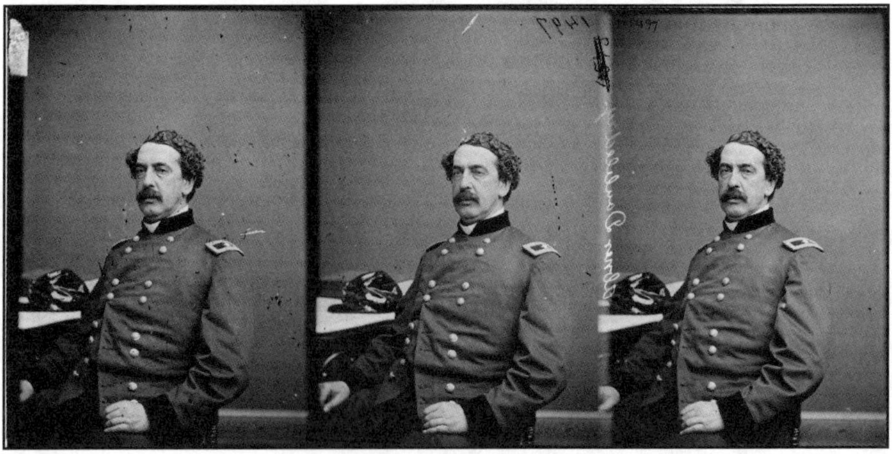

Abner Doubleday during the Civil War.

(8)

Fort Sumter

The sun was still somewhere in the ocean, only a sliver of orange light hinted on the horizon that it would soon rise. It was just enough light for the Confederate soldiers to discern the outline of the fort against the darkness.

A little more than a mile out into the middle of South Carolina's Charleston Harbor, Captain Abner Doubleday slept, determined to get as much rest as possible. He knew what was coming and feared there would be no sleep for days to come. Someone in the darkness shook him awake. It was Major Robert Anderson, commander of the First U.S. Artillery, the only soldier who outranked Doubleday at Fort Sumter.

Anderson had in his hand a note from his adversary on shore, General P.G.T. Beauregard, commander of the Confederate forces, which warned that shelling of the fort would commence in one hour. The notice left Beauregard's hand at approximately 3:20 a.m., but by the time it reached Anderson and he was able to alert Doubleday it was already after four o'clock. The one-hour warning had only a few minutes remaining by the time the letter arrived.

Moments later, the first cannon shot exploded in the distance. Before Doubleday could move, the garrison wall shook from impact, the cannon ball embedded in the wall about a foot from his head. Technically, it was a warning shot with a lead ball that was not filled with gunpowder. Many cannonballs were not filled with gunpowder, but the damage they caused was still severe. That particular hurtling lead ball didn't need to be packed with gunpowder to do massive damage, however, because it happened to hit one of the few spots in the fort that could easily ignite. Doubleday was resting in the former artillery room were all the gun cartridges were assembled. The room was still filled with loose gunpowder and now, thanks to the artillery shot into the wall, dust and debris clouded any chance of vision in the early morning darkness. Had the cannon ball penetrated the wall inches from Doubleday's head, the stored gunpowder would have exploded upon impact.

Doubleday scrambled out of the dangerous room as nineteen batteries of Confederate soldiers firing forty-three cannons rained down a cacophony of artillery on the fort.

It was still dark, too dark to fight considering the Union soldiers in Fort Sumter were low on ammo and had prayed for provisions before a Confederate assault would cut off any chance to resupply. Any hope of that was gone now that the feared Confederate assault had begun.

So they ate breakfast instead: pork, porridge and water. Confederate shells continued to thunder during the meal, but the men where in good spirits, not happy, but ready: what they had trained for was finally commencing. The country was less than a century old, shorter than one long lifetime, and if it hoped to have a future fully realized, this fight between countrymen had to be fought, unfortunately.

After breakfast, when the sun rose high and bright enough to clearly see the shoreline, Doubleday led his men to the lower level, aimed one of the 8,000-pound Parrott rifles at the pitched roof protecting the closest Confederate battery and fired the forty-two pound artillery shell.[21]

It was April 12, 1861.

The Civil War had just begun.

(9)

Baseball Funds Civil War Efforts

On July 21, 1861, three months after Doubleday's historic shot at Fort Sumter, 4,700 Americans died in the first major battle of the Civil War, the Battle of Bull Run (Union: 2,950; Confederate: 1,750).[22] Three months later to the day, the second significant battle of the war, the Battle of Ball's Bluff, left another 1,070 men dead (Union: 921, Confederate: 149).[23] In an age of antiquated armor, where most of the killing happened in such a small amount of real estate that soldiers could see their opponent before, during and after getting shot, 5,770 Americans were killed by fellow Americans in just twelve weeks. (For generations, the total number killed in the war was believed to be about 620,000, but recent research claims a more accurate death toll was between 750,000 to 850,000.[24])

On the same afternoon of Ball's Bluff, October 21, 1861, more than 10,000 baseball fans descended on Elysian Fields to enjoy an all-star game between the Brooklyn and New York teams. It was one of the last big events at Elysian Fields, the decades-old park having fallen out of favor, replaced by Central Park.

New York City was the hotbed of all baseball activity. The sport that once was split into various factions—the Massachusetts game, the New York game and, to a lesser extent, the Washington game—was, by the Civil War, unified under what would have been regarded as the New York game. Each game variation had slightly different rules; the New York game was the one that most resembled what fans today would recognize as baseball.

New York's dominance in baseball echoed its status among American states. In 1790 (year of the first U.S. census), when there were seventeen states, New York's population (340,000) ranked fifth. By 1860, New York ranked first among thirty-three states with 3.8 million, one million more than all of Pennsylvania. The overwhelming numbers of baseball players in the country were in the New York region, giving that version of the game the momentum it needed to unify the rules of the game and alter the war.

Businessman William Cammeyer made a small fortune in the leather industry, but, noting the popularity of recreation activities and the rising New York City population figures, he invested in sports entertainment. A longtime resident of the Williamsburg section in Brooklyn, Cammeyer bought the sunken property at the corner of Marcy Avenue and Rutledge Street and, taking advantage of its sub-street level eccentricity, flooded the plot to make a public ice skating rink.

His timing could not have been better. Skating had become a rage in New York and his rink was a smashing success. Nobody can skate in the springtime; but Cammeyer knew precisely what he needed to replace skating: baseball. After skating season ended, Cammeyer built the country's first enclosed ballpark specifically for baseball and patriotically named it the Union Baseball and Cricket Grounds.

On May 15, 1862, Union Grounds debuted in a game with teams that comprised players of the three teams that called the ballpark home: the Eckfords, Constellations and Putnam clubs. The 3,000 fans who witnessed the historic game were allowed in free of charge, thanks to Cammeyer, who was eager to show off his innovative sports venue. Measuring 592 feet by 448 feet, with seating for 20,000 fans, Union Grounds was an historic first for the sport as its dimensions would translate to just about any professional ballpark by today's standards. It also provided the North an advantage in the Civil War.[25]

Whether Cammeyer was a loyal patriot, saw it as good business advertising or was—yet gain—fully in tune with public sentiment, he established another first in the ever-tightening relationship between baseball and U.S. military action by funneling funds from baseball to the war effort. During the inaugural 1862 season at the Union Grounds, Cammeyer established special game days where he contributed all funds from baseball games to the Sanitary Commission, which helped wounded Union soldiers.[26]

Local newspapers trumpeted the cause, urging fans to support the Union war effort by attending the games played between city champion Atlantics and the Eckfords. The ten cents admission fee may seem laughably small today, but the combined funds from all baseball games allowed the Union to divert monies that would previously have gone to aiding their wounded to the battle instead. Additionally, citizens, (not just sports fans) were expected to support Cammeyer's games since they aided the Union's war effort. There was no longer a difference between cheering for the Union military and cheering for baseball—they were one in the same at Cammeyer's Union Grounds. It was a shrewd tactic that many dictators, presidents and gangsters would later copy with great success, including a twelve-year-old baseball fan in Illinois named Albert Spalding.

(10)

•---- -----

Shipbuilders & Championships

William Cammeyer's success in supporting the Union's war efforts was largely due to the popularity of one team, whose connection to today is so eerie it seems worthy of a quick note. Despite the fact that teams were adamantly amateur at the time, their popularity was just as widespread as today. The only difference was the players didn't get paid. Amateur status was vogue; the notion that a man would be paid to play a game was distasteful, an insult.

"A man who does not pay his obligations and has it in his power to do so is a knave and not fit to be trusted in the game of ball or anywhere else," one proud amateur baseball insider wrote in a newspaper editorial, "and if he has not the money his time would be much better spent in earning the same than playing ball. Business first, pleasure afterward."[27]

That author was Frank Pidgeon, founder of the Brooklyn Eckfords.

The 1862 games at the Union Grounds that benefited wounded Union soldiers were between the Atlantics and Eckfords, both from Brooklyn. The Eckfords won the first match, 20-14; then the Atlantics rebounded with a 39-5 blowout. On September 18, the Eckfords defeated the Atlantics 8-3 to win the unofficial championship of New York and the nation. Since New York was the center of the baseball universe at the time, the Eckfords were unofficial 1862 "national" champions.

Pidgeon founded the team in 1855, was the team's star pitcher and a shipbuilding trailblazer, in addition to being a painter, musician, inventor and close colleague of George Steers, builder of the *America* for which the America's Cup is named. Pidgeon named the team for another naval architect, Henry Eckford, who was one of the foremost naval pioneers before he died in 1832. The members of New York's "national champion" Eckfords roster were amateur ballplayers who were all professional shipbuilders by trade.

In 1973, CBS sold the New York Yankees to George Steinbrenner, whose fortune was made from the same industry as Pidgeon's : shipbuilding.

The Yankees, whose name was an appropriated insult turned into a patriotic nickname, have been the most successful team in baseball history. Though located in the Bronx, not Brooklyn, Yankee Stadium, the home to more championships than any other baseball team, is located just thirteen miles from where home plate was located in Brooklyn's Union Grounds where the Eckfords, in 1862, began the tradition of shipbuilders building championships.

(11)

Life & Death, New York & Boston

It seems odd that one of the men who changed sports the most during his lifetime, especially baseball, is not enshrined in any Hall of Fame. Ironically, Jim Creighton was elevated to the level of baseball deity for what did *not* happen, yet the contributions he actually *did* make have gone unrecognized, save for historians.

A Brooklyn native, Creighton was one of the first two-sport stars in American sports. In 1859, the first American cricket tour pitted an all-star team of professional English players against American counterparts. While the Americans lost every game in the series, Creighton proved himself to be a rising star pitcher, in part for his ability to shrewdly bend the rules, despite being just eighteen years old. Since the Knickerbockers' rules for baseball were established in 1845, a baseball pitcher was forced to mimic a traditional cricket throw: they were allowed a two-step running start and the ball had to be released underhand with a stiff elbow and wrist. Additionally (and significantly), the pitcher was *not* allowed to put any spin on the ball.

Creighton, however, eschewed the running approach, using instead what has become a traditional pitch set up today: from a standing position, pivoting on one foot, stepping back with the other and following through with the pitching motion. Unconventional and effective, Creighton's delivery was also technically illegal as the key element of his delivery that allowed him to eliminate a running approach was a flick of his wrist, which put spin on the ball and made it rise upward, confounding the batters.[28]

In the summer of 1859, Creighton split time between pitching for the American Cricket Club and two Brooklyn baseball clubs (Niagara and Star). Learning from the success of the 1859 cricket exhibition tour, the Brooklyn Excelsiors staged the first baseball tour of the country in 1860, going to cities throughout the Northeast from Washington D.C. to Albany, New York. The tour was a wild success; the Excelsiors went 18-2-1 with Creighton pitching every game. It was a financial success for Creighton, too, as the Excelsiors broke the anti-professionalism rules of the day, secretly paying him, as well as his former Star teammates George H. Flanley, Asa Brainard and his brother, Henry Brainard, $500 apiece for the season, equivalent to approximately $15,000 in 2016.[11]

In 1861, the Excelsiors played only intramural games, forcing Creighton to focus on cricket, which he dominated, while playing baseball sporadically with other Brooklyn teams. After a year from competitive play, the Excelsiors returned to a regular baseball schedule in 1862. Like they had done on the historic 1860 baseball tour, the Excelsiors were eager to play road games, unafraid of any distance to travel. On July 10, 1862, the Excelsiors traveled to Massachusetts, defeating Bowdoin 41-15, marking the first significant game between baseball teams in New York City and Boston. (Other Massachusetts teams played baseball by the New York rules as early as 1858, but none in a game against New York squads before Creighton and the Excelsiors, which was confirmed by John Thorn in our correspondence. Forty years later, on May 7, 1903, the Boston Americans defeated the New York Highlanders, 6-2, in the first matchup between the organizations known today as the Red Sox and Yankees, respectively.)

Three months after Creighton launched the Boston-New York rivalry, he was dead, his death turned into propaganda used by American patriots to further rebel against their British forefathers.

On October 14, 1862, Creighton's Excelsiors defeated Unions of Morrisania 13-9, with Asa Brainard as the starting pitcher. Creighton went 4-for-4 with four doubles before relieving Brainard in the sixth, at which time Creighton supposedly suffered his fatal injury. Atlantic outfielder John Chapman later claimed to have been at the game and that Creighton hurt himself hitting a home run in a similar fashion to the manner Roy Hobbs (played by Robert Redford) did in *The Natural*.[30] Four days later, Creighton died at his parent's home. He was just twenty-one years old.

No definitive cause of death was revealed. The most frequently repeated reason for his death was that he ruptured his bladder. An 1887 report in the *Missouri Republican* may have been the source of this story as someone who claimed to be a spectator at the game described the scene that day and said that some of his "companions averred they heard his bladder burst."[31] The author signed the letter simply "Old Timer." Medical experts assured me that it is impossible to *hear* a bladder burst, much less from seats many feet away, so this account is highly dubious, if not ridiculous.

Henry Chadwick later claimed that Creighton injured himself in a cricket match a week earlier on October 7, which Chadwick personally witnessed, and, not realizing how serious his injury was, he played his final game a week later, reinjuring himself while pitching. Thorn supported and expanded upon Chadwick's theory, suggesting that the specific cause of death was a ruptured inguinal hernia. This last theory is the most likely culprit. While the question has been raised about how Creighton could possibly play baseball a week after a hernia, medical experts assured me that the inguinal hernia theory, proposed initially by Chadwick (though without the medical details) and later supported by Thorn made logical sense: Creighton likely gave himself a hernia from his cricket match and a week later, while going through the strenuous activity of pitching, ruptured the hernia.

Excelsior president Dr. Joseph B. Jones, along with a chorus of like-minded baseball supporters, insisted that Creighton died from his cricket activities, not from baseball. Jones's assertions should come as no surprise. Baseball officials were zealous to elevate baseball's status while simultaneously diminishing any other sport's challenge for the public affection, particularly an English sport. Baseball officials not only made Creighton a national hero, but they stressed that a "foreign" sport caused the death of an American athlete, not "our" National Pastime. Mythmaking of the highest order would help everyone in baseball, even though there was no empirical way to prove cricket's blame.

"The battle for the nation's sporting allegiance was at a crucial point," Thorn wrote, explaining why baseball officials were so eager to blame another sport. "Cricket had been the favored sport until only recently … and thus may have moved them to propagandize for baseball's spotlessness, as well as Creighton's."[32]

Little did baseball officials know at that time, but the Civil War would help the sport in ways no team owner or executive could ever accomplish.

(12)

•---- ••---

The ABC's of 1862: Anaconda, Baseball, & Christmas

Two hundred and forty-one years after one of the first recorded bat and ball games in North America, Union soldiers celebrated Christmas the same way the settlers at Plymouth Colony did, by playing ball games. In 1621, colonists celebrated Christmas by playing stool ball, an early ball game similar to cricket. Likewise, in 1862, Union soldiers in Hilton Head, South Carolina, took a break from the Civil War to celebrate the holiday by playing baseball, with Confederate prisoners and freed slaves in attendance.[33]

One Union team comprised soldiers from the 165th New York Volunteer Infantry, including Abraham "A.G." Mills, the future president of the National League. Mills and his teammates traded their Union blue uniforms for an unusual baseball choice: red pants with white spats, an ornamental jacket and instead of a baseball cap, a fez with blue tassels. The other team, assembled from members of the Forty-Seventh and Forty-Eighth New York Infantry Regiments, wore blue.

The original source of the story was none other than Mills himself, who claimed to pack a bat and ball with him when he went to war as an eighteen year old. Knowing how much of a key figure Mills was in the Doubleday creation myth, his credibility about baseball topics should always be in question, especially when he claimed that 40,000 people gathered to watch the game.

Hilton Head historians and journalists researched the Christmas 1862 game, known as the Hilton Head Baseball Championship, and found that Mills' story was mostly accurate, but the attendance figure was closer to 10,000 people.[34] (In its earliest history, Hilton Head was also called Port Royal.)

The Hilton Head Baseball Championship was a pivotal moment in the merging of baseball and military action because it allowed three distinct national groups to observe, learn and promote the New York rules of baseball: Union soldiers who carried the New York rules back to small towns across the North, Confederate prisoners of war who would teach the New York game in rural areas of the South and freed African American slaves eager to embrace American freedom in every fashion.

Doubleday and his fellow Union soldiers were forced to surrender Fort Sumter on April 13, 1861, evacuating the next day. Seven months later, a Union armada of more than 13,000 soldiers took Hilton Head, one hundred miles south of Fort Sumter, freeing thousands of slaves and establishing a southern foothold they would not relinquish for the duration of the war. After the loss of Fort Sumter, General Winfield Scott developed a three-prong attack to force the Confederate surrender, dubbed The Anaconda Plan. Securing Hilton Head was the first key part to strangling Southern resistance, followed by attacks from the Mississippi River and invading Virginia, capturing Richmond, the capital of the confederacy, then pushing further south.[35] The plan was considered to be too passive for Scott's colleagues who insisted that sacking Richmond was more vital than starving the South with naval blockades that choked the Rebels financially. Officially, the Anaconda Plan was not used as Scott envisioned. However, the Union's attack relied heavily on a vital element of his plan: a naval blockade of Southern ports.

While the North may not have used all three elements of the Anaconda Plan, the Christmas 1862 game successfully put baseball in the minds of Americans from all regions and races in three key ways:

1) Union military leaders established baseball as a key element of all future American military success;

2) Confederate soldiers spread the New York style of the national pastime to new areas;

3) freed slaves also learned the sport which would become a key factor in coming years on the road to equality

Doubleday may have lost the battle at Fort Sumter, but baseball was about to win the war.

(13)

•---- •••--

The Militarization of Baseball

A vital part of The Anaconda Plan was patience, an ingredient in short supply by many Union generals, who preferred combat to economic embargoes. However, the naval blockade and subsequent de facto control of ports of trade, the very backbone of General Winfield Scott's vision, was used to win the war. The blockade took time to implement, but the results were two-fold: the cessation of the South's cotton trade with Europe, whose funds were dire to the Confederate war effort, and the South's ability to gain food and other supplies from European allies (though smuggling of goods with Mexico, Cuba and the Bahamas was problematic for the Union to squash).[36]

Employing the largest naval blockade in human history to that point was going to take some time.[37] In any military conflict in any era of history, war-time leaders have had to find ways for troops to occupy their free time between repetitive drills, chores and, of course, battles. Both Union and Confederate leaders urged athletic activity, including ball games, to stave off boredom in a healthy manner. But there were key differences between the two factions, according to historian George B. Kirsch. The U.S. Sanitary Commission, a private organization that worked directly with the Union to assist wounded soldiers and improve daily conditions for active troops, urged Union commanders to support athletic outlets for their men, in particular baseball.

Additionally, newspapers in the North supported the idea of sports benefitting soldiers and for years had already been including sports news in daily editions. Today, the sports section is the most popular part of the newspaper in many areas. The genesis of that came from New York newspapers forced to appease the news appetite of the largest population in the country, many of whom played baseball or were fans of the game.

Having soldiers play sports during the war was urged because of the "beneficial effect they have on the spirits and health, and how they tend to alleviate the monotony of camp life," wrote one reporter for *The (New York) Clipper* at the time. "They also lead to a wholesome rivalry between companies and regiments, and augment the esprit du corps of the same, to an extent that to those who have not witnessed it would appear marvelous."[38]

Union commanders supported athletics in the free time to the extent that many of them even participated in games with the enlisted men, further strengthening the bond between superiors and subordinates. Among the many stories shared in war diaries by enlisted Union soldiers were the recounts of Union General George L. Hartsuff who was riding through Virginia on his horse, but stopped when he saw soldiers playing baseball and asked if he could play catcher for a while. General William Hays was such a supporter of the sport that he requested that bats and balls be sent to Battery A, First Regiment, Rhode Island Light Artillery division; when he returned later, the regiment captain assumed Hays wanted to inspect the men going through drills.

"No," Hays replied, "I want to see them play ball."

Later, Captain Lemuel A. Abbott of the Tenth Regiment Vermont Volunteer Infantry participated in a game against noncommissioned officers, the winners earning an oyster dinner.[39]

Through baseball the bond between officer and enlisted man was secured in the Union ranks. New York City newspapers that had begun reporting baseball scores in recent years began publishing stories about players going off to war, including ninety-one members of the Brooklyn Excelsiors. Sports fans were able to continue reading the exploits of their favorite players, they just needed to read the news section, after the Civil War started, not the sports section.

Additionally, the former ballplayers made for better soldiers, as they were accustomed to wearing uniforms, going through extensive practice drills and working together to achieve a common goal.[40]

Like seeds on the wind, soldiers dispersed to new regions with their regiments and companies in the aftermath of the Christmas 1862 baseball game, sprouting the game everywhere that military action carried them. Baseball games in military camps were "all the rage in the Army of the Potomac" and became so widespread that reports out of Virginia revealed "it was common for ball-players of one regiment or brigade to challenge another regiment or brigade. … [And] these matches were watched by great crowds of soldiers with great interest."[41]

Confederate soldiers also played ballgames, though they tended to play town ball and the Massachusetts style more than the New York rules that were preferred in Union camps.[42] Like their Northern counterparts, Southern medi-

This drawing by Major Otto Boetticher depicts Union prisoners of war playing baseball at the prison camp in Salisbury, North Carolina, in 1863.

cal professionals urged the Confederate troops to participate in athletic endeavors when free from chores or training. Dr. Julian Chisolm, one of the leading surgeons in the South who would later gain fame after the war for his work with Helen Keller, urged Rebel troops to participate daily in the "manly play of base."[43]

Where Chisolm was urging a generic playing of "base," his Northern counterparts specifically cited baseball. The difference between "base" and "baseball" was slight, but it's clear that while Union soldiers were promoting the New York rules of baseball, their Southern counterparts were already familiar with the game overall, they just needed to learn the new rules that were overtaking the nation and the game.

Though it was rare, the realms of Union and Confederate soldiers did overlap at times thanks to baseball. While some anecdotes exist of enemy teams playing against each other, there's no proof of such games occurring. In almost every case, the anecdote can be traced back to Albert Spalding or Abraham Mills, both of whom had financial reasons after the war to invent such tales.

Politics makes for strange bedfellows, as the saying goes, and so, too baseball. In 1863, Union soldiers were camped north of the Rappahannock River in Falmouth, Virginia, and across the water they could easily watch Confederate ballgames being played. John G.B. Adams of the Nineteenth Massachusetts Regiment wrote in his diary that enemy soldiers not only watched each other play baseball games, but used the Rappahannock River as a neutral zone where "our men and theirs met in the river and exchanged papers, tobacco and coffee and were on the best of terms."[44]

Other encounters were not so positive. George H. Putnam shared a famous encounter of Union soldiers playing a baseball game in Texas, unaware that Confederate fighters had spied them and were preparing an ambush. In the middle of the game, Confederate shots rang out, hitting each of the outfielders. The right and left fielders were able to scramble back to safety, but "the center field[er] was hit and was captured." The Union's return volley staved off any more injuries, but the damage had already been done: "We not only lost our center field but … the only baseball in Alexandria."[45]

What happened to that center fielder we will never know, but prisoners of war factored greatly into both the enhancement of baseball's future and the end of the Confederacy.

(14)

•–––– ••••–

POWs

Captured prisoners of war create both a boon and bane for any military. On the positive side, the numbers of enemy combatants on the battlefield have been reduced, supplies and information can be confiscated and a better understanding of the other side can be reached through interrogation and interaction. However, maintaining POWs in humane conditions can be expensive, sapping already depleted reserves of money, food, shelter and clothing.

The Union's naval blockade reduced the economic ability of the South, which had a direct affect on the day-to-day life and overall attitude of Confederate soldiers and their POWs. Tedium affected all soldiers, Union and Confederate, along with the desire to play baseball. It wasn't just a Northern sport, but Union regiments and companies were provided with real sports equipment, either through official government requests (like with General Hays) or direct shipments from manufacturers and civilians.

"Because southerners had a much harder time than their counterparts in obtaining good bats and balls, they generally had to make do with rudimentary home made equipment," historian George B. Kirsch explained.[46]

Discarded boards, fence posts, and just about anything that could be held in the hand and swung with ease was used for a bat; the ball was often nothing more than a cloth-wrapped walnut or stone. Confederate troops made due as best they could, embracing the makeshift games as a relief from boredom. Southern newspapers took up the cause, beseeching readers to send some sporting equipment to the troops.

After the Christmas 1862 game, conditions in prisons grew worse as war rations became scarce. Overcrowding and lack of food kept ballgames from physically happening in many prisons where inmates were forced to eat rats to survive. Yet baseball was still played in some prisons for both Northern and Southern inmates. Prison camps in Salisbury, North Carolina, and Johnson's Island, Ohio, were the settings for many games. The mingling of guards and prisoners from different parts of the country helped popularize the most non-violent version of baseball, the New York game. When the war ended, the rules of New York baseball pollinated the entire country when soldiers, prisoners and guards returned to their homes.

Town ball, the most popular ball game in the South, and other similar versions of baseball allowed for an out to be recorded by hitting the baserunner with the ball. The New York game forbid that and instead had the putout rules of contemporary baseball where a player or base must be tagged with the ball in a glove or hand. Given the overcrowded and ever-increasingly deplorable conditions inside prisons, it isn't difficult to imagine the violence that could erupt from a baserunner getting hit with a baseball to record an out. Josephus Clarkson, a Bostonian imprisoned at Salisbury, revealed that baseball was known across the country, but that the new rules were something that POWs and guards alike had to learn.

"Since many of the men were in a weakened condition, it was agreed to play the faster but less harsh New York rules which intrigued our guards," Clarkson wrote. "The game of baseball had been played much in the south, but many of [the guards] had never seen the sport devised by Mr. Cartwright."[47]

Aside from breathing oxygen, walking on two legs and living in the South, slaves had little in common with Confederate soldiers except for the fact that hardly any of them had seen the New York game either. That would change quickly and so would the racial makeup of baseball players and fans forever.

(15)

●▬ ▬ ▬ ▬ ●●●●●

Emancipation Proclamation

On September 22, 1862, three months prior to the Christmas Day game at Hilton Head, South Carolina, President Abraham Lincoln announced his plan to free all slaves; his Emancipation Proclamation would go into effect on January 1, 1863. Although African American baseball teams had begun playing three years earlier—the first documented game between black baseball teams was played on November 15, 1859, with the Henson Ball Club of Jamaica (located in Queens) defeating the Unknown Club of Weeksville (Brooklyn), 54-43—Lincoln's Proclamation was a catalyst for the introduction of African Americans into the National Pastime. In 1859, there were three known black baseball teams: Henson, Unknown and the Monitors, but their numbers would soon multiply.

Frederick Douglas Jr. played integrated baseball games in 1859 before starting the Alerts in Washington D.C., just one of dozens of black baseball teams formed in Washington, Philadelphia and New York in the 1860s. While free African Americans in the North organized their own teams and leagues, newly freed slaves at Hilton Head were being introduced to the game. Across the young country, black communities embraced baseball for several reasons, not the least of which was the attraction of competing with whites in a non-lethal manner, proving that they were as deserving of taking the field just as much as anyone . (An example of William James' "moral equivalent of war" decades before his essay).

"Before, during and after the Civil War black baseball was inextricably linked to the campaign for African-American civil and political rights," George Kirsch explained in *The New York Times*.[48]

The connection between baseball and civic pride, at least for Union supporters, crossed racial lines after the Emancipation Proclamation. The life of Octavius V. Catto was a prime example of the interweaving of baseball and politics that blossomed during the Civil War (and continues today). Born in South Carolina, Catto's family moved to Philadelphia when he was a teenager. Initially a cricket fan, Catto switched allegiances to baseball during the Civil War. In between fighting to desegregate Philadelphia public transportation, pushing for African American voting rights, campaigning for Lincoln's reelection and mobilizing soldiers for the Union, Catto was co-founder of the Pythian Base Ball Club of Philadelphia.[49] Though motivated by the Emancipation Proclamation to prove that blacks were as equal to whites in any fashion, Catto would soon be disappointed.

Octavius V. Catto

"African-American clubs proliferated" by 1867, and the Pythians, led by Catto, "felt confident that their club could gain official recognition from the Pennsylvania State Association of Base Ball Players, a subsidiary of the National Association" (organized baseball's leading authority).[50] Catto was wrong. Local officials made it clear that the Pythians would not be allowed in the Pennsylvania Association. Undeterred, the Pythians sought admission into the National Association of Base Ball Players' by approaching officials during the league's annual meetings held in Philadelphia.

On December 11, 1867, the NABBP's Nominating Committee recommended that black baseball players be barred from playing in the league. The vote was unanimous "against the admission of any club which may be composed of one or more colored persons."[51]

There it was in black and white: African American baseball players were forbidden from playing baseball with their Caucasian counterparts. Adding insult to the black players' dilemma, the New York Base Ball Association altered its league rules in 1870 to forbid any players of color from competing, urging "colored clubs of New York and Philadelphia" to form their own league. At the same meetings, two known gamblers and game-fixing players were reinstated. In other words, proven cheaters were OK in the NABBP, but non-white players were not.

Insult led to lethal injury a year later on Election Day 1871, when Catto was shot dead by Frank Kelly, a white man, who had attacked another black man earlier in day because of his assumed political sympathies to Lincoln.

Kelly's first attack didn't result in bloodshed, but he sought to fix that with his second assault. When he came across Catto on the street, Kelly shot Catto in the back then, when Catto turned to face his murderer, he fired a second shot fatally to the heart. Just as had happened when he tried to integrate baseball, Catto received no justice for his murder: Kelly was never punished for his cold-blooded killing and was acquitted of all chargers at his eventual trial.[52]

While private institutions such as the NABBP and individual team owners excluded African Americans from their organizations, the United States government had other plans for integration that would change baseball and the nation's war effort.

(16)

•---- -••••

Jim Crow & Buffalo Soldiers

Who was Jim Crow?

It's something of a trick question. The one-word answer is: nobody. The term *Jim Crow* does not refer to a specific person, but rather to the racist, segregation laws, codes, rules and widespread customs that dominated the United States from the 1870s until the 1960s, when Martin Luther King sparked the Civil Rights non-violent movement for equality. The origin of the term is still a mystery, though it most likely began in 1828 when a white singer/actor named Thomas Rice introduced a character named Jim Crow to his traveling shows. Rice's character costume included black face makeup, ragged clothing and he sang in an exaggerated black dialect to the delight of white audiences. The character became very popular and soon the term *Jim Crow* became a popular racial epithet for black people, less severe than *nigger,* but equal in insult to other racial terms such as *sambo, coon* and *picaninny.*[53]

Entire books are dedicated to discussing Jim Crow segregation, but for our purposes it is enough to establish the prevailing national sentiment about African Americans when the U.S. government created a new division of soldier that would amplify the relationship between military action and baseball: Buffalo Soldiers.

Beginning with the freed slaves at Hilton Head, South Carolina, more than 186,000 African Americans served in volunteer infantry, cavalry and artillery units for the Union. Their bravery and contributions could not be ignored and at the end of the Civil War, Congress changed laws that allowed black soldiers to serve in the military, not as volunteers, but as paid soldiers just like every other white recruit.

On July 28, 1866, Congress reorganized the army, expanding the cavalry from six to ten regiments, and the infantry from nineteen to forty-five regiments. Six of the new regiments were the Ninth and Tenth Cavalry as well as the Thirty-Eighth, Thirty-Ninth, Fortieth and Forty-First Infantry, which were comprised of black soldiers led by white officers. In 1869, Congress reorganized the infantry from forty-five regiments to twenty-five, with the Thirty-Eighth and Forty-First Infantry becoming the Twenty-Forth Infantry and the Thirty-Ninth and Fortieth Infantry becoming part of the Twenty-Fifth Infantry. The Ninth and Tenth Cavalry remained the same. In the ensuing decades, the Ninth and Tenth Cavalry and the Twenty-Forth and Twenty-Fifth Infantry saw action in western states (fighting against Native Americans), Cuba (against Spanish soldiers) and in the Philippines (against indigenous guerillas).

These soldiers were soon given the nickname Buffalo Soldiers for reasons that are still unclear. Government archives claim the term was first applied by Native Americans describing troops of the Tenth Cavalry, and that the nickname was quickly applied to all black enlisted men. As with the term *Jim Crow*, there is no definitive genesis of the term *Buffalo Soldier* though historians cite three reasons why the Native Americans, who revered the buffalo, created the soon-to-be-popular nickname: the black curly hair of the soldiers resembled that of the buffalo, the dogged determination and tireless marching the soldiers were willing to undergo echoed a buffalo's determination and the fact that many of the soldiers wore jackets made from buffalo pelts.[54]

Revisionist historians may want to paint a cheery veneer on the term, claiming it was a source of pride, given the high respect Native Americans had for the buffalo, but the reality was that bigotry and prejudice was as rampant in the military as it was in civilian life. Whether Native Americans meant the term as an honor or insult, the term became another racial epithet used by white soldiers and officers, many of whom refused to serve with the Buffalo Soldiers. In 1866, up-and-coming officer George Custer refused the position of colonel in the Ninth Calvary (one of the Buffalo Soldier regiments), opting instead for the lower rank of lieutenant colonel with the Seventh Cavalry, an all-white unit.[55] (In the next chapter, we'll learn that Custer's bigotry would contribute to one of the most infamous slaughters in American military history.)

Buffalo Soldiers altered baseball history beginning in 1894, when Colonel Andrew Burt began a team for the Twenty-Fifth Infantry to provide healthy alternatives to boredom while stationed in Missoula, Montana. The Twenty-Fifth Infantry's baseball team, dubbed the Wrecking Crew or Wreckers, quickly

Buffalo Soldiers, such as those in the 25th Infantry seen in this 1890 photo at Fort Keogh in Montana (top) with some soldiers wearing buffalo robes, had to battle against the negative stereotypes exacerbated by the infamous character Jim Crow (right). Even risking their lives by serving in the military did little to ease racism against the African American soldiers. For example, according the Library of Congress, on the backside of the image above is a handwritten note: "Some of the coons that are in camp at Keogh taken Sunday morning, Dec. 14th '90."

became the most dominant baseball team in the entire U.S. military. They were consistent military league champions wherever they were stationed including a four-year run as Philippine Island Champions (1899-1902), followed by a three-year run as Department of Missouri Champions (1903-1905) and Hawaiian Islands champs from 1914-1918.[56]

The undisputed domination of the Wreckers led to accounts of their games being reported in black newspapers across the nation. Their games attracted thousands of fans of all races and were so popular that a new ballpark was built in Hawaii, paid for by local companies eager to advertise their businesses at the only events to consistently draw thousands of spectators.[57]

More than a dozen future Negro League players filled the Wreckers' roster, including future Hall of Famer Wilber "Bullet Joe" Rogan, and baseball greats like Walter "Dobie" Moore, Oscar "Heavy" Johnson, Andy Cooper, Bob Fagan, Lemuel Hawkins and Hurley McNair. But the Buffalo Soldiers' success didn't come without backlash. Military officials gave preferential treatment to members of the Wrecking Crew, often excusing the soldiers from their military duties to practice and play baseball. This did not sit well with white soldiers on other military baseball teams, particularly when one of the regiment's Buffalo Soldiers openly stated that the Wreckers were more of a professional baseball team that occasionally participated in military exercises than a military unit that played baseball. Government officials didn't help ease the situation when they confirmed in 1915 to a local Hawaiian newspaper that the Wreckers were, indeed, professional baseball players, not merely amateurs who were good at the game, with each team member receiving $20 for the season.

"Our ball players are professionals," Lieutenant Charles Wyman told the *Hawaiian Commercial Appeal.* "They have received pay for playing."[58]

In 1920, Rube Foster began the Negro National League; he was its first president and treasurer as well as being owner and manager of the Chicago American Giants. Competition was fierce in the NNL, prompting Kansas City Monarchs owner J.L. Wilkinson to sign six players from the Wreckers to his team: Fagan, Hawkins, Rogan, McNair, William Linder and Moore.

The heyday of the Buffalo Soldiers baseball team was over due, in large part, to the rise of the NNL as a viable option for players who didn't need to enlist to play professional baseball.

(17)

●▬▬▬▬ ▬▬●●●

Custer's Last Stand

A decade after refusing to lead one of the newly-created Buffalo Soldier regiments, Lieutenant General George Custer and 261 members of his Seventh Cavalry were slaughtered by Sioux, Cheyenne and Lakota warriors on June 25, 1876. Though armed with machine-built rifles and munitions, Custer and his men were killed by Native Americans armed with only hand-made bows, arrows and hatchets. Recent revelations indicate that Custer's real undoing was not enemy combatants, but a combination of egotism and tepid support, underscored by the regiment's baseball history.

"It's a good thing he didn't take us with him," said one African American descendent of the Buffalo Soldiers about Custer, whose baseball bias would factor into his own undoing.[59]

Buffalo Soldiers and their supporters weren't the only ones who had a problem with Custer, who was widely disliked by subordinates, superiors and peers. Even his apologists concede, "few men had more enemies than Custer."[60] No description of Custer would be complete that doesn't point out his narcissism and vanity, a blatant desire to achieve fame and glory through exaggerated acts of bravery that left colleagues and commanders divided between admiration and annoyance. Even his telltale hat, wide-brimmed and often worn askew, was an affectation created by Custer so that he could easily be recognized on the battlefield.

"At times the general could be a pompous ass, as pretentious and flamboyant as a modern-day rock start," wrote one historian of Custer. "He was especially vain about his clothing and appearance—even in the field. Custer, it appears, was fated to be loved or hated by his men, his superiors and posterity. General Ulysses S. Grant, later President Grant, his commanding officer, referred to him as a "strutting peacock.""[61]

Custer's devil-may-care bravado advanced his career during the Civil War, but rolling the dice on fate caught up with him at the Battle of Little Bighorn when he decided to attack a Sioux camp by breaking the 600-man Seventh Cavalry into thirds, giving command of one-third to both Major Marcus Reno and Captain Frederick Benteen. The Indian camps were located on the western side of Little Bighorn River. Custer ordered Reno and his men to cross the river and attack from the south while Custer led his column north along the eastern side of the river. Benteen and his men were ordered to stay out of the action and to cover Custer's flank and rear. Unaware that they were charging into a trap, Reno's column attacked first. The overwhelming number of Native Americans lying in wait slaughtered nearly all of Reno's men. After realizing Reno's men were in trouble, Custer led his third of the regiment into battle, but it was too late.

By hesitating, Custer gave lethal advantage to the opposition. Not only was Custer going against greater numbers, but the warriors who slaughtered Reno's men were now able to turn and join their comrades and help annihilate Custer and his men. Meanwhile, Benteen realized he had been sent on a fool's mission and raced his men into battle. Reno's few retreating soldiers were aided by Benteen's timely return, but the Native American forces pinned down Reno, Benteen and their men for the next thirty-six hours, preventing them from helping Custer and his men. It wouldn't have mattered; Custer and his soldiers were all killed in less than an hour.[62]

"Custer should have held his men together," reported White Man Runs Him, a Native American scout employed by Custer and an eyewitness that day. "Some would have been killed, but not all. Custer was reckless. Instead of Custer going ahead and starting at the same time as Reno, Custer held back and did not start until he saw Reno fighting. That was poor generalship. We do not cut up our command when we fight and say, "While you wait I will fight, and while I wait you will fight." … I have been with other officers of the Army and they attacked differently than Custer did. It did not look right. It was just as if he [Custer] said, "Reno, you go ahead and let them whip you and then I will go ahead and they will whip me." Only seven who crossed the river with Reno came out alive."[63]

Why Custer divided his regiment into thirds has been questioned for more than a century. If White Man Runs Him was correct, that keeping the Seventh Cavalry intact was the only option for survival, why would Custer purposefully send Benteen on a useless mission away from the action?

Shockingly, baseball is a part of the answer.

Years earlier, Custer developed an "Indian Killer" reputation on the East Coast after leading his soldiers into the 1868 Battle of the Washita River that left more than one hundred Native Americans slaughtered. Not only was Benteen unimpressed with Custer's notoriety, he considered the flashy General to be

Some of the important individuals in the Battle of Little Bighorn included (from left to right): Captain Frederick Benteen, General George Custer and White Man Runs Him.

an embarrassment to the military.

"I am only too proud to say that I despised him as a murderer, thief and a liar—all of which I can prove," Benteen once wrote about Custer. What Benteen knew, and would later reveal, was that most of the Washita River Battle victims were women and children who were asleep at the time of Custer's attack. Even worse, they were on reservation lands and were visibly displaying a white flag of peace.[64] Custer's murderous actions went beyond being merely deplorable and amoral, Benteen claimed, they were traitorous. Benteen claimed that Custer remained at the Washita camp, wasting ammunition to kill dogs and ponies as a form of useless revenge instead of defending nineteen soldiers who were killed less than two miles away by Native Americans incensed at Custer's senseless Washita attack.[65]

The *St. Louis Democrat* published Benteen's account of Custer's savagery which enraged Custer. Clearly, Benteen and Custer would never be friends. But baseball further widened the gap between the two.

The differences between Custer and Benteen could not have been more exaggerated. Custer was flamboyant of actions and clothing, with a manicured mustache and soul patch, he was often aloof from his troops, insisting on high moral standards while he secretly suffered from gonorrhea. On the other end of the spectrum, Benteen was clean-shaven, his clothing never a concern, he often got dirty playing baseball with the troops and was known to enjoy drinks with the soldiers. (In his later years, Benteen was court-martialed for, among other issues, being drunk and disorderly).[66]

As the Seventh Cavalry moved west in the late 1860s, baseball became part of their daily life. Bats and balls, due to their scarcity, were valued possessions and protected by Benteen, who was an avid fan and player. Popular with the enlisted men, Benteen was welcomed where Custer was shunned. The chasm between the two led to two baseball teams being formed in the Seventh Cavalry:

the Actives and the Benteens. No records indicate what position Benteen played, leading historians to speculate he was the team manager. An assumption supported by Custer's refusal to never watch games that involved the Benteen nine.

"Intensely hated by the Benteen players, Custer watched only the Active ball games," historian Robert Elias explained. "While the Actives remained north and played baseball in North Dakota, the Benteens were sent in 1874 to help suppress civil unrest in New Orleans."[67]

In 1875, the two teams were reassembled in the Dakotas months before the Battle of Little Bighorn.

"Custer anticipated an easy victory and split his forces [at Little Bighorn]," Elias explained. "To rob his detested subordinate of the glory (possibly due in part to a baseball rivalry), he sent Captain Benteen on a scouting mission."

The Benteens baseball team never played again after that bloody day, though five players survived the infamous battle. Second baseman William "Fatty" Williams had already signed to play for Pittsburgh, but was so injured at Little Bighorn he never took to the baseball field again. Pitcher Joseph McCurry, the best Benteen player who planned to play professionally after his commission, survived, but was wounded in the shoulder, killing his baseball hopes. Likewise, Alex and Charlie Bishop were wounded that day and never played baseball again.[68]

The fifth survivor was shortstop Andrew Burt. Though there's no evidence Burt played baseball again, he changed baseball history in a way that would likely rile the bigoted Custer. In 1892, Burt was made colonel and, two years later, was given command of the Twenty-Fifth Infantry. One of Burt's first acts for his famous Buffalo Soldiers was to do what he learned from Benteen: he began an infantry baseball team. Burt's team became the famous Wrecking Crew that dominated military leagues before Negro League owners signed all the best players to professional contracts.

(18)

•▬▬▬▬ ▬▬▬••

President of Fantasy Baseball

Tommy Wilson was an average boy growing up in Augusta, Georgia, a teenager who enjoyed sports and the outdoors. If there was one thing that stood out about the boy it was his propensity for detail. His friends didn't seem to mind because his fastidiousness actually came in handy at times, like when the second baseman would make the lineups for their baseball games.

The Light Foot Base Ball Club was formed in the late 1860s as an informal neighborhood group, a boys-only club of teens looking to have fun after school. In 1870, Wilson became the group's president and official record keeper. It was around this time that his unusual attention to detail began to surface. Wilson wrote formal bylaws for the club, which he insisted must follow Parliamentary Procedure during their meetings. It may have been a little extreme, but that was nothing like what Wilson did in his free time once he got a taste for baseball.

For the baseball-loving fourteen year old, the 1871 season was a dream come true. A new league had been launched, the National Association of Professional Base Ball Players (NA) which changed the entertainment landscape across the nation. The NA replaced the National Association of Base Ball Players, which began in 1858, but was comprised almost entirely of amateur teams from the Northeast, primarily New York and Pennsylvania.

Created by players eager to be paid for their work, the NA featured teams outside of the Northeast (Chicago, Illinois; Rockford, Illinois; and Cleveland, Ohio) and gave the players more control of salaries and schedules.

Tommy Wilson was president of the Light Foot Base Ball Club as a child before becoming President Woodrow Wilson as an adult. In this photo, President Wilson is throwing out the first pitch of the 1916 season.

On May 4, 1871, nineteen-year-old pitcher Bobby Mathews led the Kekiongas of Fort Wayne to a 2-0 win against the visiting Forest City of Cleveland in the league's debut game. In the end, the NA proved to be more of a semi-pro league at best, with uncertain payments and schedules, teams seemingly coming and going overnight. There was no way to know that the NA would only stumble forward for just a few years during that inaugural 1871 season that was so magical to Wilson that he created what is believed to be the world's first fantasy baseball league.

"[He] created a whole universe of players, statistics and a pennant race, with or without the aid of dice," MLB official historian John Thorn explained. "Wilson did not create players or teams. He used only the cast of characters in the real-world National Association of 1871, which he surely read about in the sporting weeklies."[69]

The amount of detail he created for his fictional season was astonishing, even extrapolating his make-believe statistics out to four decimal points. Every pitch, hit, run scored, putout recorded and final score was Wilson's fantasy. In the real world, the Philadelphia Athletics won the 1871 NA championship with a record of 21-7, topping the Chicago White Stockings' mark of 19-9. Wilson didn't appear to like that version of reality and moved the Athletics to the middle of the pack with a record of 11-16; and he gave Chicago a record of 16-11, which trailed only the Kekionga Club of Fort Wayne's 16-9 record (in the real 1871 season, Kekionga was a disappointing 7-12).

Wilson never lost his love for baseball, not when he played at Davidson College in North Carolina for a year before transferring to and graduating from

Princeton, or even when he went into his eventual profession, politics.

If you never heard of Tommy Wilson the politician that's because while at Princeton he stopped using his first name and began using his middle and last name for all his correspondence: Woodrow Wilson.

In 2013, a reference librarian at the Library of Congress unearthed Wilson's 1871 fantasy baseball league. After much research, Thorn concluded that while it may seem far-fetched, the twenty-eighth president of the United States was the creator of fantasy baseball: "I believe Wilson commenced his work here in March-April of 1871," Thorn wrote. "This was the record of a magical mystery tour, played between the young Wilson's ears."[70]

Even in death Chicago's William Hulbert was bigger than life. More than a century after his burial, Hulbert made sure than anyone who sees his massive gravestone in Graceland Cemetery knew that baseball was a big deal to him. His baseball-shaped gravestone stands approximately four feet tall and is still one of most popular markers in the Chicago cemetery known as the final resting spot for many celebrities.

(19)

Going Global

While Native Americans were having their future forever altered by the western migration of American society, a businessman in Chicago was similarly altering the future of sports.

William Hulbert, who was born near Cooperstown, New York, was one of the founding members of the National Association of Professional Base Ball Players. Though originally from the East Coast, Hulbert made his fortune in Chicago and loved the city so much he was fond of saying that he'd "rather be a lamppost in Chicago than a millionaire elsewhere."

The Great Chicago Fire of 1871 decimated Chicago's hopes of maintaining its first-place standing in the inaugural NA season. The team's uniforms, equipment, clubhouse and ballpark all burned, Hulbert's baseball dreams literally going up in smoke. Rebuilding Chicago forced Hulbert's team out of action until the 1874 season, and when the successful businessman returned to league action he was determined to win the championship that was lost to him thanks to Mrs. O'Leary's cow and the fire it allegedly set in Chicago.

Aggressive and impatient, Hulbert grew frustrated with league rules that he felt favored Eastern teams and by an organizations run by amateurs, not seasoned businessmen. Though the NA was technically the first professional league in sports, it was a "fledgling" enterprise with "fly-by-night clubs" that consistently cancelled games or even the remainder of a season without notice.[70] The only thing professional about the NA was that players were paid money, but the overall management of the league was amateurish by any definition. Fueled by a combination of baseball passion and concern about his financial investment in his team, the Chicago White Stockings (later renamed Cubs), Hulbert decided it was time to create a *real* professional league that was run by businessmen who had an eye on long-term success, not players just happy to be paid for one day's efforts.

From the first baseball games at Elysian Fields, debates about which teams and players were professional and which were amateurs raged in every town. The establishment of the National Association of Professional Base Ball Players in 1871 drew a line in the sand forever between amateur and professional players, launching a first in global sports: the first professional sports league, albeit "fledgling."

But five years later, on February 2, 1876, at the Grand Central Hotel in New York City, Hulbert took the NA one step further by launching the world's first *successful* professional sports league. Fraught with business problems from the beginning, the NA successfully separated professional from amateur ballplayers, but it was Hulbert's team, the White Stockings (not to be confused with the White Sox created years later in the American League), and his new league, the National League (the same NL that plays today), that would successfully turn a sport into a sustainable business. The NL left no ambiguity or want for amateurs: it was the world's first fully professional sports league from top to bottom, run by businessmen as a money-making venture, not merely a form of entertainment with teams that may or may not exist a day, week or month later.

At the end of the 1875 NA season, Hulbert began his coup of the NA by poaching the best player in Boston, pitcher Albert Spalding, for the princely sum of $4,000 to be player/manager for the Chicago White Stockings. Spalding wasn't the only player that Hulbert cherry-picked from the other NA teams during that 1875 season. Philadelphia's top player, Adrian Anson, agreed to join Hulbert's new league and became a Chicago icon for decades where he was known as Cap Anson, in deference to his lengthy tenure as team captain. Knowing that NA officials would certainly cancel the 1876 contracts Hulbert signed with players while they still played the 1875 season with their current teams, the Chicago owner secretly sought out other team owners who wanted to start a new league, allowing them the freedom to ignore any decisions by NA officials, too. Hulbert found like-minded team executives in Boston, Cincinnati, Hartford, Louisville, New York, Philadelphia, and St. Louis; and the NL was born.

Hulbert bet his organization's future on Spalding because the pitcher was no simple player. In addition to being the best player in the game, the native of Rockford, Illinois, was also one of the most innovative businessmen in the game and was eager to stop playing baseball and start selling it.

Spalding led Chicago to the first NL championship in 1876, going 47–12 with a 1.75 ERA. The burgeoning city of Chicago was the perfect location from which to launch the sporting goods empire of which Spalding dreamed. On February 12, 1876, Spalding and his brother, J. Walter, borrowed $800 from their mother to open a sporting goods store at 118 Randolph Street in Chicago.

Her investment proved wise as Spalding soon convinced NL officials to contract his company, Spalding & Bros., to supply the league's official baseballs. Spalding's company held the contract for a century, until Rawlings replaced them in 1977. (The American League also used Spalding baseballs from 1888 to 1973.)

Spalding left the playing field after the 1877 season to become secretary of the White Stockings. As the right-hand man to Hulbert, a successful businessman in coal and real estate, Spalding learned business tactics that would change professional sports globally.

By his late twenties, Spalding was a sports tycoon. His company's contracts with the NL and AL made him the most influential man in baseball and then other sports. Spalding & Bros. was constantly expanding: in 1878 they were the first publisher of baseball's official set of rules; in 1887 they manufactured the first football; in 1894, they became the official manufacturer of both the rules book and the ball for professional basketball.[72]

When Hulbert died in 1882, he left a massive void at the top of baseball's hierarchy; his foresight and guidance had changed the landscape of American sports forever, ushering in the era of true professional sports. Spalding stepped in as the White Stockings owner and president of the team until 1891. During his tenure as secretary and then owner, Spalding proved himself to be one of the smartest men in baseball, as well as the richest. Though the Cubs would become known for more than a century without a championship, the organization, known then as the White Stockings, dominated baseball during the last decade of the nineteenth century, taking first in the NL five times and second twice.

But dominating the American landscape was only the beginning. Spalding's company needed more markets in which to grow. While pitching for Boston in 1874, Spalding was part of the first baseball tour abroad. The tour of Great Britain was a failure, in no small part because most British fans considered baseball to be merely a form of their childhood games, only played by men who took themselves too seriously.

Learning from that experience, Spalding created the first true global tour for any professional sports team or league. Between the 1888 and 1889 seasons, Spalding, whose team was in the midst of baseball's first pro championship dynasty, took a select group of his White Stockings around the world to play exhibition games against handpicked players from other teams. Spalding's All-Star World Tour played exhibition games in Australia, making stops along the way in Hawaii, Sri Lanka, Egypt, Italy, and France, showcasing the sport to would-be fans worldwide.

Globalization is a common term in sports today, but it all began in 1888 with professional sports' first true dynasty that led to the world's first global tour which sought to create markets for Spalding to sell equipment in every time zone.

The business lessons Spalding learned from Hulbert allowed the former pitcher to secretly consolidate baseball's manufacturers in a similar fashion to the way Hulbert clandestinely created the NL right under the noses of NA officials. Boston's Wright brothers beat Spalding to the merchandising market, but eventually either became part of Spalding's empire or trampled by it. In 1871, both Harry and George Wright launched competing sports manufacturing companies. Harry Wright and partner Charlie Gould, his former teammate, launched a sports goods store at 18 Boylston Street in Boston. The company lasted only two years; and by the time Wright was able to launch a new company with different partners in 1879, Spalding & Bros. was dominating the marketplace. Harry's younger brother, George, also launched his sports company in 1871, partnering with Henry Ditson to form Wright & Ditson, a sporting goods manufacturer that still exists today.

In Philadelphia, Al Reach established his own successful sporting empire as well. Both Reach and George Wright surreptitiously sold their companies to Spalding, who insisted that both firms continue to do business under their own names to create the appearance of competition. Spalding eventually asked both Reach and George Wright to be two of the seven members of his infamous Mills Commission in 1905.[73]

(20)

Proud to Pirate

Lou Bierbauer in 1888

When life imitates art, the results can be surprising and even funny. Such was the case with an infamous example of appropriation of a name, this time with a humorous angle, unless you're a fan of the old Philadelphia Athletics. Two of the short-lived leagues in baseball history were the American Association from 1882 to 1891 and the Players Association of 1890.

By the end of the 1889 season Philadelphia's Lou Bierbauer had established himself as arguably the top second baseman in the AA. Shortstop John Montgomery Ward was the player/manager of the Brooklyn Ward Wonders. Ward was not only the creator of the PL, but he saw Bierbauer as a great double-play partner who would entertain the New York fans.

The PL lasted only the 1890 season. Due to the reserve clause that existed then, most players had no choice but to return to the team that held their rights from the 1889 season. The Philadelphia Athletics, however, had not filed the paperwork to retain Bierbauer's rights for the 1891 season. Realizing he had leverage in negotiating with any team, Bierbauer reached terms on a more lucrative agreement with the Pittsburgh Alleghenys.

Philadelphia executives cried foul, but arbitrators awarded Bierbauer's rights to Pittsburgh. Newspaper stories and baseball fans everywhere claimed the Alleghenys "pirated" Bierbauer from Philadelphia.

Embracing the media firestorm, Pittsburgh appropriated the pejorative being labeled on them anyway and officially changed its name from Alleghenys to Pirates beginning with the 1891 season. Since then, the organization has been known to baseball fans everywhere as the Pittsburgh Pirates.

Section III:

•–• ––– ••– –• –•• •• –• ––•

ROUNDING THE BASES

– •••• • –••• •– ••• • •••

(21)

●●▬▬▬ ●▬▬▬▬

Which Roosevelt Is That Again?

"Well, that's George Washington and that's Thomas Jefferson and that's Abraham Lincoln," the elderly man explained to his wife as they walked toward Mount Rushmore. "The other's Roosevelt."

"Which Roosevelt?" She asked.

"FDR!" He yelled, full of annoyance (and ignorance). "Why would it be the other one? What did he do?"

That was a real conversation I overheard on the observation deck at Mount Rushmore National Memorial in South Dakota years ago. The elderly couple could have used a refresher on the Roosevelt family, but for baseball fans the achievements and differences between the two presidents were enormous and important to the advancement of the game around the world. Both Franklin D. Roosevelt, the thirty-second President of the United States, and his cousin, Theodore Roosevelt, the twenty-sixth, advanced baseball and American politics during wartime, but for very different reasons.

We'll talk more about FDR's contributions to the game when we get to World War II. But for now we will focus on Teddy Roosevelt, who hated baseball but, ironically, was a catalyst to the sport's global reach. Everything about Theodore Roosevelt was a contradiction to the point that someone could easily question his true feelings on many topics.

Roosevelt's visage appears on Mount Rushmore, in part, for his contributions as a conservationist (his aggressive expansion of the National Park System earned him the nickname "the conservation president"), soldier (his vol-

President Theodore Roosevelt would be honored to learn that his image was etched into Mount Rushmore, but he would likely be displeased to learn that his actions in the Spanish-American War helped baseball expand around the globe.

unteer cavalry unit, the First Volunteer Cavalry, took San Juan Hill, a key battle in the Spanish-American War) and sports hero (his direct intervention saved American football). Yet at every turn, Roosevelt was baffling. Part of his personal motivation to create many new national parks was due to the fact that while he was big game hunting, he couldn't find enough animals to kill.[74] While he did resign his post as Assistant Secretary of the Navy on May 6, 1898, in order to volunteer for battle, he made sure that his uniform was unique and better-tailored than other volunteers, hemmed specially by experts at the famous Brooks Brothers company.[75] His involvement in sports is equally bewildering. A sickly child who suffered from asthma and was not allowed to play outdoors, much less participate in sports growing up, Roosevelt craved a masculine persona as he matured, favoring football versus baseball, a sport he detested so much that his hatred for the game exacerbated American political rifts that still run deep today.

Though Roosevelt hated baseball, the Spanish-American War, which was a significant part of his career, did as much to cement the relationship between patriotism and the American Pastime as any other event.

(22)

●●▬▬▬ ●●▬▬▬

A Splendid Little War

Spain's reign in the Western Hemisphere ended with the short but important Spanish-American War. Detested by the indigenous people they ruled, Spain's domination from Cuba to South America and the Philippines began in the late fifteenth century, but ended in 1898.

In the aftermath of the Civil War, America was primed for expansion. The raw resources abundant throughout Central and South America were too appealing to a country that sought to spread its power and influence. Throughout most of the Americas, centuries of brutal Spanish rule had primed furious subjects for revolution.

Cuban students studying in America during the Civil War, returned to their homeland with bats, balls and a sense of freedom, all of which were new to the island nation. Before William Hulbert created the National League in 1876, Cuba's first professional baseball team, the Habana Baseball Club, was founded in 1872. In 1873, the Matanzas Baseball Club was begun. In 1878, the Liga General de Base Ball de la Isla de Cuba (Cuban League) began, the island's first professional baseball league, which spread across the country faster than a good rumor.

"Virtually every town and city of any size organized at least one team," wrote Cuban historian Louis A. Perez Jr. "In all, more than two hundred baseball teams were organized in Cuba between the late 1870s and early 1890s."[76] Cuban-born player Esteban "Steve" Bellán learned the sport while attending school in New York and helped found the Cuban League. American baseball teams began barnstorming Cuba in 1879; and in 1889 the Cuban Giants announced plans to play regular games at the famous Elysian Fields, the alleged birthplace of modern baseball. The Cuban Giants were created in 1885 by combining the players from four black baseball teams shunned in the U.S., but welcomed in the island nation (Keystones, Orions, Manhattans, Argyles).[77]

Expanding American interests in Cuba led to the deployment of the *USS Maine* in the waters outside of Havana. Launched on November 18, 1889, the *USS Maine* was built in the Brooklyn Navy Yard, the same shipyard that gave rise to the famous Brooklyn Excelsiors baseball team.[78] The baseball roots that the *USS Maine* was built upon continued while the battleship was deployed along the east coast. In December 1897, a baseball team from the *USS Maine* defeated a team from the *USS Marblehead*,18-3, in Key West, Florida, earning the Navy baseball championship. The star southpaw pitcher for the *USS Maine* team was William Lambert, the only African American player on the team. Weeks later Lambert and all but one of his teammates were killed when the *USS Maine* exploded under mysterious circumstances on February 15, 1898.

The explosion killed 260 of the 350 men aboard that night. Despite Spanish ships immediately lending aide, Spain was accused of causing the explosion with a mine. (Other theories included a Cuban mine planted to draw the Americans into war or an accidental combustion of coal reserves in the ship's hull. The precise cause of the explosion has never been identified.)

Emotions quickly escalated and on April 24 Spain declared war on the United States, which declared war on Spain the following day, though made retroactive to April 21. On May 1, U.S. ships decimated the Spanish fleet in Manila Bay in the Philippines. By July 17, Spanish ships and forces in Cuba were similarly destroyed. On December 10, Spain and the United States signed the Treaty of Paris, which ended the war and awarded all sovereignty of Cuba, Puerto Rico, Guam and the Philippines to the U.S. in exchange for $20 million dollars. Hawaii, previously an independent state, was also annexed as part of the treaty.

Though it lasted less than eight months, the Spanish-American War changed the U.S. from a country based solely in North America to a world power with far-reaching possessions. Secretary of State John Hay described the conflict as a "splendid little war."[79]

Baseball fans and American military strategists could not agree more because, thanks to the Spanish-American War, the sun no longer set on either's far-reaching empire.

(23)

••▬▬▬ •••▬▬

Dogs, Defiance, & Revolt

In 2008, while on a trip to Peru, one of my goals, aside from climbing Machu Picchu, was to learn more about the terrorist group Shining Path (*Sendero Luminoso*) directly from citizens, not history books. Fearful of backlash, nobody would speak about the organization. One woman heard my questions and she raised her skirt just enough to reveal her calf and ankle, her entire lower leg covered in scars: *"Esto es Sendero Luminoso,"* she said. ("This is Shining Path.")

As a child, she was on a bus that exploded from a hidden bomb planted by members of Sendero Luminoso. She was lucky to survive with just scars to her legs, she said, adding that several people died. The money to be made in narcotics turned the political group into something more akin to drug lords than political protestors, she explained. Sensing someone I could trust, I asked her an off-the-wall question that had fascinated me my entire time in Peru.

"Why are there so many dogs everywhere?" I asked.

"Because we hate the Spanish," she said. "Dogs are Peru. Cats are Spain. Burros are Peru. Horses are Spain."

Even in the twenty-first century, she explained, a Peruvian who possessed horses and cats instead of burros (or donkeys) and dogs was not to be trusted. So too, she added, was anyone who still attended bullfights.

Active defiance against government leaders takes many forms and baseball has been key among them. Just like the Peruvians who own dogs, not cats, and refuse to attend bullfights as a sign of native solidarity, Cubans used baseball to defy their Spanish rulers.

"Cubans celebrated the modernity and progress implied in baseball, associated with the United States, and denounced the inhumanity and backwardness suggested by the bullfight," explained Louis A. Pérez, Jr., a professor at the University of North Carolina. "Baseball became another way to express disaffection with Spain. … Baseball as an expression of change and as an agent of change."[80]

As soon as they saw Cubans supporting baseball, not bullfighting, Spanish rulers immediately sensed revolt and viewed baseball as a threat. Their fear of the new sport proved to be well-founded. When the Matanzas Baseball Club was formed in 1873, Spain banned the sport for a year as "anti-Spanish." Spain also banned baseball team names like *Yara* and *Anacanoa* that blatantly incited Cuban resistance. (A revolt by indigenous Cubans in the town of Yara sparked the Ten Years' War for independence that led to the popular chant *'Grito de Yara'* (Cry of Yara); Anacanoa was a princess executed by Spanish officials centuries earlier.) In 1881, Spanish authorities stopped the creation of a team in Cardenas for fear that it was teaching Cubans to fight against the government.

They were correct.

Cubans were using baseball as an act of defiance. It may have been the first time the island nation did so, but it wouldn't be the last. In fact, Cuban officials have repeatedly used baseball as an international act of rebellion. Defiance and banning specific sports can work both ways: one of the first actions taken by General Leonard Wood, commander of Theodore Roosevelt's First Volunteer Cavalry who became Military Governor of Cuba after the Treaty of Paris, was to ban the Spanish "sport" of bullfighting.[81]

The Spanish-American War allowed Cuba to use baseball as a weapon against their oppressors, but in other theaters of the war—Hawaii and the Philippines particularly—American military commanders learned how to weaponize the sport formally, using it as a means of both social control and widespread distraction. Cuba's use of baseball was so vital to the country's development that we will examine this topic in detail in the final chapter, but first we will discover how baseball saved lives and helped build the foundation for other countries under American domination.

(24)

••▬▬▬ ••••▬

Starting & Ending Revolutions

Hand grenades, Hawaiian history, the political conflict between British and American interests and the future of China were all altered by baseball prior to the 1898 annexation of the island nation by the United States. The hand grenade's history began more than a millennium earlier when Roman and Chinese armies hurled gunpowder encased in a fragmentary shells with a wick that could be lighted, causing mayhem, damage and death from a safe distance. But early grenades were closer in size to a cannon ball than anything that could be manually tossed. Technological advancements reduced the size of a grenade and gave rise to grenadier companies in British and French armies that specialized in the hand-tossed weapon.

In 1778, British Captain James Cook landed on the Hawaiian Islands, establishing the first European presence in the Pacific. By 1820, American Protestant missionaries began arriving from the United States. In 1841, the Punahou School was founded in Honolulu to give American families a local school for their children instead of sending them to the mainland for a good education. The alumni of Punahou were the children of some of the wealthiest and most powerful families in Hawaii, and their influence over the inhabitants would soon be revealed by the sporting entertainment they introduced to the islands.

In 1863, bishops from the Church of England founded the 'Iolani

School (also referred to as Bishop's College School), giving British families a school where English ideals were instilled. 'Iolani's founders were "staunchly critical of the United States and its growing influence on the Hawaiian islands."[82]

In 1866, Punahou alumnus William Castle returned to Hawaii after studying for two years at Ohio's Oberlin College and brought back with him the New York rules of baseball. Later that year, the first two baseball teams formed anywhere in the world outside of the United States began in Hawaii: the Pacifics and Pioneers. By 1870 the Whangdoodles, Pensacolas and Athletics expanded Hawaii's first baseball league to five teams and were soon followed by the Stars and Honolulus.[83]

To the chagrin of British loyalists and 'Iolani supporters, the American sport took hold with islanders, drawing thousands to see games. In June 1871, King David Kalākaua became the first Hawaiian royal family member to attend a game, watching the Athletics and Pensacolas take the field.[84]

The Reciprocity Treaty of 1875 drove the wedge between American and British sentiments even deeper. All sugar in the United States originated from Southern states, but the Civil War reduced sugar production, which escalated prices. Though sugar production resumed at the end of the Civil War, American demand was more than what national companies could provide. The Reciprocity Treaty between Hawaii and the U.S. allowed sugar to be shipped tax-free to the mainland in exchange for the American Navy to use the deep-channel Pearl River, giving the United Staters a strategic military advantage.

British and French inhabitants were infuriated at the treaty, which further married the interests of American and Hawaiian industry at the expense of other nations. Baseball cemented American and Hawaiian interests even more after locals quickly adopted the sport as a new favorite pastime. While the 'Iolani School's British roots kept it from fielding a team initially, it couldn't stop students from learning the game.

In 1879, 'Iolani's most famous future alumnus began his studies. Though he wasn't able to learn baseball from 'Iolani teachers, the student became a fan of the game in his free time and when he eventually returned to his homeland three year later, he took the game with him. Back in his native country, that 'Iolani alumnus used baseball to build and train a revolutionary army which ended China's imperial dynastic rule that had governed for more than 4,000 years.

In 1911, Sun Yat-sen established the Republic of China, using baseball as a two-fold weapon: the new American sport undermined Qing Dynasty rulers, allowing Chinese citizens a taste of the modern world, and, on a practical level, the sport helped Sun teach young revolutionaries how to throw hand grenades.

"His [Sun Yat-sen's] baseball club masked its revolutionary purposes, and throwing baseballs had practical application for future grenade tossers," explained historian Gerald R. Gems. "Eight clubs played baseball in the Shanghai league in 1912, and only a year later there were leagues in six provinces."[85]

Baseball Helps End Hawaiian Revolt

Baseball and hand grenades were also a key aspect of "the only rebellion in history ever put down by a baseball player."[86] By 1889, the 'Iolani School succumbed to the popularity of baseball and fielded its first squad. Ironically, that same year baseball helped squash rebel forces attempting to undo the domination of Hawaii by foreign-born people (predominantly American and British). Known as the Bayonet Constitution of 1887, the revolt stripped Kalākaua of his power, rendered him a figurehead and granted excessive power to land owners, who were almost entirely foreigners.

Robert Wilcox in the Honolulu police station after his arrest following the 1889 revolt attempt. Though faint in this old photogrpah, the prison bars are visible behind him.

Though the coup was bloodless, it was unpopular with Hawaiian natives and sympathizers. Robert Wilcox, a Hawaiian who graduated from an Italian military academy, led a revolt against the usurpers of Kalākaua's reign. On July 30, 1889, Wilcox and his supporters stormed the 'Iolani Palace to liberate Kalākaua and end the Bayonet Constitution. Though he initially agreed to help Wilcox, Kalākaua betrayed him. When Wilcox and his men entered the palace, they found it empty: Kalākaua went into hiding nearby instead of allowing Wilcox to free him. Honolulu militiamen surrounded the palace, forcing Wilcox and his men to retreat to a royal bungalow that was protected by an eight-foot coral wall. With no clear shot at Wilcox or his men, the Honolulu militia needed a plan to draw the insurgents out into the open.

Hay Wodehouse, a catcher for the Honolulu baseball team, hatched a simple plan: he would use his baseball skills to hurl bombs onto the bungalow from a safe distance. Wodehouse enlisted the help of another baseball player, Arthur C. Turton, to light the dynamite explosives that Wodehouse threw. After Wodehouse's third bomb exploded on or next to the bungalow, Wilcox surrendered.

Wodehouse's baseball affection and his use of it to squash Wilcox's insurrection were both ironic because Wodehouse's father, James Hay Wodehouse Sr., was the British consul to Hawaii and president of a local cricket club. Hay Wodehouse's baseball skills not only led to Wilcox's capture, but also bolstered indigenous support of American baseball, which diminished the British influence in the Hawaiian Islands that his father had fought for years to establish.

(25)

●●▬▬▬ ●●●●●

Headhunters & Arctic Home Runs

Manila, the capital of the Philippines, may be more than 5,500 miles away from Herschel Island in the Arctic waters north of the Yukon, but the two locations became forever linked in the aftermath of the Spanish-American War due to Brigadier General Frederick Funston. Though the U.S. paid Spain for the rights to the Philippines as part of the Treaty of Paris, nobody had bothered to ask the native Filipinos what they thought. As it turned out, the Filipinos were not interested in trading one foreign ruler for another.

Resistance to American domination led to the Filipino Insurrection from 1899 to 1902. Led by Emilio Aguinaldo, Filipino resistance fighters battled Americans for control of the Philippines' future until Funston captured Aguinaldo on March 23, 1901. President Theodore Roosevelt issued a proclamation that officially ended the insurrection on July 4, 1902. Taking control of the Philippines extended the American empire far into the Pacific, leading to encounters with very different cultures which flamed an exaggerated American attitude of Social Darwinism. The racist attitudes that gave rise to Jim Crow rules were even more blatantly stated in the Philippines. American diplomats and missionaries alike aimed to civilize America's new "Brown Brothers in the isles" who were "genetically inferior" through the use of baseball. Major Arlie Pond, a former pitcher, and Reverend George W. Dunlap, a former catcher, led the baseball instruction and were supported by Funston, who had become an American hero for capturing Aguinaldo.[87]

Though standing just 5-foot-5 and weighing only 120 pounds, Funston believed in the unifying force of baseball. His belief in the sport during wartime was born out of his experiences while stationed in Alaska years earlier. In 1894, Funston embarked on a 600-mile round trip to help stranded whaling ships in the Arctic waters around Herschel Island. He was stunned by what he found upon his arrival on March 29, 1894. The crews of the seven stranded whaling ships were playing baseball, competing fiercely for the Arctic Whalemen's Pennant, a competition they had devised to pass the idle time. The prized first-place "pennant" was merely a strip of fabric nailed to a broom handle.[88] The whalers took the games seriously, insisting that all games be played no matter the weather conditions or else the loser forfeited. Playing in thick fur garments with temperatures dropping to forty degrees below zero, errors and mistakes were abundant. But that wasn't the point.

Brigadier General Frederick Funston

Spirits were high because of the games, which fostered deep camaraderie between rival ships because teams were composed of men working in similar professions, not by their ship of origin. Cooks teamed with other cooks, officers with other officers, firemen with other firemen, and so on. Official officer rankings meant nothing on the icy ball "field" where a lowly sailor may coach or "boss" his captain without fear of reprisal, which created a positive atmosphere despite the brutal conditions.[89]

In the Philippines, baseball again would be used to create positive relations. The Twenty-Fifth Regiment (Buffalo Soldiers) dominated the baseball action that began in Manila, but soon spread to every corner of the Philippines. Thousands of native Filipinos turned out to watch the African American players of the Twenty-Fifth Regiment, and soon learned the finer points of gamesmanship. As an act of rebellion, some Filipino natives pretended to know nothing about the game when invited by American soldiers to play. Only after urging their American counterparts to wage heavily on the game did the Filipinos reveal that they had indeed learned to play the game and beat the Americans.[90]

But it was the involvement of a future president, William Howard Taft, who may have had the most important role in baseball and the Philippines. Taft was directly involved in numerous scandals involving baseball, largely based on his family's ownership of the National League baseball team in Chicago known today as the Cubs, which we will investigate in upcoming chapters. As the acting Governor-General of the Philippines, Taft was dismayed by the hostile natives who still participated in headhunting. The Igorot and Ifugao tribes in the mountains were still very active headhunters in the early twentieth century. Members of both tribes would decapitate another for a variety of reasons from avenging a slight to blessing the crops. Hoping to end the savagery of the headhunters, Taft instructed soldiers to introduce baseball to them. The strategy worked, exemplified by the headhunters' alleged amendment to an ancient marriage custom thanks to the sport.

An Ifugao warrior proudly poses with some prized possessions, including several human heads that can be seen on the platform above him. Photo taken in 1912.

Another reason for decapitating an enemy tribesman was, oddly, for love. One headhunting custom was that a warrior could not marry until he presented the head of his enemy to his future bride. That tradition was altered, however, after the tribes learned about baseball. Tribe elders changed their decapitation marriage custom, allowing bachelors to marry their bride-to-be after hitting a home run, instead of killing a man. Reports claimed that American players would purposefully bobble easy plays, allowing a sure out to become a miraculous home run, in order for a wedding to occur and a beheading avoided.

"The one who profited the most by the switch in tradition were the suitors' enemies," recalled Ernie Harwell, the former Detroit Tigers announcer. "Under the new custom they managed to keep their heads while yelling, *"Kill the umpire!"*"[91]

Just as Spain had attempted to ban baseball in Cuba, America tried to subdue the Filipinos' lust for sports other than baseball. In 1902, the American-guided Philippine Commission banned some of the most popular pastimes in the Philippines, notably boxing and cock fighting.[92] Under Taft's direction, baseball was to become the nation's new favored sport. Manila's Paco Baseball Park was built in 1903, and within a decade there were more than 1,200 baseball teams in the island nation. Though initially played by soldiers, baseball became a way for Filipinos to compete against their new American dictators and was an added way to non-violently compete with other Asian nations. The Far Eastern

Games were played every two years from 1913 to 1938 with the Philippines winning the initial competition, before taking second to China for the next six consecutive games.

Old habits die hard, however, and America's sports bans didn't last. Cock fighting is still one of the most popular (and infamous) pastimes in the Philippines, which was home to one of boxing's biggest events, the 1975 "Thrilla in Manila" bout between Muhammad Ali and Joe Frazier. In 2010, boxing champion Manny Pacquiao became a member of the Philippine House of Representatives after creating a new political party (People's Champ Movement) that helped him win the election in a landslide. The only Philippine native known to have played in the major leagues was pitcher Bobby Chouinard who debuted for Oakland in 1996.

(26)

●●▬▬▬ ▬●●●●

Destined to Rule the World

While the United States was using baseball to control the Philippines, Japan was doing the same as they conquered Korea and eastern Russia. By 1905, baseball was sprouting throughout all of Asia. The Philippines created the country's first organized youth baseball league in Manila; two Chinese teams played in the country's first game on the mainland; missionaries introduced baseball to Korean communities and Japan, mimicking America's ongoing expansion, conquered rival countries with baseball games and gunpowder.

Tokyo's Waseda University dispatched its baseball team on a goodwill mission to the West Coast of the United States, playing twenty-six games against American teams (Waseda won seven) to create positive American sympathies for a country that was at war with Russia. Similar to the surprise attack on Pearl Harbor decades later, Japan launched a surprise attack on Russia's naval base at Port Arthur on the Liaodong Peninsula in China in 1904 and by early 1905 had taken control of the port. In August 1905, President Theodore Roosevelt's advisers negotiated the Treaty of Portsmouth, which gave Japan control of the peninsula, Korea and parts of Manchuria. Ten years earlier, in 1895, Japan defeated China in the First Sino-Japanese War, which forced China to grant Korean independence. During the ten years between the two wars, Japan's influence over Korea steadily grew and the Treaty of Portsmouth confirmed the island nation's dominion over Korea. It also allowed Japan to expand into Manchuria, doing so by aggressively improving the South Manchurian Railway.

Thousands of Japanese workers flocked to the cities on the Chinese peninsula, bringing baseball with them. By 1908, Dalian, a major city on the peninsula, had nineteen baseball teams, conducted annual tournaments and became the preferred destination for Japanese university baseball teams to travel to for exhibition games. Baseball teams from Korea, Taiwan and the Philippines flocked to Dalian over the ensuing decades as well, making the peninsula not only important for military control but a hotbed of baseball as well.

Built to connect Dalian with Vladivostok, the South Manchurian Railway ran parallel to the Korean border. To ensure they could play baseball in their free time, Japanese railway workers built ballparks in towns along the railway, eventually creating at least twenty new ballparks throughout Manchuria in addition to the nearly two dozen in Dalian.[93] Meanwhile, Chinese and Korean youth were being taught the game by the Japanese.

"Chinese students flocked to Japan to learn how a once-humble Asian land had grown so mighty," explained historian Joseph A. Reaves. Twenty thousand Chinese students studied in Japan in 1905, but the number grew to 30,000 within a couple years. Baseball was already Japan's national sport and the Chinese students "absorbed baseball as thoroughly as their other subjects, bringing the game back with them."[94]

Though American missionary Philip L. Gillett was credited with introducing baseball to Korea in 1905 by way of his work with the YMCA, it was Japan's daily domination over Korean society that fueled the baseball passion therein. As a colony of Japan until the end of World War II, Koreans embraced baseball as an outlet of personal and regional pride just as their Japanese rulers had.

"Baseball matured from an obscure distraction for a few students at missionary schools in the 1900s," Reaves explained, "to a manic passion for millions by the end of the twentieth century."

Baseball played the same role in Korea's development and relationship with Japan as the sport did within many countries under America's sovereign: it was a way for the indigenous inhabitants of the subjugated nation to battle aggressively with their oppressors, a civil version of disobedience and defiance. African American soldiers flourished on Buffalo Soldier squads, proud to defeat their white counterparts, the same way that Filipino, Hawaiian, Cuban and, later, Mexican players delighted in beating American teams.

Baseball has always been and will continue to be a battle that leaves no wounds, a safe way for opposing sides to physically battle to dominate another without bloodshed. A civilized version of warfare, baseball has been used for generations as a way to give groups in society a way to vent both physically and emotionally. But the advancement of weapons, particularly hand grenades, turned baseball from a form of exercise and entertainment, into a weapon all its own. Simultaneously engaging young men away from negative distractions (drugs, alcohol, womanizing, crime, laziness, etc.) while building individual

For decades, Waseda University's baseball team was Japan's unofficial amabassadors to the United States, playing games against the University of Chicago for years in addition to barnstorming of mainland U.S. Waseda's games were as much about establishing diplomatic relations between nations as they were in proving Japan could compete with American power on and off the field.

and regional pride, baseball increasingly became a tool used by militaries just as much as battle plans and rifles. Other countries soon learned the sport from Americans, but, in the process, they also learned how to weaponize the sport, too.

"[Baseball] tapped the militaristic tendencies in Japanese society," Reaves explained. "It rewarded self-discipline, loyalty, a fighting spirit, filial piety, and the ability to endure in the face of adversity. It punished chaos, sloth, surrender, and rampant individualism. Perhaps most important, baseball provided a practical and peaceful outlet for Japan's immense national pride – a way to measure, head-to-head, Japan's place in the world. … The Japanese believed they were destined to rule—on the baseball field and around the world."[95]

The Japanese were not the only Asians who saw baseball as a way to topple governments and dominate the world. For China, the path to becoming a superpower began with baseball.

(27)

●●▬▬▬ ▬▬●●●

China's Hand Grenade Pitchers

After four millennia of dynastic rulers, a baseball fan put an end to China's ancient ways and opened the country to new ideas. Sun Yat-sen, who learned baseball while attending 'Iolani School and Oahu College in Hawaii in his youth, used baseball as a way to lead his countrymen in the 1911 Republican Revolution. Sun was not a player nor manager, but he supported the use of baseball as a way to gather Chinese youth to ostensibly learn the sport that was raging throughout Asia. In reality, baseball practice "gave them practice in throwing hand grenades."[96]

Sun Yat-sen

As we will see in other countries (particularly in Central America), baseball teams and organizations were used as an excuse for young men to meet and prepare for war. Chinese historians credit Huang Xing for organizing baseball clubs in China, beginning with the Yangtze River Baseball Team before establishing the Changsha Yeqiu Hui (Changsha Field Ball Society) in 1911, which was famous for being affiliated with Sun.[97]

Huang worked with Sun's revolutionary party, Tongmenghui (Revolutionary Alliance or United League), to create the baseball organization in Changsha, which was just one of several such sports schools Huang and other revolutionaries created so athletes could "learn the basic skills of throwing hand grenades and tactical skills for armed insurrection."[98] A student at one of the sports schools in Shaoxing recalled his time at the sports academy: "although the school kept it secret, we knew that we were there for the coming revolution."[99]

By October 1911, the Qing Dynasty was forced to cede power. In its place was created the Republic of China with Sun elected as its first president. Though Sun died of liver cancer in 1925, baseball did not die with him.

In 1927, Mao Zedong began leading communist uprisings that would eventually lead to the 1949 communist revolution and create the People's Republic of China. Tensions with Japan escalated in the two decades prior to the 1949 revolution, culminating in the Second Sino-Japanese War from 1937 to 1945. The affections Chinese people held for baseball and athletics during Sun's life multiplied in the second war with Japan. Athletics, baseball specifically, helped Japan defeat China in the first Sino-Japanese War, but China was not going to let that happen again.

"Sport and physical education were added into military training in the army," Chinese historians revealed, much the same as had happened in the United States. "Athletics became part of the military program."

One popular song during that time reflected the elevated role sports held in China at this time, unifying the country against Japan:

The sun is setting and the wind is cool,
Let's go to the sports field and do exercises.
Play baseball, practice parallel bars, do high jump and long jump,
Throw a hand grenade, practice shooting and bayoneting.
Let's check! Whose shoulders are wider? Let's check! Whose body is strong?
Crude iron can be turned into steel after a long time smelting,
A weak person can become a strong fighter after a long time exercising.
Improve our physical strength. Kill the enemies on the battlefield,
We are strong as tiger. No one wants to be a lamb.[100]

One of the most famous Chinese leaders during this period was Marshal He Long, who used baseball more than any other Chinese leader to improve his country. Under He's direction, the People's Liberation Army fielded baseball teams (mimicking, again, the practices of the American military) with tens of thousands of soldiers taking to the baseball diamond during its heyday in the 1940s. One of the star players for the popular Fighting Sports Brigade was Du Kehe, a staff sergeant at the time who, in the 1990s, became a coach for the Chinese national team. Du recalled how He was so intent on making Chinese baseball better that he offered better treatment to any Japanese POWs willing to coach the Chinese soldiers.

"My first coach was a Japanese POW," Du said. "[He] used to say, "Baseball and sports are pillars of national defense.""[101]

By the end of World War II, baseball was popular throughout China. The sport galvanized a nation to end 4,000 years of imperial dynasties, helped Chinese soldiers finally push their enemies out of their borders in the Second Sino-Japanese War and created one of the most popular non-political movements in the nation's history. In 1959, more than thirty teams from across the nation competed in the first New China Baseball Tournament.

He Long

The next year, Mao banned baseball in China, denouncing the sport as a decadent Western influence. To stay alive, baseball players were forced at gunpoint by Mao's Red Guards to humiliate their former coaches. Du recalled watching one of his Chinese coaches get "struggled" to death, which meant that victims were publicly beaten, harassed and tormented until they died.

But as we've seen, defiance has always been a part of baseball's roots, allowing players to defy authority in any way they could no matter their nationality.

"Some of us still played in secret in the countryside," Du said. "We posted guards to whistle if someone came. Then we hid the bats and gloves and pretended to be doing exercises."[102]

Defiant until his death, He loved baseball and criticized Mao's Cultural Revolution that forbid the sport. As a result, Mao had He, one of the Fathers of Chinese Baseball, imprisoned in an isolated jail where he died when doctors purposefully injected him with insulin knowing that He suffered from diabetes. There was no funeral for He, whose wife was forced to simply identify his body at the morgue before she was allowed to return home alone.[103]

Public love for baseball in China died with He, but in the 1970s the sport began a slow return. In 2001, the Chinese Baseball League was founded; and Chinese teams have competed regularly in the World Baseball Classic since its inception in 2006.

This political cartoon titled "Lonesome" appeared in the Washington Evening Star on August 2, 1915. It depicts former President Theodore Roosevelt, dressed in a baseball uniform, but sitting out of the action, studying the GOP League News with stories about all the candidates in state elections. Roosevelt is pondering his own future and comes to the conclusion that he should stay in nation-wide politics and not consider a state-level bid for office because "After all, a fellow's foolish to jump from the big league." It's doubtful that the artist, Clifford Berryman, knew about Roosevelt's intense hatred of baseball, but used the sport, instead, to explain the complex political situation in a manner the public could easily understand.

(28)

●●▬▬▬ ▬▬▬●●

Baseball Divides the White House

Passionate politicians have always been at odds with each other, but many historians regard the 1912 presidential campaign as the start of the rift in the political fabric of the United States.

"Before 1912, presidential elections were low-key affairs, with candidates rarely campaigning in person, and never attacking each other directly," Neil Steinberg of the *Chicago Sun-Times* explained. "Then former president Teddy Roosevelt leapt into the race between President William Howard Taft and Woodrow Wilson, calling Taft a "fathead" with the "brains of a guinea pig." Taft returned fire, calling Roosevelt supporters "neurotics." [Taft] became the first sitting president to actively campaign for re-election, determined, he said, "to keep a madman [Roosevelt] out of the White House."[104]

Why the acrimony? Remarkably, part of the answer was a difference of preferred presidential sport: baseball or football.

After eighteen football players died during the 1905 season (fifteen at the high school level, the rest at universities), Roosevelt personally intervened to save the sport. Without the forward pass or any significant equipment to protect the head and body, the number of seriously injured or dead players escalated every year. Fearing that his favorite sport would soon suffer a lethal blow, too, if nothing was done, Roosevelt summoned the head coaches from Princeton, Harvard and Yale to Washington D.C. to discuss how to save football. The result was the establishment of the National Collegiate Athletic Association as well as rule changes, including the advent of the forward pass.

The president's passion for football was the complete opposite of his summary about baseball. Roosevelt "hated baseball, a game much too slow for his impetuous nature."[105] His hated of baseball (and anyone affiliated with the sport), was no secret, infamously referring to the sport as "mollycoddle" (wimpy). Even worse, Roosevelt had a massive ego and never forgot a slight, whether real or imagined.

Theodore Roosevelt in 1898 wearing the uniform he had altered by Brooks Brothers.

Meanwhile, Roosevelt's successor, Taft, was an avid baseball fan. A former pitcher at Yale University, Taft used baseball to civilize headhunters in the Philippines and, after succeeding Roosevelt as president, set numerous baseball milestones including attending three games in 1909, six in 1910, and fourteen while in the Oval Office, each a presidential first.[106] Taft was one of the first presidents to use baseball as a subtle element of propaganda when shaping his public image. On May 29, 1909, Taft became the first president to watch a game in a city other than Washington, D.C., attending a Pittsburgh Pirates game. Instead of meeting with local business leaders as planned, Taft attended the Pirates game in an effort to portray himself as an average fan like other citizens.

Charles Phelps Taft, publisher of the *Cincinnati Times-Star* (which merged with the *Cincinnati Post* in 1958), a former U.S. Representative from Ohio, owner of the Chicago Cubs and President Taft's older half-brother, was a shrewd businessman and political adviser who helped his brother easily win the 1908 presidential race against Democratic nominee William Jennings Bryan. Charles Phelps Taft was such a supporter of baseball he had ownership investments in both the Philadelphia Phillies and the Chicago Cubs. (In 1905, Charles Phelps Taft loaned $125,000 to Charles Murphy to buy the Chicago Cubs. In 1914, Charles Phelps Taft bought out Murphy to become the team's sole owner, before selling the Cubs to Charles Weeghman and his ownership group, which included Harry Sinclair, an oil baron. The relationship between the Taft family and Sinclair will become a key scandal that will be discussed in more detail later.)

Roosevelt detested the involvement of Taft's brother in the 1908 presidential race. The former president believed that he alone was responsible for

Taft's easy victory. Roosevelt also expected President Taft to advance many of his personal projects, primarily the extension of the national park system, which Roosevelt bolstered during his administration. However, the first act Taft did upon entering the White House in 1909 carved a divide between himself and his predecessor that was never bridged and would only worsen, resulting in the fiasco of the 1912 three-party presidential race.

Charles Phelps Taft, left, and his brother William Howard Taft, who became the only person to be both president of the United States and Chief Justice of the Supreme Court. At the time of this photo the future president was the Secretary of War.

What did William Howard Taft do that infuriated Roosevelt, who turned his back on his former friend and political colleague forever? President Taft dared to put Roosevelt on equal plane with his baseball-loving brother. The first letter William Howard Taft wrote after winning the election was to Roosevelt, which said, in part: *"The first letter I wish to write is to you, because you have always been the chief agent in working out the present state of affairs and my selection and election are chiefly your work. You and my brother Charley made that possible, which in all probability would not have occurred otherwise."*[107]

Taft had no idea how his simple letter of thanks would alter the course of American politics. Roosevelt was incensed that anyone else would be given equal credit for getting his handpicked successor elected. Years before Taft reversed many of Roosevelt's presidential achievements, the rift between the two was created when Taft elevated a baseball person to be equal with the football-loving Roosevelt. It took time for Roosevelt's anger to become evident, but when it did Taft asked intermediaries what the source of their split was; and the answer shocked him. Archibald Butt, who had the rare distinction of being an aide and adviser to both Roosevelt and Taft, told Taft that Roosevelt deeply resented the letter that gave credit for his election to both Roosevelt *and* Taft's brother, a man who worked in the ignoble and "mollycoddle" sport of baseball. Acclaimed Taft biographer Herbert S. Duffy summarized President Taft's disbelief at Roosevelt's anger: "That Roosevelt should regard this letter as an occasion for feeling bitter toward Taft, because he had dared to include his brother in the same class with Roosevelt, surprised [President Taft]. It seemed petty that a letter written in the fullness of gratitude, as this letter was, should hurt his vanity because Taft had included his own brother as entitled to gratitude. Taft could hardly believe that a man of Roosevelt's capacities would stoop to such a trifling excuse for breaking with him."[108]

Trifling or not, the chasm between the two was real and would only get worse. In the months leading up to the 1912 presidential race, Roosevelt reversed his previous assertions that he would never again run for president. When the Republican Party nominated Taft for a second term, Roosevelt started the Progressive Party, nicknamed the Bull Moose Party in reference to Roosevelt, and in so doing split the Republican party in two, which handed Democratic nominee Woodrow Wilson, another ardent baseball fan, the presidency in a landslide.

As the only president to also serve on the Supreme Court, Taft has the unique distinction as being widely considered the ultimate lawman in America's history. However, we will learn in the next few pages that Roosevelt may have been correct when he accused Taft of secretly selling out his presidency to big business. Aside from the Watergate affair during Richard Nixon's administration decades later, the biggest scandal of the twentieth century centered on Sinclair, the former co-owner of the Cubs, who was part of the group that bought the team from Charles Taft. By the time Sinclair was revealed to have bought off the White House years later, Taft was out of the Oval Office and had become Chief Justice of the Supreme Court, where he helped change baseball's future forever. As Chief Justice from 1921 to 1930, Taft's Supreme Court term overlapped with the infamous ruling by the Supreme Court on May 29, 1922, that declared Major League Baseball was a sport, not a business and was thus immune from antitrust laws. Though still controversial nearly a century later, the suspect ruling still grants baseball its unique status among all American sports as "the only professional sport in the country to enjoy an antitrust exemption."[109]

Baseball was not the only rift between Roosevelt and Taft. But the lines in the sand were drawn that fateful day when Taft dared to put his brother, a baseball person, in the same sentence as the former president, who saved football.

(29)

●●▬▬▬ ▬▬▬▬●

Mexican Revolution

Two military conflicts dominated Woodrow Wilson's two-term presidential tenure, both of which he wanted to avoid for the country's sake and both of which he used his passion, baseball, to alter. By the time Wilson reluctantly led America into World War I, baseball had become an institutionalized part of American military life; and the lessons Wilson and his military leaders learned during the Mexican Revolution shaped how they used the sport to prepare for World War I.

Credit for introducing the sport to Mexico goes to both American and Cuban citizens working there in the 1880s during the reign of Porfirio Diaz, whose presidency ran for thirty years from 1876 to 1911. (Manuel Gonzalez was considered Diaz's personal puppet during his presidency from 1880 to 1884 when "Gonzalez continued the corruption and repressions that was Diaz's hallmark."[110])

As early as 1882, American employees in Mexico City played baseball games for amusement, but Mexican interest was tepid at best. Albert Spalding's company began aggressively selling equipment in the capital city in 1888, intent on sparking local interest in the sport. His efforts mostly failed and baseball initially existed solely on the fringes of Mexican entertainment. Another Chicagoan, Charles Comiskey, became the first owner to hold spring training in a foreign country when he took his team to Mexico City in 1907. Though the White Sox were the defending champions (against the Cubs in the All-Chicago 1906 World Series), Comiskey's Mexican tour did little to bolster baseball fever south of the border. The reason for Mexican apathy was simple: baseball was expensive and considered elitist. Only the wealthiest could afford to attend baseball games because tickets cost as much as seven times the admission price to a bullfight, resulting in crowds consisting of "largely upper-class Mexicans and foreigners, and seldom numbered more than one thousand before the revolution."[111]

International games between teams based in Texas (Uvalde and El Paso) and Mexico (Monterrey and Juarez) were some of the most popular games in the 1890s, but were not enough to overcome the elitist connotation baseball had in the minds of most Mexicans. In 1910, Mexican workers began social uprisings across the country intent on stripping Diaz and the upper echelon of their stranglehold on the country. Though born in New York, Cubs pitcher Floyd "Rube" Kroh left the major leagues and joined the insurrection for two years before playing one final season in Boston. The revolution led to years of turmoil where rival factions battled for more than a decade to control the country with more than 250,000 Mexicans dying in the process.[112]

Mexico's instable government was a valid concern for Wilson's administration, not just for the skirmishes along the border with rebels such as with Francisco "Pancho" Villa, but also for the safety of thousands of Americans living and working within the country. While Wilson weighed his options, Comiskey and New York Giants manager John McGraw set out in 1913 on another baseball world tour. Before departing across the Pacific, the Comiskey-McGraw tour played games in the border town of Douglas, Arizona, before venturing across the border into the town of Aqua Prieta to see the Mexican conditions. What they reported wasn't good: "The Mexican village bore the scars of its nation's troubles in the form of bullet-ridden doorways, vandalized buildings, and tales of marauding border bandits."[113]

Wilson used baseball as a peacekeeping force a year later with the Third U.S. Cavalry baseball team playing a Mexican squad at Fort Ringgold, Texas, where both the Mexican and American flags were flown. Though American sentiment believed "baseball would civilize the country" it, in fact, became a method for spreading the socialist message of the revolution.[114]

As early as the 1890s, Cuban baseball players introduced Mexicans to the sport on the Yucatan peninsula. Where American influences in Mexico City created a fan base of wealthy aristocrats, Yucatan baseball became a way for socialist rebel Felipe Carrillo Puerto to train socialist ideals to children through the sport. With communist-inspired team names such as the *Marx*, *Soviets*, *Zapata*, *Gorki*, *Agraristas* (the Land Reformers) and *Los Martires de Chicago* (the Chicago Martyrs), Carrillo Puerto's goal was to turn the Yucatan into a "baseball mecca" by getting children fascinated with communist teachings through baseball. However, even in that socialist effort, American commercial baseball interests prevailed. Carrillo Puerto became the Yucatan governor in February 1922 and, knowing his region lacked essential baseball equipment for the youth to use, ordered his revolutionary administration to purchase $18,000 of baseball gear from American manufacturers. Mexican children used the equipment for free, but only for a matter of months because Carrillo Puerto was assassinated on January 3, 1924, plunging the region into conflict and rendering baseball insignificant.

After succeeding Wilson as president, Warren G. Harding continued to use baseball as a peacemaker with Mexico. Encouraged by Harding's administration, American League president Ban Johnson attended games in Mexico City in 1921 and was so impressed by his experience that he presented a bronze statue to Mexican president Álvaro Obregón to be used as a baseball award. When Obregón left office in 1924, however, he absconded with the statue. Johnson replaced it with a second, larger statue made of silver to be given to the best Mexican squad. To honor and thank Johnson for his efforts, Mexican officials invited the AL president to attend the amateur championship series in 1928 where Johnson donated new uniforms to the winning team.

Though some baseball people chided Johnson for his gift-giving publicity stunts, Harding insiders considered Johnson a vital ambassador whose efforts prevented further military conflict with Mexico.[115]

(30)

●●●▬▬ ▬▬▬▬▬

STD's & Pancho Villa

One of the biggest boosts that baseball received was due to sexually transmitted diseases and the worst mainland terrorist attack in U.S. history prior to 9/11.

The Mexican Revolution heightened tensions along the American border where as many as 140,000 U.S. soldiers were stationed.[116] Striving to remain neutral on the growing Mexican unrest, President Wilson hoped America's southern neighbor would resolve its problems without U.S. interference. But that changed in early 1916 when Francisco "Pancho" Villa, a Mexican revolutionary, killed dozens of Americans in brazen defiance of what he felt was Wilson's support for Villa's opponent, Venustiano Carranza.

On January 8, 1916, Villa and his men removed eighteen Americans from a train and executed them in cold blood. Seeing no clear retaliation from American forces, Villa upped the ante eight weeks later when, on March 9, at approximately 4 a.m., he led a charge of an estimated 500 horseback soldiers (some accounts have the number as high as 1,500) into the town of Columbus, New Mexico. The Mexican cavalry burned much of the town and killed eighteen more Americans, including eight soldiers who were stationed at the nearby Camp Furlong (death totals vary, from seventeen to twenty-four deaths).

Villa's predawn raid on New Mexico was the last time that a foreign land force invaded mainland America. Though Villa's assault on American forces and citizens in New Mexico was essentially a terrorist act, the day has become an annual festival in the region. Every year on March 9, Mexicans and Mexican Americans celebrate "Raid Day" (*Cabalgata Binacional Villista)* with approximately one hundred Mexican horseback riders, led by a Villa impersonator, who cross the border and ride into town, where a day-long celebration commences. Today, the site of Camp Furlong is a national park named Pancho Villa State Park.

Pancho Villa in 1911.

Forced to take action against Villa and his cohorts, Wilson made two decisions, both of which had long-term ramifications for baseball. In March 1916, Wilson named Newton Baker his Secretary of War; and one of Baker's first acts, under Wilson's direction, was to direct General John J. "Black Jack" Pershing to lead a retaliatory force of 10,000 soldiers into northern Mexico to extract Villa. Dubbed the "Punitive Expedition," Pershing's Mexican invasion included the Tenth Cavalry Buffalo Soldiers and the First Aero Squadron.[117] Pershing's "Punitive Expedition" was the first time that airplanes were used by American forces in combat, and two members of his squadron included former Senators pitching prospect Pat Flaherty and future Negro League star and 1998 Hall of Fame inductee Wilber "Bullet" Rogan.[118]

Baker and Pershing would both soon alter baseball's future, forever braiding their fates. While Pershing was pursuing Villa, Baker, dispatched Raymond Fosdick to the international border to determine if rumors were true about how and why American forces could be overrun by Villa and his men. During the summer, Fosdick determined that the rumors were, in fact, true: widespread sexually transmitted diseases were wrecking havoc on military life

Three of the key members of President Wilson's administration who used baseball to improve the state of the U.S. military were (left to right): Secretary of War Newton Baker, Raymond Fosdick and General John J. "Black Jack" Pershing.

along the border.

Venereal disease, drunkenness and overall undisciplined behavior permeated military life along the border, Fosdick wrote in his August 1916 report to Baker; making matters worse were military leaders who adopted a laissez-faire "boys will be boys" attitude toward the entire matter. One commanding general who resented Fosdick's investigation was noted for his devil-may-care attitude about the soldiers' lasciviousness, claiming: "anyone interested in a mission like Fosdick's was an impractical idealist or a do-gooder." The same general undermined Fosdick at every chance and referred to the "do-gooder" as "Reverend" behind Fosdick's back. That general was none other than Frederick Funston, the Philippine war hero.[119]

While Funston didn't take the topic seriously, Fosdick did and his report to Baker stressed the need to create healthy outlets for soldiers to help avoid drunkenness and womanizing in their down time. The Wilson administration adopted Fosdick's suggestions and America's "Fit to Fight" campaign was quickly put into place despite loud protestations to the contrary from soldiers.

Central to the "Fit to Fight" campaign would be baseball, which passed all the tests that Fosdick and others demanded: it offered physical exercise, helped with practical military skills (running and throwing hand grenades), and taught the men teamwork and self-sacrifice. Thanks to Pancho Villa and sexually transmitted diseases, baseball was about to become the American military's secret weapon.

(31)

•••-- •----

Unfit Americans Off to War

By the time the 1917 MLB season started, preparing for war was the national pastime, not baseball. The Mexican Revolution reached a quiet end in February 1917, when Mexican officials signed a constitution that officially ended the conflict (though it would continue to simmer for decades). That allowed President Wilson to call off Pershing's "Punitive Expedition" and put him in charge of America's troops in the European war that wouldn't go away no matter how much American politicians wished that it would without any U.S. involvement.

Though it was physically thousands of miles away, the war in Europe was on the minds of everyone in America. Preparing for war became a matter of everyday life. Since war with Germany began in 1914, the European war had a minor influence on most players. Fans were reminded of the war in small ways initially, such as when Heinie Zimmerman and Heinie Groh both changed their names to Henry, appropriating popular American names instead of their Germanic ones.

In March 1917, American League president Ban Johnson ratcheted up his growing role as human bridge between the worlds of baseball and war by declaring that AL teams would conduct military drills during spring training, using bats instead of rifles. One of the New York Yankees owners, Colonel Tillinghast L'Hommedieu Huston, a veteran of the Spanish-American War, embraced Johnson's idea. Newspaper reports quickly chided the Yankees players as Ban and Till's Tin Soldiers. Although Johnson offered a $500 prize to the team

MLB players in World War I action included (from left to right): Grover Cleveland Alexander, Eddie Grant and Christy Mathewson. Alexander and Mathewson experienced poisonous gas during the war and Grant died in action in France.

that won a drill competition, ballplayers balked at the military drills. By mid-March, several teams voted to end the drills. But on April 6, 1917, five days before Opening Day, the U.S. declared war on Germany. By then the war had grown from being a minor influence on the league a few years earlier to having a major impact: attendance in 1916 was 6.5 million, but in 1917 it dropped to 5 million and then 3 million in 1918.

On May 18, 1917, the Selective Service Act was passed (also called the Draft Act) that gave President Wilson the power to increase the American military by drafting soldiers. MLB officials feared the draft would end the league; players feared the draft would end their lives.

During the 1917 season, military ceremonies became an almost daily occurrence at ballparks, where war bonds were sold and officials had to agree to donate a percentage of all profits to the Red Cross to continue the season.[120] In the first week of the season, General John J. Pershing and Raymond Fosdick were appointed to their new roles by Secretary of War Newton Baker: Pershing was put in charge of the American Expeditionary Forces (AEF, the U.S. forces in Europe); Fosdick became chairman of the Commission on Training Camp Activities (CTCA). The first move that both Pershing and Fosdick made was to employ baseball to help.

Needing healthy men for war, Pershing supported Fosdick's "Fit to Fight" campaign. Both men had experienced the lackadaisical attitudes along the Mexican border and were determined to change a national attitude by using baseball as a way to improve overall health, teamwork and mental attitude for soldiers. In April 1917, with the baseball season barely underway, Fosdick and the CTCA held meetings with private welfare organizations including the Knights of Columbus, the Jewish Welfare Board, the American Library Association, the Playground and Recreation Association and the Young Men's Christians Association (YMCA) "to ensure a wholesome environment for the enlisted men."[121]

Following Fosdick's suggestions, several new laws were included in the legislation, in particular making it illegal to sell alcohol to a soldier in uniform and creating zones around every military base and training camp where prostitution was outlawed. In addition to keeping American men away from prostitutes, alcohol and gambling, military leaders realized the same thing that Chinese revolutionaries were aware of at the same time on the other side of the world: their men were physically out of shape.

Football innovator Walter Camp

Apparently being fat and lazy isn't new to Americans, at least according to the Father of American Football, Walter Camp, a member of the CTCA in charge of the Navy's athletic improvement. Camp described the physical state of Americans going off to war as "appalling conditions of unfitness" adding that many draft boards were forced to reject as many as "one in three" men due to their horrible physical shape.[122]

Knowing he needed strong men to win the war in Europe, Pershing echoed Fosdick's approach and met with the YMCA, which built thirty-two YMCA training camps across the nation through which approximately seventy-five percent of all soldiers were processed on their way to war. The thirty-two YMCA camps focused on athletic conditioning, preparing men for the rigors of daily battle: running, jumping and overall strength, as well as increased arm strength to throw hand grenades. Trench warfare was everyday life in World War I, and they were typically built to be six feet wide. If a soldier had to either chase or escape the enemy, being able to leap a six-foot trench was as equally important as having the stamina and speed to run. There was also the need to relay messages by hand when technology broke down, doing so the old-fashioned way of running the message from one bunker to the next across the battlefield.

On May 30, 1917, after just a few weeks of training, the YMCA held a special presentation for military officials to prove the positive results that would be possible from their athletic training. That day 375 soldiers participated in a pentathlon of events (broad jump, relay races, medicine-ball throw, hundred-yard dash and tug-of-war) to the overwhelming delight of military leaders.[123]

Though neither side realized it, the pentathlon demonstration on that Memorial Day married the U.S. military with the MLB as both organizations mutually benefitted from stronger participants: if the former didn't win, the second wouldn't continue to exist. Talk of cancelling the baseball season heightened after the Draft Act for good reason: even if baseball teams could replace drafted players with minor leaguers, would fans want to attend a game, having fun, knowing that American men were dying in Europe?

To survive, Organized Baseball needed all the help it could get. Yes, military leaders were impressed with the Memorial Day pentathlon and the results that athletic training could produce. But wars need soldiers and America sent 4.4 million to Europe before the war was over (65 million total soldiers worldwide saw action in World War I.)[124] By the war's end, 247 major leaguers served in World War I, twenty-five of them eventually becoming Hall of Famers.[125] Many of the inductees were stationed stateside and never saw action. Notable exceptions were Grover Cleveland Alexander, who was gassed during battle and never fully recuperated, and Eddie Grant, who died in the Battle of the Argonne Forest in France. Like Alexander, pitcher Christy Mathewson was also gassed, but his occurred during a training exercise, not on the battlefield.

Hoping to keep the number of baseball players drafted into war as low as possible, baseball officials and supporters launched an aggressive campaign to promote baseball as an essential element of American life. Billy Sunday, the former Cubs outfielder who became the most popular and powerful evangelist in the world, wrote a laudatory column for *Baseball Magazine* in July 1917, writing: "Let's have baseball, plenty of it, all the more because we are at war." Sunday, like most other baseball supporters, could sense that something bad was coming and sought to stave it off.

"The idea that baseball is a luxury that ought to be postponed until the war is over is ridiculous," Sunday wrote. "It is just as useful to the average spectator as to the soldier. The clerk who is working long hours for small pay needs something like baseball to put a little red blood in his veins once in a while. The American people need it as a mental and physical tonic."[126]

(32)

...-- ..---

Germany Sinks Baseball

At the same time Billy Sunday was writing his love letter to baseball, the owner of the Washington Senators created an ingenious way to further insert baseball into military life to preserve the sport's future. The Clark C. Griffith Ball and Bat Fund, named for the team owner and former player, was created to send baseball equipment to servicemen around the globe to help them cope with their down time in a healthy manner. Each package of baseball equipment contained three bats, twelve balls, three bases, three base pins, a rule book, twelve score cards, and a catcher's mask, mitt and chest protector. Costing approximately $30 per kit, the Ball and Bat Fund shipped roughly 30,000 kits worldwide at a cost of $95,104.41. It was an enlightened move to preserve baseball's future. While many of the Ball and Bat Fund packages were sent to stateside locations such as the San Diego Naval Training Camp, Kelly Field (Texas), Camp Dodge (Iowa), Great Lakes Naval Station (Illinois), Eighty-Fifth Division (Michigan) and Second Naval District (Rhode Island), their initial shipments went to France, where German submarines cemented the burgeoning relationship between baseball and the American military by sinking the first shipment.[127]

On July 10, 1917, a German submarine torpedoed the steamship *Kansan* en route to Saint-Nazaire, France, sending the Ball and Bat Fund's first European shipment to the oceanic depths off the coast of France. Griffith used the opportunity to enlist patriotic support, both financially and emotionally, for baseball in national publications, asking Americans to donate to his effort, beseeching them to not just respond emotionally to knowledge that Germans sunk the first Ball and Bat Fund but to "let it creep in and unloosen your purse strings."[128]

Weeks later, Ban Johnson announced that the St. Louis Browns were the winners of his $500 prize "for the best drilled team in military tactics" with Lieutenant Colonel Raymond Sheldon judging the competition. Griffith's Senators took second place.[129]

Meanwhile, Secretary of War Baker was lending his public support to sporting events and boosting war donations by granting furlough privileges to athletes who competed in events that donated to the Red Cross. In October 1917, the American War Department worked with the YMCA to broadcast the results of the World Series to troops worldwide (the Chicago White Sox defeated the New York Giants in six games). Recognizing the positive impact baseball updates had on the soldiers, the military continued the tradition and continue to do so today.[130]

(33)

●●●▪▪ ●●●▪▪

Freshest Man on Earth

Spreading the gospel of baseball wasn't limited to only Americans. In 1917, Canadian soldiers began to teach the sport to British and Australian counterparts, creating as many as 101 teams that competed for the Canadian overseas military championship.[131] The Canadians' success motivated the "Freshest Man on Earth" to start the Anglo-American League in London the following year.

Arlie Latham, a former infielder for the St. Louis Browns and Cincinnati Reds, earned his unusual nickname as a brash and outspoken player who always seemed to be around whenever anything unusual happened. Which was the case in 1918 when he helped launch the Anglo-American League in Great Britain. Comprised of four Canadian and four American teams, the Anglo-American League played games every weekend in Scotland and England. With several former pro players on each team, the Anglo-American League provided so much entertainment to locals that the season was extended for three weeks after its scheduled end. Additionally, America's 471st Aero Construction Squadron, located in England, created its own eight-team league.[132]

Arlie Latham aka "The Freshest Man on Earth"

Baseball was more than just a physical and mental distraction, it prepped soldiers for the fog of war, according to one Army general. One key play often alters the narrative of a game. One bad inning or individual play can change a team's game strategy, forcing them to alter their approach on the fly. Requiring improvisation and teamwork to succeed, baseball, according to U.S. Army Major John L. Griffith, taught American soldiers "unique leadership qualities during difficult situations," a skill needed on the battlefield when plans need to be readjusted in real time. Griffith elaborated further: "German soldiers often became disoriented and discouraged by unplanned disruptions in their operations, such as when an officer was killed, whereas Americans improvised, persevered and maintained high levels of morale under similar circumstances."[133] (After the war's end, Griffith became the Big Ten's first commissioner in 1922.)

More than 1.3 million French soldiers died in World War I, the second-highest total for any Allied country behind Russia's 1.7 million fatalities. Desperate to aide their soldiers, French military leaders incorporated baseball into their training regimens, creating dozens if not hundreds of teams in the French army.[134]

Eager to spread the gospel of physical fitness and baseball, the YMCA created a baseball haven in the Bois de Boulogne (Boulogne Woods) in Paris with a league of thirty teams playing scheduled games every weekend. Officials translated the rule book into French, expecting the game to take root. However, when the war ended, baseball hysteria in France ended too. Many people invested in baseball's future believed France was a likely future destination for the sport, including the Yankees owner with a French ancestry, Tillinghast L'Hommedieu Huston, who claimed until his death in 1938 that if World War I had lasted just a little bit longer, baseball would have become as popular in the country as the Tour de France.

(34)

•••–– ••••–

General Pershing: Baseball Apostle

As it turned out, European interest in baseball was on the rise at a time when America gave the sport a gut punch. On May 24, 1918, the "Work or Fight Order" was issued, dictating that all men working in non-essential jobs were open to possible drafting into the war. Anyone employed in a field considered vital to the war effort was excluded from the draft, but men employed in what the government deemed "non-essential" jobs were no longer protected from the draft. The list of non-essential jobs included: the food service industry; elevator operators and doormen; ushers at events; domestic services; sales clerks and baseball players.[135]

While ushers to performances were open to being drafted, the "Work or Fight Order" excluded the actual singers and actors on the stage. Which raised a legitimate question for ballplayers: if other performers were exempt from the draft, why weren't athletes as well?

While baseball officials appealed for special consideration from government officials, military baseball teams expanded the game in Europe. On July 4, 1918, the American Army and Navy teams played in front of 40,000 fans, including the King of England.[136] As the war drew to a close, General Pershing became the Johnny Appleseed of baseball, using the sport as a synergistic way to allow his soldiers a physical and emotional outlet that also gave them pride in teaching the sport to enthusiastic French, Scottish, British, Polish, Dutch and Belgian citizens. As Allied forces tightened the Nazi noose, Pershing's soldiers established baseball leagues across Germany (in Koblenz, the Moselle Valley, and along the Rhine River), followed by leagues in neighboring countries (The Netherlands, Poland and Belgium).[137]

After the war ended, Pershing elevated his athletic support to new heights, creating the Inter-Allied Games. Taking a lesson learned from the Far Eastern Games begun a few years earlier in the Philippines, Pershing intended to use sports as a way to foster friendship between nations. Like the Far Eastern Games, the Inter-Allied Games (also called the Military Olympics) began with baseball as its core sport, but other sports were added for diversity.

General John J. Pershing with Army enlistee Babe Ruth in 1924.

Though the Inter-Allied Games were announced in January 1919, Pershing and his advisers had planned them weeks before Germany's surrender on November 11, 1918. A classified memo sent on October 15, warned Pershing that when the war ended, the soldiers would flock to amoral activities and that athletics, again, would be the cure.

"Peace, whether it comes tomorrow or many months from now, should find us in a state of preparedness against the inevitable period of relaxation," the now-declassified memo read. "This period will bring about an increased danger from moral temptations."

Four suggestions were proposed, all four involved athletic competition for the soldiers.[138] The Inter-Allied Games ran from June 22 to July 6, 1919, with more than 1,500 athletes from eighteen countries competing in nineteen sports at Pershing Stadium in France.

(35)

•••-- •••••

Aviation, Music, & Corruption Milestones

While baseball was being played extensively overseas, it was coming to an end in the United States. Negotiations between MLB officials and the government reached a compromise that benefited both players and fans: the War Department allowed an early World Series so long as the season ended by Labor Day and that ten percent of all gross income from the games was donated to war charities. There was no way to know that the end of World War I was just weeks away when the Chicago Cubs and Boston Red Sox met for the championship. The pressure of the looming war contributed to the 1918 World Series being one of the lowest moments in the sport's history.

In addition to the government taking a cut of all receipts, league revenue was low overall for the 1918 season for many reasons. Not only did worry about the impending war reduce attendance figures, but thousands of soldiers filled seats thanks to free tickets given to servicemen for better public relations. Consequently, the World Series bonus payments to individual players were shockingly small. The winner's share that the Red Sox players received was the lowest in history: $1,102.51 apiece (it was $3,669.32 in 1917, and $5,207.07

King George V (above) presents the game ball to one of the American baseball players at the special baseball game on July 4, 1918, where the American Navy team defeated the Army, 2-1. Dignitaries from Australia, South Africa and New Zealand joined King George, Queen Mary and many American officers in attendance. Servicemen were awed by the action and a special aerial appearance (opposite page).

in 1919). For the Cubs players the news was even worse: just $671.09 apiece (compared to $2,442.21 in 1917, and $3,254.36 in 1919).

Adding insult to financial injury, General Pershing publicly claimed that the military had the best baseball players in the world and suggested that the 1918 World Series winner should play the winner of the Army-Navy series to determine the *real* baseball champion. (It never happened.)

Before the start of Game 5 of the World Series, players from both the Cubs and Red Sox refused to take the field, demanding their shares be increased. The work stoppage didn't last long, however, after Ban Johnson reminded the players that Americans were dying in Europe and that the grandstand was filled with wounded soldiers who wouldn't be sympathetic to their financial demands. The players reluctantly took the field.

Rumors have circulated for years that frustrated Cubs players threw the

On July 4, 1918, the American Army and Navy baseball teams played a game at Chelsea Park in England. A huge dirigible flew over the field during the game, causing the players on the field to momentarily lose interest in the ballgame to join the spectators in watching the blimp fly overhead. Two months later, during the 1918 World Series between the Red Sox and Cubs, the U.S. Air Force had the first flyover of military airplanes during a sporting event, which was likely inspired by the captivated attention of the players and spectators at this amateur game.

1918 World Series in an attempt to earn back the lost income from their small World Series bonus. Eddie Cicotte was a member of the infamous 1919 Black Sox, the White Sox team that took payments to purposefully lose the championship. In his 1920 deposition about the Black Sox scandal, Cicotte said that the Sox players got the idea to throw games after seeing the Cubs do so in the 1918 World Series.

Questions still linger about whether or not the Chicago Cubs threw the 1918 World Series.

Two patriotic firsts did occur during the series, however, both happening before or during the first game of the series on September 5, 1918. The world's first public event with a coordinated airplane flyover happened before the start of Game 1 with sixty Army biplanes flying overhead to bolster support for the war effort. The inspiration for the pregame flyover was more than likely the July 4 celebration game months earlier in England that was another first in aviation and left the American players and spectators in awe.

On July 4, 1918, Arlie "The Freshest Man on Earth" Latham umpired a special baseball game between Army and Navy squads in England. In addition to the thousands of British and American servicemen in attendance was British royalty: King George V and Queen Mary along with many other dignitaries. During the game a dirigible flew overhead of the action. After years of fighting in the war, British citizens may have been accustomed to the sight of huge blimps in the sky, but it was still a new sight for Americans, who had only recently entered the conflict. The stunned baseball players on the field stopped the game to gape at the sight overhead, before finally resuming action.

Undoubtedly inspired by the awe generated from the first blimp flyover of a baseball game in England, American Air Force commanders created the first airplane flyover for Game 1 of the 1918 World Series. Aviation flyovers are so popular they have become a traditional part of pregame ceremonies for all major sporting events every year, not just baseball games.

During the seventh-inning stretch of Game 1 in the 1918 World Series *The Star-Spangled Banner* was played to rousing cheers. Though the song had been played previously for special occasions (most notably before the first game at Union Grounds in 1862), it wasn't until Game 1 of the 1918 World Series that it became a consistent part of the Fall Classic. *The Star-Spangled Banner* was played at the rest of the games in the 1918 World Series and all World Series games until 2001 when *God Bless America* replaced it after the 9/11 attacks.

(36)

●●●▬▬ ▬●●●●

Get the Kaiser!

Innovation comes in many varieties and Leland "Larry" MacPhail was one of the most creative minds not just in baseball, but also in punitive justice, well, almost. MacPhail was inducted into the Hall of Fame in 1978 for ushering in new elements of the game that contemporary baseball players and fans take for granted: night games, airplane travel, batting helmets, and player pensions.

Long before he was general manager for the Cincinnati Reds (1934-37) and Brooklyn Dodgers (1938-42) or president/minority-owner of the New York Yankees (1946-47), MacPhail was an Army captain disappointed in the outcome of World War I. MacPhail's particular disgust was that German Kaiser Friedrich Wilhelm II was able to escape capture and cloister himself in a Dutch castle. MacPhail and several accomplices decided to do something about it.

In January 1919, while Pershing was announcing his upcoming Inter-Allied Games, MacPhail and seven collaborators, posing as journalists, approached Amerongen Castle in the central Netherlands, where the Kaiser had retreated after his abdication.[139] Their plan was to kidnap the Kaiser so he could stand trial. Security protecting the Kaiser discovered the ruse and chased away MacPhail and his colleagues, including Colonel Luke Lea, who would become a U.S. Senator after the war, but not before MacPhail was able to pocket an ashtray that bore the Kaiser's emblem.

The Dutch government was furious at the border breach and demanded punishment for MacPhail and his associates. With the potential to spark an international conflict, the matter worked its way to Pershing, who quietly squelched it without punishing the soldiers.

"I am not a rich man," Pershing said later, "but I would have given a year's pay to have been with those boys in Holland."[140]

The ashtray became MacPhail's prized possession throughout his life and was prominently on display in his offices with the Reds, Dodgers and Yankees.

Landis Oversteps

Another baseball executive was determined to get his hands on the Kaiser as well. Germany's sinking of the *RMS Lusitania* on May 7, 1915, escalated global tensions and was a significant factor in America's eventual involvement in the war. Though it was a British ocean liner, 120 Americans died in the sinking, including a thirty-four-year-old from Chicago, Michael Gibbons. Years before he became famous as MLB's first commissioner, Kenesaw Mountain Landis was an Illinois district judge who swore he was going to try Kaiser Wilhelm II for the murder of Gibbons. There was only one problem: it wasn't legal. Government officials had to explain to Landis that under existing international treaties, extradition of the German Emperor was impossible.

Kaiser's Revenge

But "The Kaiser" did get his revenge on baseball, well, sort of.

Since it took America years to enter into World War I, headlines about the European conflict caused plenty of heated debates, especially with people of German ancestry who tended to sympathize with their distant relatives. One such person was a minor league pitcher for the Boston Red Sox, Wallace "Toots" Shultz. While playing for the Providence Grays, Shultz expressed sympathies for Germany, which prompted his teammates, including a young southpaw named George "Babe" Ruth, to nickname him "The Kaiser." After a newspaper article reported that 75,000 Germans had been killed during a battle in France, Ruth and his teammates cut out every copy of the article they could find and left them for Shultz to discover in his shoes, clothes, locker, bed and under his dinner plate.

Quietly, Shultz collected and saved every article, waiting for his revenge. The moment presented itself weeks later when infielder Matty McIntyre, one of Shultz's most vocal harassers, was eagerly awaiting a shipment from home. Shultz took the dozens of articles and wrapped each one around a brick. He put the collection of wrapped bricks in a box and shipped them C.O.D. to McIntyre, who enthusiastically paid for what he thought was his long-anticipated package from his family. McIntyre was incensed, giving "The Kaiser" a small (and hilarious) victory for Germany.

(37)

●●●▬▬ ▬▬●●●

Homers for the IRA

In the bottom of the first inning, George "High Pockets" Kelly belted a grand slam home run and the cheers could be heard all the way to Dublin, Ireland. Kelly's homer led the New York Giants to a 7-5 win against the St. Louis Cardinals in front of 12,000 fans, nearly all of them sons of Erin, including a mayor, a general, two governors and dozens of government officials all with presidential support.

Nearly every immigrant community in U.S. history has used baseball as a way to fit into American society, particularly the German-, Jewish-, Italian-, and African-American communities. But none have used baseball to alter their status in the U.S. to the extent that the Irish did. The Irish dominated baseball rosters for decades and by the time the American League was formed in 1901, historians claim they comprised one-third of all rosters.[141]

After centuries of English rule, Irish immigrants to America used baseball as much to assimilate into their new country as to diminish any British influence on their daily lives in their new country. Irish participation in baseball simultaneously promoted the National Pastime and removed English games such as cricket, two-cat, three-cat and other derivatives from American society. The reciprocal, symbiotic relationship between American-Irish politics and baseball climaxed on May 12, 1921, when John McGraw's Giants and Sam Breadon's Cardinals donated all profits from their game to the American Committee for Relief in Ireland (ACRI), which helped finance the on-going Irish Revolution.

Both McGraw, the Giants manager, and Breadon, the Cardinals owner, were born of Irish immigrants and raised in New York, so there should have been no surprise that they wanted to support their distant relatives back in Ireland. Little did McGraw and Breadon know in May 1921 that the Irish War for Independence, which had begun with the Easter Uprising in 1916, was just months from ending. The IRA's guerrilla war reached a truce with British authorities on July 11, a peace treaty was negotiated on December 6 and Irish independence was officially ratified by a vote on January 15, 1922.

By late winter of 1921, however, the war was depleting Irish coffers and the ACRI was eager to find new ways to finance the IRA's efforts. Traditional political supporters with the financial means to help had already been donating for years, so ACRI leaders determined that they needed to "reach beyond the usual pool of political sympathizers" and identified baseball as one of the perfect options.[142] Given the huge Irish population in New York, the Polo Grounds had become a popular destination for the Irish, and not just because of McGraw's influence. In November 1920, more than 40,000 Irish descendants packed the Polo Grounds beyond its 38,000-seat capacity for a ceremony to honor the death of Terence MacSwiney, Lord Mayor of Cork and Irish revolutionary who was imprisoned after the Easter Uprising. The massive turnout made the Polo Grounds, the New York Giants' home, a tempting option for the ACRI. (Though other major-market teams could make a similar argument given the extensive influence Irish owners held in their respective cities such as Chicago's Charles Comiskey, Boston's Bob Quinn and Philadelphia's Connie Mack.)

The only disappointment the day of the Cardinals-Giants game was the threat of bad weather which limited fan turnout. Bad weather didn't diminish the political clout on hand for the game, however, which was widely advertised as a fundraiser for the ACRI. Attending the game were General Douglas MacArthur, New York Mayor John Hylan, Governor Nathan L. Miller (N.Y.), former New York Governor Al Smith, as well as the Sixty-Ninth Regimental band led by their chaplain, Father Francis Duffy. Even the White House was represented at the game. A baseball signed by both President Harding and General Pershing was auctioned off to raise more money for Irish relief.[143]

While the game supported Irish relief in the short term, the 1921 Cardinals-Giants fundraiser would come back to haunt McGraw. In 1924, McGraw's Giants and Comiskey's White Sox went on their final world tour. With games only scheduled in Europe, the 1924 "world" tour was a mislabeled and disastrous event. Hostilities between English and Irish politics were still very contentious in 1924 (and for decades to come) and McGraw's involvement in the Cardinals-Giants IRA fundraiser game in 1921 created such a negative backlash that the 1924 "world" tour had to be halted after just a few games. Despite playing in front of King George, Queen Mary, the royal family and the U.S. Ambassador, the McGraw-Comiskey tour drew such small crowds in England, Ireland and France, that games in Belgium, Italy and Germany were cancelled.[144]

Despite Pershing's efforts, baseball was lightly embraced in Europe by Allied countries. Conversely, Germany's Adolf Hitler and Italy's Benito Mussolini soon joined Japan's Hirohito in embracing the National Pastime.

(38)

●●●▪▪ ▪▪▪●●

Teapot Dome Scandal

The Teapot Dome Scandal of the 1920s revealed the truth behind the long-suspected practice of big business "buying" politicians through campaign financing and bribes. Which was perfect for oil baron Harry Sinclair, the former Chicago Cubs owner, who never hid his desire to be the world's richest person and was willing to unleash the most destructive scandal in American political history to achieve his goal.

Though the Watergate scandal that doomed President Richard Nixon's administration was the only White House scandal to compare with the Teapot Dome fiasco, the latter was much more damaging to the nation despite being dwarfed in media coverage by the former. (Baseball was also deeply involved in Watergate, which is discussed at length later.)

"We followed the path of corruption right up to the White House door," said Senator Burton Wheeler (D-Montana), who led the Senate investigations into the Teapot Dome scandal. "But President [Warren] Harding was dead by then, so we never attempted to go any further."[145]

Watergate and Teapot Dome were the two worst White House scandals of the twentieth century (and arguably of all time), but Wheeler, who served in the Senate from 1923 to 1947, made it clear that between the two, Teapot Dome was the "worst U.S. scandal" ever. "Watergate involved idealists who resorted to these things [phone taps, break-ins, etc.] for political power," Wheeler explained. But the Teapot Dome conspirators "severely damaged democracy while taking part in every crooked deal imaginable. … They stole everything they could. They were corrupt and were real traitors to our country. … They would resort to any means, to corruption of any kind to get what they wanted. And they were willing to try and crush anyone who stood in their way."[146]

Sinclair aimed to step out of the economic shadow cast by his biggest business competitor, John D. Rockefeller, the founder of Standard Oil, who was one of the richest men in history and a pioneer in buying the White House. In 1896, Rockefeller contributed more than $250,000 to Republican presidential candidate William McKinley, the governor of Ohio. His single contribution equaled half the entire funds raised by McKinley's Democratic opponent, William Jennings Bryan. The Democratic nominee sought to curb the monopolies of Rockefeller and other tycoons such as Andrew Carnegie and J.P. Morgan. McKinley won the presidential election, ensuring Congress never passed legislation that hampered big business monopolies.[147]

Due to failing health, Jim Hart sold the Chicago Cubs to former Cincinnati sports reporter C. Webb "Charlie" Murphy and his financial backer and newspaper boss, Charles Phelps Taft, in 1905. Charles Taft was the older half-brother of future President William Howard Taft, who entered the White House four years after his brother helped buy the Cubs. Chicago's NL team experienced some of its best (and worst) days during the Murphy-Taft era, winning the 1907 and 1908 World Series thanks to eventual Hall of Famers Mordecai "Three-Finger" Brown, Frank Chance, Johnny Evers and Joe Tinker. By 1912, however, the team was on the decline and Murphy began unloading some of the team's best players.

In 1914, Charles Taft bought out Murphy, becoming the sole owner of the Cubs and was immediately forced to deal with a serious threat to the organization. Taft's Cubs were located close to downtown where the smell of nearby slaughterhouses wafted through the crowded streets. Six miles north of the city, however, a new baseball Mecca was being built that promised fans a chance to escape the city while watching the best team in town, thanks to the acquisition of players the Cubs were forced to trade or couldn't sign to contract.

Built the same year that Charles Taft took control of the Cubs, Weeghman Park was an immediate success years before it was eventually renamed Wrigley Field. Home for the Federal League's Whales, Weeghman Park gave team owner Charles Weeghman enough leverage—the best team *and* the best stadium—to make MLB owners and executives nervous across the country, not just across town. Weeghman built his team by signing many former Cubs players, who brought with them to the upstart league a legion of dedicated fans who flocked to the new ballpark that allowed for larger crowds in a safer environment than almost any other professional ballpark in the world.

Only Chicago's Comiskey Park, built of concrete and steel in 1910, rivaled Weeghman Park in both safety and size. Boston's wooden Fenway Park, constructed in 1912, was a public safety concern until renovations replaced timber with steel. In 1935, a five-alarm fire destroyed much of Fenway Park during renovations. Though the stands were empty at the time Fenway Park burned, the Cubs were not so fortunate when they experienced the horror that fire presented to the fans packed into wooden grandstands. In 1894, fire engulfed the crowded seating area at Chicago's West Side Grounds, home ballpark for the Cubs (then named the Colts), forcing panicked fans to scramble over barbed wire and onto the field for safety, leaving the wires "strung with bits of hair and strips of skin and flesh."[148] Weeghman Park, by contrast, took advantage of new construction materials and was built mostly of steel and concrete, making it a far less hazardous environment for public gatherings.

Harry Sinclair

If Charles Taft continued to downsize his team the way that Murphy had in recent years, every AL and NL team was at risk of falling victim to the expanding Federal League, not just Chicago-based ones. Lawsuits between the Federal League and Organized Baseball where filed in 1914 and 1915, and on December 22, 1915, the fighting ended with a $600,000 buyout of the Federal League by Organized Baseball with the agreement that two Federal League owners would be allowed to buy existing major-league franchises and merge their baseball interests. St. Louis Terriers owner Philip Ball bought the AL's St. Louis Browns (which became the Baltimore Orioles in 1953) and the Chicago Whales owner, Weeghman, bought the NL's Cubs and moved the team into their beautiful new ballpark in January 1916.

While Weeghman recognized the great opportunity to buy the Cubs for $500,000, as the agreement called for in the Federal League buyout, he couldn't afford it. A restaurateur who pioneered fast food in his popular Chicago Loop lunch counters, Weeghman claimed to be worth as much as $8 million, but given his tendency for grandiose gestures and lack of ready cash, his claim proved to a massive exaggeration. Undaunted by his lack of cash, Weeghman approached some of the wealthiest businessmen in Chicago and convinced them to become investors in the ballclub, including: J. Ogden Armour (meatpacking tycoon), William Walker (fish monger who later became team president), Julius Rosenwald (partner in Sears and Roebuck), Albert Lasker (advertising pioneer) and William Wrigley (chewing gum magnate). One non-Chicagoan was among Weeghman's partners: Sinclair, an oil mogul and former owner of the Federal League's Newark franchise, who invested the $100,000 he received from the negotiated demise of the Federal League into the Cubs as a minority owner.

Despite having high-powered partners, Weeghman's empire crumbled thanks to World War I, which simultaneously improved Sinclair's fortunes. Government food rationing caused Weeghman to close his restaurants and bakeries, eroding his ability to finance the Cubs. But for Sinclair, the war was a blessing because it vastly increased consumption of oil, gas and petroleum-based products beyond anything he could have envisioned. Sinclair founded the Sinclair Oil and Refining Corporation in 1916, eventually becoming the leader of a billion-dollar company and one of the wealthiest men in the country before he died in 1956.

Many baseball historians contend that Sinclair's only interest in baseball was monetary and that he, unlike Weeghman or Wrigley, never had a passion for the game. Whether Sinclair loved baseball or not, his investment in the Cubs ended by 1921, when Wrigley took ownership control.

Parting ways with Sinclair proved to be fortuitous for Weeghman, Wrigley, and the rest of the Cubs owners when it was later discovered that Sinclair had bribed a member of President Harding's Cabinet to gain oil rights in the largest American land lease scandal to date. By the fall of 1923, details emerged that Sinclair paid Alfred Fall, Harding's Secretary of the Interior, $100,000 to secure the rights to drill for oil on portions of land owned by the government in Wyoming (named the Teapot Dome oil field) and California (Elk Hills and Buena Vista oil fields). Fall resigned his Cabinet position in January 1923, but not before giving Sinclair a five-year contract to the oil rights in the Teapot Dome reserves, amounting to roughly two million barrels of oil per year. Even worse, the contract was renewable.

On August 2, 1923, Harding died from a stroke. Biographers and researchers have differed for decades about whether or not the former president was aware of Sinclair's illegal acquisitions of oil fields in Wyoming and California. But, as Laton McCartney explained in his book *The Teapot Dome Scandal: How Big Oil Bought the Harding White House and Tried to Steal the Country,* the fact that Harding's widow, Florence, immediately returned to the White House after the president's funeral to burn any papers that might besmirch her dead husband's legacy does not shed a positive light on Harding's role in the scandal.[149]

Vice President Calvin Coolidge replaced Harding, knowing that the Teapot Dome scandal was a mess that would likely doom his political career. Unsure how to handle the situation in order to minimize its impact on both his future and the Republican party, Coolidge turned to former president Taft, whose brother, Charles, had sold the Cubs to the Weeghman-Sinclair ownership group seven years earlier. Taft's suggestion to Coolidge was terse: "Do Nothing."[150]

Taft's advice to Coolidge, to keep the Oval Office out of the matter, benefitted Sinclair, who recently had bought the MLB team Taft's family had controlled for more than a decade.

An official government investigation into the Teapot Dome scandal began in October 1923. After years of deliberations, Fall became the first Cabinet member sent to prison for his actions in office, eventually serving nine months in a New Mexico jail in 1930. Fall was also fined $100,000, the amount of

Political cartoonist Clifford Berryman used baseball to put the 1920 presidential race into perspective in this cartoon titled "Ambitious Home Run Hitters." Democratic candidate James M. Cox (left) was soundly defeated by Republican Warren G. Harding. While the two Ohio newspaper publishers were battling to reach the White House ("The Real Home Plate"), they were the second biggest story in the nation that summer because it seemed that all everyone was fascinated with was Babe Ruth's historic first season with the New York Yankees, leaving both politicians to ask: "How does he do it?" Though Ruth belted thirty-eight home runs at the time this cartoon ran, he would eventually hit fifty-four for the season, a new record.

Sinclair's bride. He got off lightly, however, considering Sinclair's bride to Fall totaled as much as $269,000, according to McCartney.[151]

But the heart of the scandal was Sinclair, the former MLB and Federal League owner, who refused to cooperate with authorities and investigators. He and his lawyers did everything possible to draw out the investigation. In the end, he was found guilty of contempt of the U.S. Senate and contempt of court. In May 1929, Sinclair went from being known as one of the richest men in the nation to being known as inmate No. 10520 in the District of Columbia Jail & Asylum. Sinclair served seven months in prison where he wore silk pajamas to bed at night.[152]

Despite his jail sentence, Sinclair had the last laugh. After departing jail in November 1929, his fortune multiplied. At the time of his death in 1956, his net worth was estimated at more than $400 million and Sinclair Oil had annual revenue well over one billion dollars. Though Sinclair never accumulated the mountain of wealth Rockefeller amassed, the latter was never convicted of a crime and had to be incarcerated.

The Teapot Dome scandal revealed that elected officials and their powerful offices were for sale to the highest bidder, making the rich even richer while denying average Americans access to, and the government profits from, valuable public lands. At the center of this dark period in U.S. history stood a former MLB owner, Sinclair, who proved he would use any and all means at his disposal to secure what was best for his own interests. Had Sinclair spent as much time, effort and money focusing on baseball fields as he did oil fields, the history of the Chicago Cubs just might include more World Series titles, instead of possessing the ignoble distinction of having the longest non-championship streak in professional sports history.

(39)

●●●▬▬ ▬▬▬▬●

Hunter's Tours

As a "moral equivalent of war," baseball has long been a political tool used by public leaders to give people an entertaining distraction and physical outlet that fosters regional and national pride. But baseball's role in altering geo-politics matured during the 1920s and 1930s with an institutional belief system and set of goals that was nearly identical to the American military's at the time: physical ability was no longer questioned, but assumed, and preparing for global domination was the new directive.

Between the First Sino-Japanese War (1894-1895), Spanish-American War (1898), and World War I (1914-1918), the major players in global conquest had changed considerably, with Japan and the United States assuming control of areas previously held by Spain, China, Russia and Great Britain.

Hand-wringing around the globe about eminent military conflict in the aftermath of World War I proved justifiable given that the Second Sino-Japanese War (1937-1945) and World War II (1939-1945) were just beyond the horizon. By the time World War II commenced, baseball was not only integrated into the physical aspect of military training, but was also involved in the war's planning and propaganda. After World War I, baseball's role in global relations was no longer just the physical introduction of the game to new regions, but the specific use of the game as both a means to gather information about future military allies (or enemies) as well as a way for countries to communicate unspoken messages of goodwill to each other through international acts of propaganda.

Baseball became a way for Japan and the United States to continue communications despite a clear escalation of distrust between the two nations. The Immigration Act of 1924 limited the number of immigrants allowed to the U.S. and specifically restricted Japanese natives and anyone born in other "Asiatic" countries from becoming citizens.[153]

Baseball tours between Japan and America had occurred for decades with collegiate teams from both countries crossing the Pacific Ocean several times. In 1905, Waseda University played twenty-six games on American soil during the Russo-Japanese War. In 1908, the Reach Sporting Goods Company sponsored a seventeen-game tour of Japan, and in 1913 Charles Comiskey and John McGraw made Japan a key stop on their world tour. The University of Chicago and Waseda University played each other ten times between 1912 and 1936.[154]

A lousy hitter who scraped together a four-year career with the New York Giants, Chicago Cubs, Boston Red Sox and St. Louis Cardinals, Herb Hunter became a vital cog in American-Japanese relations during this period thanks to the baseball tours of Japan he coordinated. Between 1920 and 1934, Hunter helped assemble a roster of major-league talent that he took on tours of Japan. The response was massive with Japanese baseball fans swooning for players they had only previously read about in newspapers.

Playing against mostly Japanese college players, Hunter's all-star teams easily won all twenty of their games in 1920 and went 15-1 in 1922 (there was no tour in 1921). America's Immigration Act of 1924 curbed Hunter's abilities to continue full rosters during the rest of the decade, with many of his "tours" comprised of just a few players who went to Japan to teach the game to young athletes. Hunter maintained his visits to Japan and though some historians claim he made as many as seventeen trips to Japan between 1920 and 1934, the exact number is difficult to pinpoint as some visits were unofficial and included only himself and a couple companions. What was obvious, however, was that Hunter had become baseball's unofficial ambassador to Japan.

In 1931, Matsutarō Shōriki, an influential Japanese newspaper publisher, asked Hunter to set up another all-star tour of Japan to play local college teams. Japanese fans were eager to see the biggest players in the game, begging specifically for Babe Ruth. MLB commissioner Kenesaw Mountain Landis, still angry that the 1921 team had lost a game to Japanese college players (reports that American players didn't take the game seriously that day and loafed around the field, embarrassed and angered both American and Japanese tour leaders), made sure two things would happen: the U.S. team would be stocked with some of the game's best players and that Hunter was not going to be in charge any longer.

(40)

....- -----

JAPANESE BENCH GEHRIG

Fred Lieb, a New York sports writer, was given the reins of MLB's 1931 Japan tour, with Herb Hunter as his right-hand man. Landis padded the roster with future Hall of Famers Mickey Cochrane, Frankie Frisch, Lou Gehrig, Lefty Grove, Rabbit Maranville, Al Simmons and pitcher Lefty O'Doul, who fell in love with Japan and would soon take over as tour leader.

Much like when the United States unleashed the Dream Team of NBA all-stars in the 1992 Olympic games, America's athletic show of force during the 1931 tour led to blowout victories. After Japanese teams lost three consecutive games by more than fifteen runs (20-3, 22-4 and 19-1), Japanese tour officials asked if the American team would consider handicapping their Japanese opponents twenty runs to start the game. While that didn't happen, the U.S. team did handicap themselves with something that no American baseball fan ever saw during a fifteen-year span: an injured Lou Gehrig sitting out a game.

Before Baltimore's Cal Ripken broke his record in 1995, Gehrig was known as The Iron Horse for playing 2,130 consecutive games from 1925 to 1939. However, Gehrig's streak would have never been anywhere near that long had his exhibition games counted in Japan. In a rare close game against Keio University (Americans won 2-0), Gehrig was hit by a pitch and broke two bones in his right hand. To the great disappointment of Japanese baseball fans, Gehrig did not take the field the rest of the tour. The games he was forced to sit out in Japan were the only ones the first baseman missed during his historic streak.[155]

In other words, in 1931, a Japanese pitcher and Commissioner Landis combined to do what no other MLB team could: force Gehrig to sit out a game.

(41)

••••– •––––

The Spy Who Wore Cleats

The 1931 tour drew more than 450,000 Japanese fans to games, which exceeded the total attendance that seven MLB teams had for the entire 1931 season. The outpouring was so large that many ballparks opened gates nine hours before the first pitch to satisfy the fans' demands.[156]

That success allowed a 1932 tour to commence, this time with a marginal backup catcher on the roster who was one of the most interesting people in the history of baseball and international espionage: Morris "Moe" Berg.

While playing for Princeton University, Berg studied seven languages: French, German, Greek, Italian, Latin, Sanskrit and Spanish. Berg also spoke Portuguese, Japanese, Hebrew and Yiddish; and would eventually dabble in Arabic, Bulgarian, Mandarin Chinese, Polish and Russian.[157] As a backup catcher for the Brooklyn Robins (later renamed Dodgers), Chicago White Sox, Cleveland Indians, Washington Senators and Boston Red Sox, Berg only appeared once every four or five games for his team (663 games in 15 years). Berg's mark in history, however, was not for what he accomplished on the ball field.

Invited by Lefty O'Doul to join the 1932 Japan touring team, Berg jumped at the chance. While in Japan, Berg taught classes in Japanese and even began developing a linguistic solution to help the Japanese speak English easier.[158] He loved Japan and was eager to return. No tour occurred in 1933, but when asked to join the 1934 tour, Berg enthusiastically agreed.

It was during the 1934 tour that Berg's biggest claim to fame happened. The highlight of the 1934 Japan tour was Babe Ruth, who had just finished playing his last season for the New York Yankees. Fans worldwide knew his career was going to come to an end soon, which only heightened the hysteria in

Japan. (Ruth retired in the middle of the following season.) With the collective attention of all of Japan and most of the world on Ruth, Berg was allowed to perform the duties off the field he was there to accomplish for the U.S. government.

By 1934, relations between Japan and the U.S. were worsening. Japan's ongoing conflicts with the rest of Asia had American officials on high alert. Though World War II was still years away, Berg sensed that his country needed him. Determined to use his celebrity access in Japan to help U.S. interests, Berg packed his weapon of choice in the suitcase: a 16mm Bell and Howell film camera. He was not recruited by government agents to do this work, Berg merely saw an opportunity that he could exploit. His daring and ingenuity, however, would soon make him an official member of the American intelligence network.

Berg used his camera to capture as much film about Japan, Russia, China and Korea as he could to share with American military officials. The Tsugaru Strait in the northern region of Japan has been a vital focus for Japanese military defense for centuries. After decades of war with neighboring countries, Japanese officials considered any information about the waterway as top secret information of the highest order, especially photographs of military installations and equipment protecting it. Security was so tight in the region that when O'Doul and his MLB teammates toured the area, inspectors even subjected Ruth to close inspection. Undaunted by the tight security (possibly inspired by it), Berg secretly filmed the straight while Japanese officials focused their attention on his more famous teammates.

Bolstered by his success, Berg stepped up his daring days later when, on November 29, 1934, he and his 16mm became part of military legend. Thanks to his career as a backup catcher who rarely took the field, Berg managed to slip away from his MLB tour team unnoticed. (Who was going to miss a backup catcher sitting on the bench when the mighty Ruth was on the field?) While his teammates were busy defeating the All-Japanese team 23-5 at the stadium in Ōmiya, Berg carefully dressed in the spy costume he had decided was best: a kimono and wooden clogs. To blend into the crowd, he parted his dark hair down the middle and carried with him a bouquet of flowers and his camera hidden under the garments. Days earlier, the granddaughter to U.S. Ambassador to Japan Joseph Grew was born at Tokyo's St. Luke's Hospital. One of the tallest buildings in Tokyo, the hospital offered an uncommon and militarily-valuable sight from its roof: a full panorama of Tokyo Bay. Disguised as a local citizen delivering flowers to the Ambassador's granddaughter, Berg calmly entered St. Luke's Hospital and asked for directions to Grew's room. En route to the room, Berg discarded the flowers in a trash can and took the elevator to the seventh floor. There he climbed to the highest point on the roof, removed the hidden camera from his kimono and captured unobstructed footage of Tokyo Bay.

When the tour ended weeks later, Berg stayed in the Far East, deter-

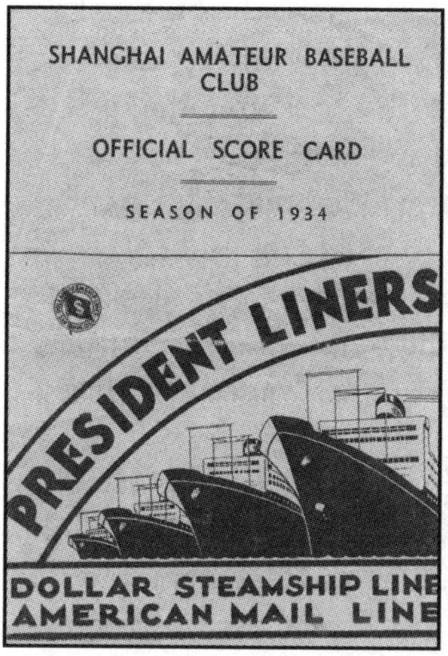

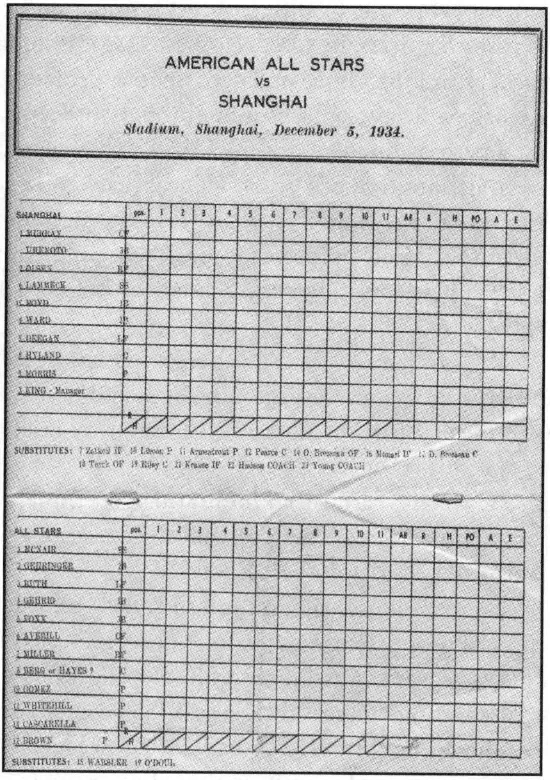

Six days after etching his name forever in espionage lore by secretly filming Tokyo Bay, Moe Berg was slated to bat eighth for his MLB All-Star team when they played at Shanghai Stadium.

mined to travel to Moscow via the Trans-Siberian Railway. While crossing from China to Korea on a train, Berg took extensive photos of more potentially high-value military targets, particularly the bridges crossing the Yalu River that connected both countries. When the train reached Korea, government officials confiscated his film, but allowed him to continue his trip. Undeterred, Berg continued filming across Siberia, using every railroad stop to film the barren countryside. When the train reached Moscow, Berg filmed several locations in the Russian capital, including Vladimir Lenin's tomb, but Russian officials confiscated his film and nearly deported him.[159]

No American military officer ordered Berg's photographic reconnaissance missions. The ballplayer merely realized that his extraordinary access was something that could possibly help his government. As it turned out, his personal secret mission was a successful audition for even bigger official espionage assignments. Berg's bravado and willingness to put himself in harm's way without being asked to was precisely the attitude that William J. Donovan, the new head of American spy activities, would covet in the coming years, allowing Berg to become a formal member of America's spy network.

In July 1941, President Franklin Roosevelt created two new departments that Berg would work for, using baseball as a military weapon for undercover work: the Coordinator of Information (soon renamed the Office of Strategic Services; the OSS was predecessor to today's Central Intelligence Agency) and the Office of Inter-American Affairs. With a background in pro baseball, which was blossoming throughout Central and South America, Berg was a perfect candidate for the OIAA, which was created to build solidarity between nations in the Western Hemisphere. Seeking to build rapport between all countries in the Americas as a way to improve defense of the U.S. borders, the OIAA specifically used sports, arts, entertainment and other cultural influences to foster better relations throughout the hemisphere in the advent of another global war.

On January 5, 1942, Berg accepted a position with the OIAA. His initial assignment sent him to Central and South America to ostensibly consult with the governments there to help improve their athletic development, but that was just his cover story.

"Berg was instead infiltrating governments and collecting information about Latin American leaders and their relations with Germany and Japan," explained historian Robert Elias.[160]

Six month later, on June 13, Berg transferred to the OSS, which sent him to Europe. Berg was just one of several celebrity spies employed by Donovan's OSS, which used their unique connections to gain access to important but small meetings around the globe. OSS agents ranged from Julia Child, before becoming a celebrity chef, to circus baron Henry Ringling North, Hollywood director John Ford, as well as alleged mobsters and members of the wealthiest families including the Morgans, Mellons, Du Ponts and Vanderbilts.[161]

Donovan loved brave and daring actions such as what Berg did in 1934 when filming secret areas in Japan, Korea, China and Russia.

Immediately upon joining the OSS, Berg told military leaders about his Tokyo Bay footage, eager to share it with high-ranking officers. On July 28, Berg conducted a private film screening of his Tokyo Bay footage for OSS leaders from every branch of the military. Though the general assessment of his footage was positive, there's no conclusive evidence it was used in any military attacks on Japan. Many stories claim that Berg's footage was used to plan the famous Doolittle Raids on Japan that were launched in retaliation for the Pearl Harbor attack. But Lieutenant Colonel Jimmy Doolittle led U.S. Air Force planes on a mainland attack of Japan on April 18, 1942, three months before Berg showed his footage to OSS leaders.

Berg's combination of intellect, knowledge of foreign languages and daring earned him his most important official assignment. In December 1944, Berg, along with OSS partner Leo Martinuzzi, attended a lecture by world famous physicist Werner Karl Heisenberg in Zurich, Switzerland. Standing barely 5-foot-6 and weighing just 100 pounds, the diminutive Heisenberg was working with the Germans on a huge project: development of an atomic bomb. Berg's

OSS mission was simple: if he learned from the lecture that Heisenberg was close to having a German A-bomb completed, the former MLB catcher was to kill the scientist with his pistol. If the mission became compromised, Berg was ordered to commit suicide instead of being captured by ingesting an "L tablet" (lethal cyanide pill) given to him by his commanders. Berg determined that Heisenberg was not on the verge of launching an atomic bomb and spared his life.

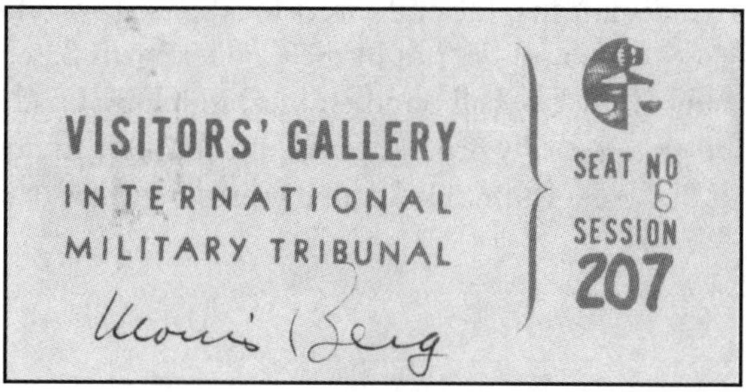

Though he never expressed a desire in the final years of his life to profit from his vast government and baseball connections, Morris "Moe" Berg did manage to obtain a rare ticket that no fortune could purchase: admission to the International Military Tribunal. Known more commonly as the Nuremberg Trials, these trials were conducted between 1945 and 1949 in Nuremberg, Germany, to bring Nazi war criminals to justice. Berg signed his ticket, which is the prized possession of a private collector.

Historians have questioned whether Adolf Hitler would have allowed Heisenberg to discuss anything in public if the scientist was, indeed, still part of the Nazi war machine. One keen observation Berg made during Heisenberg's talk appears to indicate that the physicist and his colleagues were not only closer than previously thought concerning Germany's development of an A-bomb, but that the German wasn't the only powerful Nazi within a short bunt of where the former MLB catcher sat taking notes. In that cold Zurich lecture room where less than two dozen attendees listened to Heisenberg's thoughts on S-matrix theory, Berg noticed one shivering man: Carl Friedrich von Weizsäcker, a key member of Nazi Germany's atomic bomb research team.[162]

The OSS was disbanded after the end of World War II and with it went Berg's secret espionage missions and moments of fame. Though he later served as a staff member on the Advisory Group for Aeronautical Research and Development for the North Atlantic Treaty Organization (NATO), Berg never worked again in baseball or espionage full-time. Unmarried and broke, Berg spent the final two decades of his life living with family members who supported him. Though destitute with a secret background few knew about before his death, Berg never leveraged his vast baseball or government connections to gain regular work in his final years. Personal pride was one area he never compromised.

In the last few years before his death, Berg agreed to write his autobiography for Doubleday Books. When Berg went in to sign the contract, a Doubleday editor enthusiastically greeted the former spy and baseball player in a playful manner that at first confused, then enraged, him. The young editor incorrectly mistook Moe Berg for Moe Howard, the comedian leader of the famous Three Stooges. Insulted, Berg stormed out of the office and never wrote his life story before dying penniless in 1972.

The National Baseball Hall of Fame doesn't enshrine mediocre backup catchers like Berg. Instead, baseball fans would need to visit the CIA Museum to see memorabilia that honors Berg's achievements. Before he died, Berg summarized his unusual life and career for the CIA with humility and humor:

"Maybe I'm not in the Cooperstown Baseball Hall of Fame like so many of my baseball buddies, but I'm happy I had the chance to play pro ball and am especially proud of my contributions to my country. Perhaps I could not hit like Babe Ruth, but I spoke more languages than he did."[163]

(42)

••••_ ••___

Assassins & Japan

During the interwar years between World War I and World War II, baseball became a political topic for many countries. Eager for a way to show either their support of or animosity toward the United States, several countries established national laws based on the sport's American affiliation.

One of the highlights of the (in)famous 1934 Moe Berg Japan tour was the eleventh contest the Americans played when a Japanese teenager pitched one of country's most important games. Just seventeen years old at the time (some accounts list him as being eighteen), Eiji Sawamura was a high school hurler who agreed to join the Japanese team even though it meant sacrificing his amateur status and ability to pitch in college. But on November 18 (some reports date the game November 20), Sawamura became a national icon to his countrymen, handcuffing the Americans with his precision in the only close game of the tour. Though the U.S. team won 1-0, Sawamura stole the headlines by striking out Hall of Famers Charlie Gehringer, Babe Ruth, Lou Gehrig and Jimmie Foxx in succession in the first and second innings.

The star of the tour was unquestionably Ruth, who, according to Ambassador Grew, did more by himself to improve relations between the two countries than any elected politician or "100 ambassadors" could.[164]

"All Japan has gone wild over him," Grew wrote about Ruth in his journal on November 6, 1934. "He is a great deal more effective Ambassador than I could ever be."[165]

The 1934 tour was a rousing success, but before the 1935 season began, MLB owners, kowtowing to mounting political pressure, voted to terminate any future tours abroad due to growing concerns about Japan's escalating war efforts. Eager to curate continued American support, Japan sent a baseball squad on tour to the American mainland in 1935. The tour, however, did more to strain international relationships then mend them.

Eiji Sawamura

Sawamura was the star of the U.S. tour and many MLB teams were eager to woo the teenager despite growing anti-Asian sentiment in many American regions and government sectors. The Pittsburgh Pirates exacerbated relations by blatantly attempting to "steal" Sawamura. Posing as an autograph hound, a Pittsburgh scout approached the pitcher and asked him to sign some papers that Sawamura, who didn't know any English, could not read. The paperwork was a player contract, not some random papers off the scout's desk. An attentive translator intervened and prevented Sawamura from signing the contract.

After Japan's hero returned home, he explained, to the delight of his countrymen, why he didn't want to play in the United States: "I hate America and I cannot make myself like Americans."[166]

Sawamura served several tours of duty in World War II. Before his transport boat was sunk by an American submarine, Sawamura used his baseball fame to help raise war funds and bolster Japanese pride by working with media outlets to broadcast his message beyond the crowds he was able to speak to in person. Thanks to his baseball and military exploits, Sawamura became a legendary figure in Japanese culture. He was an inaugural inductee into the Japanese Baseball Hall of Fame, statues of him were erected across the nation, his face was on a postage stamp and Japan's equivalent of the Cy Young Award is named for him.

Years before the December 7, 1941, bombing of Pearl Harbor, baseball fans knew that something was going on in Japan that wasn't good for American interests. In the aftermath of the Pirates' attempt to pilfer Sawamura, Japanese baseball officials were determined to remove all American influences from "their" game. By the late 1930s, Japanese baseball officials replaced all English terms with Japanese phrases, replaced any team names that sounded American, altered colorful team uniforms into military-inspired clothing and the same baseball fans who once cheered on Ruth and his tour-mates still yelled Ruth's name, but in a different way: "To hell with Babe Ruth!" and "Fuck Babe Ruth!" could be heard on baseball fields across Japan.

"I hope every Jap that mentions my name gets shot," Ruth responded, when told of the change in attitude toward him from the same Japanese fans that adored him only a few years previous. "And to hell with all Japs anyway!"[167]

Japanese aggression during the 1930s wasn't limited to foreign enemies. Matsutarō Shōriki, the newspaper publisher who funded the 1934 tour and is regarded by many historians as the Father of Japanese Baseball, survived an assassination attempt by a sword-wielding national furious that American baseball players were allowed to play near sacred grounds. The assassination attempt left a sixteen-inch scar on the side of his head, giving Shōriki "a badge of honor for his love of baseball."[168]

Two of the most unexpected supporters of baseball were Benito Mussolini and Adolf Hitler. The Italian dictator (left) used baseball to strengthen Italy's soldiers in preparation for World War II, while the Führer used the sport to bridge diplomatic relations with the United States while doing the same with his countrymen in Germany.

(43)

●●●●▬ ●●●▬▬

Mussolini's Men in Tennessee

Individual physical fitness was never a real concern for European leaders until American intervention in World War I forced them to realize that stronger soldiers made for stronger armies. U.S. and Canadian forces created hundreds of baseball fields, teams and leagues during and immediately after the war prompting one infamous dictator to use the sport to help Italy prepare for future battles.

In 1919, Italian-American Max Ott (Mario Ottino before his name was changed) returned to his homeland and introduced his Italian friends to baseball. Ott stayed for two years and the many games he organized during this period are considered the first organized Italian baseball games.[169] In 1920, YMCA leaders organized baseball games in Rome to further teach the game. But it wasn't until Benito Mussolini became prime minister in 1922 that baseball became politicized in Italy.

The fascist leader was consumed with the idea of a new Roman Empire, one that extended Italy's influence and power around the world. Equally megalomaniacal was American health guru Bernarr Macfadden, who desired to dominate the world of physical fitness. Between his seminars, products and publications, Macfadden was the most famous fitness proponent in North America, if not the world. In 1930, Macfadden, looking to expand his sporting empire, went to Italy to discuss his ideas about fitness regimens with Mussolini, who embraced the idea of a stronger Italy.

"Your soldiers eat too much," Macfadden bluntly told Il Duce. "If I had a few of your men for three weeks, I guarantee you they'd be better soldiers."[170]

Claiming that a healthy and strong nation was the best way for Italy to live in peace, Mussolini agreed to send forty Italian troops to Macfadden for physical fitness training. Macfadden trained the soldiers for six months in Tennessee. Part of the physical regimen was learning baseball, which proved to be the Italians' favorite sport. When the troops returned home in 1931, Macfadden made sure to send plenty of baseball equipment with them to teach the sport to their countrymen.

Bernarr Macfadden

Italy's new affection for baseball didn't go unnoticed. American equipment manufacturers were eager for a new market and sports magazines predicted a wave of Italian players to reach the big leagues soon.

Upon their return home, the Macfadden-trained soldiers played several exhibition games around the nation, but the future of baseball in Italy was halted on June 15, 1935, when new laws were installed under a directive straight from Mussolini that became known as *Sabato Fascista* (Facist Saturday). Under Mussolini's new laws, all Italians, especially boys and young men, were required to participate in military, educational and sporting regimens designed to defend the country every Saturday afternoon at 1 p.m.[171]

Baseball was forbidden on *Sabato Fascista* because of its American affiliation. Moving inexorably toward another global war, both Japan and Italy embraced America's pastime to prepare for battle. As war loomed, Japan removed all American influence in the game, making it a modern-day samurai training regimen. Italy simply banned the sport.

Their future Axis partner, Germany, also embraced baseball as a way to achieve their common goal: world domination.

(44)

●●●●▬ ●●●●▬

Adolf Hitler's Baseball Record

On May 13, 1931, the International Olympic Committee announced that the 1936 Games would be held in Germany. Less than two years after the announcement, Adolf Hitler was appointed chancellor of Germany on January 30, 1933.

One of the key reasons IOC members awarded the games to Germany was to help the nation rebuild after years of economic struggles following World War I and exacerbated by America's Great Depression, which had a cascading negative affect on markets around the world. When whispers of Germany's anti-Jewish campaigns began spreading internationally, American officials talked about banning the 1936 Olympics, but in the end chose against it.

For Hitler, the 1936 Games provided a chance to do two things simultaneously: bolster national pride and endear Germany to foreign leaders who were suspicious of Hitler's true intentions. Much like Benito Mussolini had done in Italy just a few years earlier, Hitler made sports a key element of his administration. Nazi supporters across the country were ordered to promote sports as "a vital part of being a good National Socialist." Hitler ordered an Olympic convoy of trucks to travel the nation, spending two or three days in more than 500 towns where the message delivered was a hopeful mandate to the people: the 1936 Olympic Games were a "national task for the German people."[172]

Two exhibition events were scheduled for the 1936 Olympics: gliding and baseball. German leaders endorsed both sports for military reasons. The 1919 Treaty of Versailles limited German use of military equipment, notably

Eva Braun and Adolf Hitler in 1942. Braun had two Scottish terriers named Negus and Stasi (undetermined which one is pictured) and Hitler's German shepherd was named Blondi. As Allies closed in on the Fuhrer's bunker, Hitler and Braun allegedly committed suicide. According to official reports, Hitler grew suspicious that the cyanide pills he was given were fake, so he tested one on Blondi, killing the dog. Negus and Stasi were shot to death before Hitler and Braun committed suicide. A 2015 television series named "Hunting Hitler" revealed that Federal Bureau of Investigations operatives worked for decades following up on stories that Hitler and Braun actually faked their suicide and managed to escape Germany undetected.

airplanes. Creative German aviators and military leaders turned to the glider as a viable weapon and used them very affectively to silently invade Holland and Belgium in 1940. Germany's interest in baseball, however, was almost purely propagandistic.

Germany went out of its way to embrace the American Pastime, primarily as a way to diminish suspicion about the country's future military plans. Hoping to ensure that there was nothing to suspect from Germany, Hitler's baseball propaganda machine included using himself and his own girlfriend and future wife, Eva Braun, who claimed to be working on a documentary about the sport. The subterfuge allowed the couple to attend practices and meet with the American baseball team ostensibly to learn more about the game. While the Nazis filmed much of the Olympics, no recordings have ever been discovered that featured or were filmed by Braun.

The most likely explanation for their visit was simple reconnaissance and propaganda. While we'll never know what information Hitler and Braun gathered from their visit, there's no question that the propaganda part of their mission was a success.

Pitcher Carson Thompson recalled nothing but positive things from their visit, recalling later that Braun was "fascinating" and "beautiful." Though we know now that Hitler was on the verge of unleashing World War II, when he met with the Americans, Hitler was "polite and seemed like a nice man," and that he and Braun "both had this fixation with American ballplayers."[173]

On August 12, 1936, the American baseball team (the only one at the games) played a split-squad exhibition game in front of 125,000 spectators. Though few Germans understood the rules, it didn't matter. Hitler wanted to show support for the American Pastime and he did so in record-setting fashion: it was the largest crowd to ever witness a baseball game. After the Olympics baseball continued to be played around the nation until the 1939 invasion of Poland.

Many sports fans remember the 1936 Olympics as Jessie Owens' personal highlight reel, winning four gold medals in front of Hitler, whose Aryan philosophy dictated that black (and Jewish, gypsy, communist or homosexual) individuals were inferior to their white counterparts. Another African American member of the U.S. Olympic team was Matthew "Mack" Robinson who finished second to Owens in the 200-meter dash. The Robinson family would arguably do more for race relations than any other family in sports. Mack's younger brother was Jackie Robinson, who, eleven years later, after his older brother showed Hitler that black athletes were every bit as worthy as white ones, did the same thing to baseball fans and officials when he joined the Brooklyn Dodgers and won the inaugural 1947 Rookie of the Year Award.

First Lady Eleanor Roosevelt (left) with Rafael Trujillo and his wife in 1934, three years before Trujillo ordered one of the worst acts of genocide in the Western Hemisphere.

(45)

●●●●▬ ●●●●●

Genocide: Parsley Massacre

"Como se llamas esto?" The Dominican Republic soldier asked suspiciously of the dark-skinned farmer, holding up a sprig of parsley. The soldier's question ("What do you call this?") was childishly simple, yet lethal in its true implications.

"Pe'yil," the nervous farmer replied.

The Spanish term for *parsley* is *perejil* yet Haitians, who predominantly speak French, have difficulty trilling the *r* in the word that their Spanish-speaking island neighbors do not. In 1937, mispronouncing that one word was a death sentence. The Dominican soldier had heard enough to be convinced that he had found another Haitian who, according to his orders, must be eliminated. The soldier removed his machete and sunk it into the sweaty scalp of the Haitian. As brutal as it was, death by machete was quicker and less painful than the other common options: stabbed by bayonet or bludgeoned by clubs that in another time and another place could have been mistaken for baseball bats.

Baseball bats were not necessarily used as a manner of execution in the Parsley Massacre of 1937 (machetes were a much quicker and more intimidating form of murder), yet baseball had a very key role in the genocide that killed more than 20,000 Haitians.

"It's good to have people [watch] baseball [so] they don't pay attention to politics," said Dominican Republic dictator Rafael Leónidas Trujillo Molina, who ordered the Haitian slaughter along the shared border between the two countries.

Supported militarily by the United States and financially by local sugar companies, Trujillo assumed power in 1930 and soon renamed many of the streets, bridges, buildings, regions, and cities after himself. Santo Domingo, the capital and oldest city in North and South America, became Ciudad Trujillo. Eager to eliminate any Haitian influence on the island both nations shared, Trujillo created one of the best baseball team's money could buy to "help maintain control and to distract the masses from his government's rigged elections, repression and murder."[174]

"The dictator did not give a whit about baseball," explained Larry Tye, a Satchel Paige biographer. "Yet he knew his people were mad about baseball and he saw an opportunity to exploit that passion."[175]

On the eve of launching his massacre, Trujillo rearranged the four-team Dominican Republic baseball league into a three-team league by combining two squads, Licey and Escogido, into a single squad: Los Dragones de Ciudad Trujillo. Officers of the two teams unanimously agreed (more likely they were forced) to name Trujillo the newly-combined organization's "honorary president and protecting partner."[176] In addition to using baseball to distract his citizens from all the bloodshed, Trujillo also made it clear that his team was expected to bring the championship to his namesake city.

Paige was targeted by Dragones officials as the best way to ensure a league title and they approached the Negro National League pitcher with $30,000 and a proposition: Paige could pay himself what he wanted, but he needed to bring as many of his fellow players with him as possible. Paige agreed; and Cool Papa Bell, Josh Gibson, Cy Perkins, Leroy Matlock and Sam Bankhead joined him in the Dominican Republic.

When games began in April, the black players were treated like rock stars: women flocked to them, local restaurants named dinner specials in their honor, and newspapers focused on the *norteamericanos* in their reports. Though Paige and his teammates knew nothing about Trujillo's bloodthirsty side prior to their arrival, they quickly learned the truth and wasted no time leaving when the season was over. During the season, armed guards escorted the players everywhere with the claim that it was for the players' protection, though the real mission for the escorts was to prevent information about bloodshed and politics from reaching the ballplayers. Paige was even locked in jail before big games, not as punishment but to be sure that the pitcher remained safe, sober and rested so the Dragones would have a better chance of victory. As the Dragones approached the championship, Trujillo reportedly ordered that any citizen who sold alcohol to one of his ballplayers would be shot on sight.

"We were guarded like we had the secret combination to Fort Knox," Paige recalled later.[177]

When the forty-four-game season ended, the Dragones defeated the Estrellas de Oriente in the championship with armed guards ringing the field.

The next day, a Pan Am plane flew the American players home.

"We never did see Trujillo again," Paige said. "I ain't sorry."[178]

Dominican Republic baseball fans didn't see any more professional baseball for almost a generation. The 1937 season financially ruined the professional league and professional baseball didn't reappear again until 1951. Ten years after professional baseball returned to the nation, seven men assassinated Trujillo on May 30, 1961.

"The only way to get rid of him was to kill him," said General Antonio Imbert Barrera, who is considered a national hero in his country and proud of his involvement in the assassination conspiracy. "I killed the cruellest dictator in the Americas."[179]

Trujillo wasn't just a despicable dictator, he was also, at least for one season, baseball's most bloodthirsty executive in history.

American government officials process incoming Mexican braceros into the U.S. farm labor program circa 1943.

(46)

●●●●▬ ▬●●●●

The 80,000-for-2 Trade

Today's contentious, expensive and never-ending debates about maintaining the U.S.-Mexican border escalated quickly during the 1940s thanks to two Negro League baseball players: pitcher Theolic "Fireball" Smith and catcher Quincy "Big Train" Trouppe. Decades before they spent billions of dollars annually to restrain Mexican immigration, American policy makers begged the help of Mexican migrant workers.

The U.S. entry into World War II deprived American farmers of necessary laborers to harvest crops. To offset the farmhand shortage, U.S. and Mexican officials began the Bracero Program on August 4, 1942, in which *braceros* (Spanish for "manual laborer") would be loaned to American farmers. In its first year just 4,203 *braceros* reached American soil, but that would quickly change thanks to Jorge Pasquel, a Mexican businessman who, as Mexican League president, was the country's top baseball executive.

Heading into the 1943 season, Pasquel sought both Smith and Troupe to play south of the border only to learn that both players had received letters from the U.S. government detailing that their draft eligibility prevented them from playing. Pasquel's close friend was Mexican politician Miguel Alemán, who helped Pasquel negotiate one of the most unusual trades in baseball history: Mexico would loan the United States 80,000 migrant workers in exchange for Smith and Trouppe being allowed to play in the Mexican League. American officials agreed to the deal.

"It staggers my mind how he was able to bring about this exciting exchange," Trouppe later said.[180]

The result was nearly instantaneous: in 1943 approximately 44,000 *braceros* became American workers, in 1944 the number rose to 62,170.[181]

By simultaneously securing work for more than 80,000 Mexicans and improving the level of play in the Mexican League, Alemán's popularity soared and he was elected president in 1946. Emboldened by both the 1943 trade and his friend's ascension to the presidency, Pasquel approached white baseball players in 1946 to further improve the Mexican League. Though he failed to sign such luminaries as Ted Williams and Stan Musial, Pasquel did sign twenty-three white players to contracts for the 1946 season as well as luring Hall of Famer Rogers Hornsby to manage.

Baseball officials considered Pasquel's actions a declaration of war. Signing Negro League players was one thing, but making offers to white players like Williams and Musial was too much. (In part because the white players used their offers to secure pay raises from MLB teams.) In June 1946, MLB commissioner Happy Chandler banned any players who signed to play in the Mexican League. Outfielder Danny Gardella, who signed to play in Mexico, but changed his mind after finding substandard conditions, found himself blackballed by MLB officials. He was forced to sue MLB for lost wages because of Chandler's ban. Though an initial court ruled on behalf of MLB, the Second Circuit Court of Appeals determined that the ban was "shockingly repugnant" and awarded Gardella $300,000. The MLB planned to take the matter to the Supreme Court to review the Second Circuit's decision, but before the case could reach the Supreme Court, lawyers for both sides quietly reached a settlement, preventing MLB from being forced to accept the game-changing ruling that the Court may have handed down.[182]

Though Chandler's ban was eventually rescinded, the negativity generated by the blackballing of players polluted the political waters for many bureaucrats. For one of the first times in American history, lawmakers viewed baseball's partnership negatively. Chandler's ban was unwelcomed by politicians who worked to create global peace in the aftermath of World War II.

"Baseball is making it tough on us," one politician lamented. "We try to build up goodwill and this sort of thing tears it down."[183]

In the end, baseball's "Mexican War" was an elaborate propaganda tool waged at first by Mexican politicians to ensure Alemán's presidential election, than by American baseball executives eager to publicly prove their patriotism by banning players they to be traitors.

"The whole thing was strictly a political deal," said Donald Honig, one of the players lured to Mexico. "After the election Pasquel started cutting everybody. He cut me from $20,000 a year to $10,000. That's when we started jumping back to the United States."[184]

(47)

....- --...

World War II & Global Changes

There are probably more books written about baseball's multifaceted role during World War II than any other sports category in the library, so delving deeply into the myriad ways the two commingled isn't possible in just a couple chapters. With 500 major leaguers and more than 4,000 minor-leaguer players having served (some estimates run as high as 5,400 professional baseball players eventually served), baseball and the war effort were intertwined on a personal level. Many servicemen trained with and, on rare occasions, fought along beside star players, which popularized the sport on a personal level even more with soldiers, sailors, officers, and civilians. Other professional athletes served in the war, but baseball benefitted the most.

"According to studies conducted by the War Department, approximately 75 percent of American fighting men enjoyed participating or viewing baseball or softball games, far outdistancing the second-place sport, football," explained history professor Steven R. Bullock. "Military leaders, including [General George] Patton, often relied upon baseball to placate the athletic appetites of servicemen because of its popularity."[185]

The codependent relationship even reached the White House. Conservative to the core, MLB commissioner Kenesaw Mountain Landis needed the approval of President Franklin Roosevelt, a popular democrat. The two men

President Franklin Roosevelt (above) welcomed National League president Ford Frick (middle) and Washington Senators owner Clark Griffith to the Oval Office, where Frick and Griffith presented the POTUS with his annual MLB pass to all ballparks for himself and his wife, whose pass is inside the new handbag held by Griffith. Notably absent from the 1939 meeting was MLB commissioner Kenesaw Mountain Landis, a vocal Republican who was unwelcome in the office of the popular Democratic president. To curry support for baseball in the aftermath of the Pearl Harbor attack, Landis enlisted the help of Robert Hannegan (left), a powerful Democratic kingmaker and eventual minority owner of the St. Louis Cardinals, who secured, with Griffith's assistance, the famous "Green Light Letter" FDR wrote giving baseball permission to continue play during World War II.

openly disliked each other, the commissioner unwelcomed in the Oval Office. A personal friend of the President's was Robert Hannegan, a St. Louis native who was a baseball lifer and would eventually become a minority owner of the St. Louis Cardinals. A star player in school before he became a significant force in politics, Hannegan spent a decade as the Chairman of the Democratic City Committee of St. Louis before being Roosevelt's pick for Internal Revenue Service Commissioner in 1943. The height of Hannegan's power and prestige, however, occurred in private meetings that nobody ever witnessed. In the weeks after the Pearl Harbor attack, Hannegan became the secret liaison between the President and the Commissioner and helped preserve baseball's war-time existence.[186]

After the Pearl Harbor attack on December 7, 1941, all able-bodied men were being shipped to war. To determine how best to proceed, Landis wrote a letter to Roosevelt asking if MLB should play the 1942 season. Meanwhile, the tandem of Hannegan and Clark Griffith, the Washington Senators owner and former player who, like Hannegan, was an avid Democrat, used their personal friendship with FDR to speak on baseball's behalf with the politically-aligned president. On January 15, 1942, Roosevelt wrote his famous "Green Light" letter that gave Landis permission to schedule the 1942 MLB season despite losing some of the best talent to the war effort.

The convergence of baseball and the American war effort peaked during World War II after MLB officials agreed to financial and promotional support of the military in exchange for permission to allow games to be played during the war.

Within weeks of the "Green Light" letter, Larry MacPhail, who was preparing to leave the Brooklyn Dodgers to return to the military, suggested that the MLB buy a B-17 Flying Fortress and have the plane manned entirely by major leaguers (approximate cost: $300,000). Though MLB officials didn't approve MacPhail's plan, they did begin years of special events that raised millions of dollars in war bonds and donations. Throughout 1942, weekly games offered discounted or free seats to fans who donated rationed goods and to servicemen in uniform. Both the MLB and Negro Leagues staged special all-star games at Cleveland Municipal Stadium, one of the largest in the country. On June 26, 1944, three weeks after D-Day, the Yankees, Giants and Dodgers played an unusual three-sided, round-robin game that raised six million dollars for the war effort.

Teams competed to support regiments, and servicemen gladly aligned themselves with specific teams. Pilots found that a baseball cap was a simple solution to shield their eyes from the blinding sun on most missions, but hats were hard to come by in the military at times. Marine Major Gregory "Pappy" Boyington, commander of fighter squadron VMF-214, told reporters his men would shoot down one Japanese plane for every baseball cap that was donated from the 1943 World Series-winning team. Though the Yankees won, Hannegan's St. Louis Cardinals beat them to it and outfitted Boyington's fighter pilots with Cardinals caps and paraphernalia, in addition to bats, balls and associated gear.[187] The B-24 unit of the Air Force's Eighth Bomber Group was dubbed "Cronin's Kids" in honor of Boston manager Joe Cronin after the Red Sox outfitted them with team gear.[188]

On August 6, 1945, George Caron was wearing his beloved Brooklyn Dodgers hat while he and his fellow airmen of the Enola Gay reviewed final orders for their historic flight that dropped the atomic bomb nicknamed "Little Boy" on Hiroshima, Japan.

Henry "Zeke" Bonura, a popular first baseman with players and fans alike, was one of first MLB players drafted and his actions earned him lifetime respect from servicemen of varied nationalities in the North African Theater where Bonura was deployed. Insisting that sports could do what weapons couldn't, Bonura used his MLB connections to secure enough equipment to create the "North African World Series," a tournament of forty-four teams comprised of Algerian, British, Canadian, French and American servicemen. Even enemy soldiers liked Bonura, who was Italian American and could speak enough Italian to talk with Italian prisoners of war. Bonura used the POWs to build the twenty baseball fields he needed for the tournament and though he had to teach them the game, the prisoners jumped at the opportunity.

"They had a helluva time, they all wanted to come out," said Bonura, who was such a positive influence on Allied soldiers and Axis POWs that on October 23, 1944, General Dwight D. Eisenhower awarded him the Legion of Merit award.[189]

The Great Escape

Baseball didn't just help enemy POWs, it also came to the rescue for Allied prisoners held in German prison camps.

One of the most popular war movies for generations has been *The Great Escape* starring Steve McQueen. The 1963 film was a fictionalized version of the true story of British and American POWs who attempted to escape from Stalag Luft III in Żagań, Poland, by digging three massive tunnels dubbed Tom, Dick and Harry. On March 24, 1944, seventy-six British POWs escaped through Harry, a 335-foot tunnel twenty-five feet below the surface. German soldiers captured seventy-three of the escapees and Adolf Hitler ordered that fifty of them be executed immediately. The other twenty-three were returned to Stalag Luft III. The three unaccounted escapees were never heard from again.

During construction of Tom, Dick and Harry, American POWs used baseball games as a diversionary tactic, cheering and yelling loudly to distract German guards from the construction commencing beneath their feet. Within days of learning about the daring "great escape" attempt by British prisoners, American secret service operatives located stateside amplified their efforts to assist American POWs with more than just tunneling equipment. In October 1942, the U.S. government created the ultra-secretive organization dubbed MIS-X (Military Intelligence Service-X). Based on England's successful MI-9

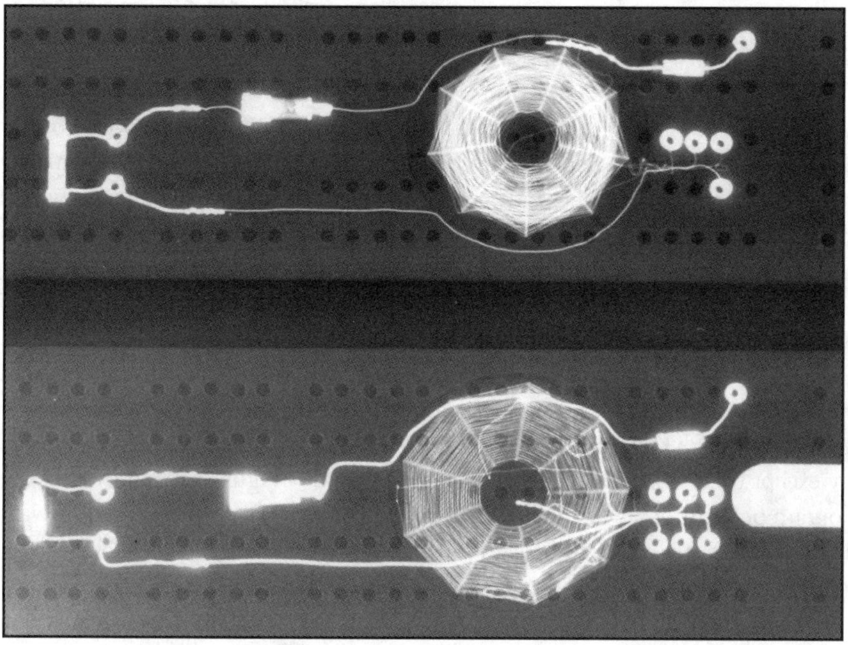

An x-ray of a cribbage board with a radio embedded within it that was created by the MIS-X program that shipped the espionage objects to POWs in Stalag Luft III in Poland. No images are known to exist of the softballs created by MIS-X operatives that contained radio parts so prisoners could hear reports from their superiors outside of the camp.

program that aided British POWs, MIS-X was created to train Air Force officers on evasion and escape techniques, to manufacture and distribute escape equipment, and manage correspondence between POWs with Allied countries, such as England, so that escape plans could be coordinated and not interfere with each other.

Lloyd R. Shoemaker was one of the key operatives at MIS-X who interfaced directly with individual companies to seek their cooperation in working with his department that turned ordinary-looking objects into packages that hid contraband and were sent to POW camps. German authorities allowed packages to be sent to POWs from special agencies and MIS-X operatives like Shoemaker saw to it that as many items as possible in those parcels contained equipment to help Allies escape or communicate with their superiors outside of the prison camp. A deck of playing cards that could be peeled apart to reveal maps of the area, cribbage boards with radio parts built into the board, chess games that had devices built into both the individual pieces and the actual board as well as Ping-Pong paddles hollowed out to hide electronic equipment were some of the successful everyday objects that MIS-X turned into espionage equipment. So, too, was a regular softball.

By mid-April 1944, Shoemaker had already convinced the F.W. Sickles

Company in Chicopee, Massachusetts, to create a miniature radio made of just four parts. Twelve complete radios were created and all forty-eight individual parts were shipped to the Goldsmith Baseball Company in Cincinnati, Ohio, where the radio parts replaced the rubber cores to forty-eight otherwise normal softballs. A discreet, colored sticker was placed on each ball to indicate which part it contained; a complete radio required the parts hidden inside balls with a green, yellow, red and white dot. The radios arrived in Stalag Luft III weeks after the real-life "great escape" and provided American POWs direct communication with superiors outside the prison. Years later, Shoemaker confirmed that all of the espionage softballs were destroyed after the war. Though occasional memorabilia collectors have claimed to posses one of the MIS-X softballs, Shoemaker emphatically stated that any such claims are fraudulent. All of the softballs were destroyed after the war. In fact, nothing from MIS-X is supposed to remain today except their stories: at the end of the war, the Pentagon ordered the MIS-X program be terminated with all evidence and equipment burned, which it was during a massive controlled fire ignited after sunset on August 20, 1945.[190]

Or was it?

One of the major topics we've discussed repeatedly in this book is that nothing is ever what it seems, especially when politics is involved—and the magnitude of deceit is many times greater when dealing with the subject of espionage. That truth revealed itself in the final stages of editing this book when the U.S. Air Force revealed an exhibit that contradicted Shoemaker's emphatic claims that all MIS-X objects were destroyed in 1945. The National Museum of the U.S. Air Force in Ohio unveiled an exhibit in 2015 ("Winged Boot: Escape and Evasion in World War II") that displayed a few MIS-X objects that the Air Force claimed had survived the war. While no softballs are in the collection, several other fascinating objects can be viewed, in particular a camera allegedly smuggled into Stalag Luft III so that Captain John Bennett, a POW in the camp, could create fake identity cards for escapees.[191] While "Winged Boot" is a fascinating exhibit, it raises more questions than it answers: Was Shoemaker wrong and MIS-X objects were not destroyed, but are still in government vaults? Are the objects on display truly originals that POWs brought home after the war or are they actually postwar replicas created for propaganda? Most importantly, what other captivating objects are secured in vaults that will never be seen by the public?

While some answers may never be possible regarding specific sports objects created by the government for surveillance purposes, what is known is that the termination of the MIS-X program didn't end baseball's role in espionage and assassination attempts. Anti-Castro operatives, located in both the United States and Cuba, used the sport several times to try and assassinate Cuban leader Fidel Castro. Cuban intelligence officials claim that there were more than 600 failed assassination attempts of Castro. Assassins disguised as members of a band

On December 8, 1941, the day after the Pearl Harbor attack in Hawaii, this store in Oakland, California, was closed by order of the U.S. government because its owner was Japanese American. Like thousands of other Americans who were of Japanese, German or Italian lineage, the owner was sent to one of many internment camps located across the country.

once planned to sneak into a baseball game attended by Castro where they were going to lob hand grenades into his seating area. Another plan mimicked the MIS-X program with contact explosives packed into a softball that would explode when the ball hit Castro's vehicle. Castro, of course, survived the hundreds of attempted assassinations and his involvement with baseball is discussed in greater detail in coming chapters.[192]

Turning baseball equipment into physical weapons wasn't limited to the mid-twentieth century. In 1990, members of the Palestinian Liberation Organization detonated a hollowed baseball bat filled with explosive at a game in Chile days before the arrival of President George H. W. Bush. In 2012, *The New York Times* revealed that President Barack Obama maintained a stack of terrorist mug shots with accompanying biographies that one insider referred to as a set of "macabre 'baseball cards.'"[193]

POWs in the U.S.

On February 19, 1942, President Roosevelt issued Executive Order 9066, one of the more notorious acts in recent American history that ordered the incarceration of German, Italian and Japanese Americans to prevent possible espionage within U.S. borders. Japanese Americans constituted the overwhelming majority of the estimated 120,000 who were forced into one of ten internment camps built around the country.

"About two-thirds of them [were] American citizens," explained presidential historian Michael Beschloss. "Inmates were crowded into barracks, with communal, unisex showers and latrines without partitions."[194]

Thousands of them lost their homes, farms and had their families splintered and sent to camps around the nation. Yet, as in POW camps in Europe, baseball was one of the few ways to maintain sanity during a difficult period in history. POWs of Japanese descent formed more than one hundred baseball teams in the camps, at least a dozen of which were all-female teams, according to Beschloss.

"Many of the inmates considered playing baseball a weapon with which, amid their hourly humiliations, they could assert their own Americanism," Beschloss revealed. "[Internee] Takeo Suo recalled, "Putting on a baseball uniform was like wearing the American flag.""[195]

The extent of the injustice became clear in 1943 when internees were allowed out of the barbed wire camps to join the armed forces. Those internees-turned-soldiers became some of the bravest soldiers, sailors and intelligence officers in the war. The 442nd Regimental Combat Team, almost entirely comprised of Japanese Americans, has been called "the most decorated unit in American history."[196] In 2011, more than 19,000 Japanese American who served in World War II were given the Congressional Gold Medal, the nation's highest civilian award.

One internment camp expert estimated that nearly three-quarters of the American population today doesn't even know that there were POW camps within the continental U.S. borders, incarcerating thousands of innocent citizens who would later become decorated war heroes. The Nisei Baseball Research Project (*nisei* is Japanese for "second generation") was founded by Kerry Yo Nakagawa to preserve the memory of brave Americans who were forced into makeshift prisons unnecessarily and to educate contemporary citizens who are unaware of what occurred.

"Through the prism of baseball, we are hopeful that they will understand what happened," Nakagawa said.[197]

SOCIAL CHANGE

The most lasting result of baseball's involvement in World War II didn't produce a single piece of equipment or weapon housed in a museum; it resulted in societal change across the country.

The Bracero Program opened America to thousands of Mexican workers who would otherwise not have reached the United States. African American soldiers who fought for their country returned to a nation that was forced to address Jim Crow segregation, leading to Jackie Robinson's historic 1947 season. Robinson's debut with the Dodgers inspired an eighteen-year-old black teenager, who would become one of the most important individuals of the twentieth

From left to right: Martin Luther King drew inspiration from the battle that Jackie Robinson and other African American baseball players fought to take the field in Major League Baseball. The gender battles women waged were symbolized by Rosie the Riveter. A Japanese American child at the World War II-era U.S. internment camp in Manzanar, California, waits eagerly for the baseball team to assemble.

century.

"You'll never know how easy you and Jackie [Robinson] and [Larry] Doby and Campy [Roy Campanella] made it for me to do my job by what you did on the baseball field," Martin Luther King, Jr. said to African American pitcher Don Newcombe, who was one of the first black players to join Robinson on the Dodgers roster.[198]

King was assassinated less than one month after his revelation to Newcombe.

Women joined Mexican Americans and African Americans as another huge societal group that reached new levels of equality during World War II thanks to baseball. One of the most iconic images of the twentieth century was Rosie the Riveter flexing her biceps in posters with the accompanying slogan: *We Can Do It!* In addition to replacing men on the factory lines that built munitions and other essential wartime products, women also replaced men on the baseball field.

The All-American Girls Professional Baseball League was created by Chicago Cubs owner Philip Wrigley initially as a way to prevent MLB ballparks from becoming white elephants during the war. More than 600 female athletes competed from 1943 to 1954, when the league finally closed. The all-female league inspired a nation of women the same way that Robinson and other African American players inspired King.

Based on the AAGPBL, the 1992 film *A League of Their Own* is still the highest-grossing baseball film in history. Having earned more than $107 million since its release, the film also produced one of the most famous lines in movie history.[199]

"There's no crying in baseball!" Coach Jimmy Dugan (played by Tom Hanks) yelled to one his sniffling female players.

While there may not be crying in baseball, there is deception and the occasional trick play.

General Douglas MacArthur, a lifelong baseball enthusiast, proved just how deceiving baseball can be when he used the sport as part of the largest military deception since the Trojan Horse was created by the Greeks to raze the city of Troy more than 3,000 years earlier.

Section IV:

-••• •-• •• -• --• •• -• --•

BRINGING IT HOME

•• - •••• --- -- •

(48)

●●●●▬ ▬▬▬●●

Biggest Deception in Military & Baseball History

"At least the Americans made it a five-game series," General Douglas MacArthur must have thought, at least momentarily, while he stood on the deck of the *USS Mount McKinley* moments away from launching military history. Instead of wearing his traditional uniform, MacArthur wore his prized possession: a bathrobe upon which was sewn the Army varsity sports letter he earned at West Point, where he scored the winning run in the inaugural Army-Navy baseball game in 1901.[200]

On September 15, 1950, MacArthur etched his name in military annals by engineering one of the largest amphibious military attacks in history, leading 13,000 Marines against North Korean forces at Inchon, Korea. Only two previous military sieges in history compared to what MacArthur unleashed: the Allies' successful D-Day beach landing at Normandy, France, on June 6, 1944, was the only larger amphibious military attack; and the Greeks' famous Trojan Horse ploy, engineered more than 3,000 years earlier to deceive and conquer the Trojans in 1183 B.C., was of equal cunning.[201]

The Inchon Landing was a military masterstroke, its craftiness still stud-

This U.S. Marines photograph from the Inchon Landing reveals the huge tidal fluctuations that had to be considered in planning the surprise assault. With as much as a thirty-three foot difference between high and low tide, vessels and support vehicles were easily trapped by receding waters which complicated the difficult mission.

ied in military academies because of the mission's daring and surprise.

Why was the Inchon Landing such a surprise?

In part, because MacArthur used baseball, the inaugural Inter-Hemispheric Semi-Pro World Series specifically, as the world's largest military distraction, dwarfing the duplicity employed by the Trojan Horse thousands of years before.

In the aftermath of World War II, the simmering global conflict between the free market economies (United States and Allies) and communist-leaning governments (U.S.S.R., China) for control of Korea directly led to the Korean War. The country was divided along the thirty-eighth latitudinal line north of the equator (the Thirty-Eighth parallel), North Korea drew support from the Soviet Union, while the southern half, closer to American-occupied Japan, was protected by U.S. forces and their allies.

Between 1945 and 1950, MacArthur had grown into one of the most powerful world leaders with a nearly unlimited budget at his disposal to rebuild Japan. Replacing traditional Japanese emperor rule was the multi-national Supreme Commander for the Allied Powers (SCAP), headed by MacArthur, whose right-hand man was Major General William Marquat, one of the most important and unheralded people in all of Asia whose name only a few non-military people knew.

A former semipro baseball player and reporter for the *Seattle Times*, Marquat was not a military lifer like MacArthur, whose father, Arthur MacArthur, was the military governor of the Philippines when the U.S. used baseball to civilize Filipino headhunters.[202] Yet, Marquat's influence over Japan's reconstruction and his involvement in the greatest deception in military history made him one of the most powerful baseball fans to ever live. As the director of SCAP's Economic and Scientific Section, Marquat was essentially in charge of the world's largest ungoverned budget, known simply as "The M-Fund" for Marquat.

The M-Fund was anything but simple or small. Before Japan had agreed to surrender terms, the Allies had already begun planning the rebuilding of the nation as a foothold to the rest of Asia. The financing of the reconstruction came from a mammoth stockpile of cash and goods Japan's government had pillaged for decades from neighboring countries and its own citizens. For years, the Japanese government had used black market operations and the sale of confiscated criminal property and goods as a major revenue stream, all of which now flowed into The M-Fund. Even greater revenues were pumped into The M-Fund from the Allies' sale of shares of dissolved Japanese companies, as well as the "sales of confiscated Japanese military stockpiles of industrial diamonds, platinum, gold, and silver that had been plundered in occupied countries."[203]

General Douglas MacArthur

Major General William Marquat

MacArthur and Marquat "looked to sports, most importantly baseball, as an instrument for pacifying and amicably ruling the occupied islands and their populace, just as the American military rulers had done in the Philippines half a century earlier." Marquat and MacArthur took sports seriously and issued SCAP directives almost immediately that banned the teaching of Japanese traditional martial arts, turning the equipment used for kyudo (archery), naginata (sharp swords) and kendo (wooden and bamboo sword-like sticks) into rudimentary baseball gear.[204] Sumo wrestling was banned, but baseball was not only endorsed it earned vocal support by MacArthur and extensive financial backing from Marquat's generous M-Fund to reestablish the sport in Japan.

Before the end of 1945, SCAP officials made sure Japanese college and pro teams entertained the war-weary citizenry. An eight-team pro league was allowed to begin play in 1946 and the league champions, the Hawks, were given a new ballpark thanks to Marquat's M-Fund.[205]

"Marquat and MacArthur were unabashed in their use of baseball as one of the many potent tools at their disposal to reshape Japan in the wake of the war," wrote historian Joseph Reaves.[206]

MacArthur and Marquat's restoration of Japan to pre-war levels of normalcy allowed Lefty O'Doul to rekindle his baseball ambassador missions. O'Doul's 1949 tour was greeted by an estimated one million enthused fans and more than 430,000 fans paid to see the major-league players tour Japan, prompting MacArthur to claim that O'Doul's trip was "the greatest piece of diplomacy ever."[207] MacArthur's praise should be taken with a grain of salt, however, because The M-Fund paid for O'Doul's trip, so in reality MacArthur was really complimenting himself and Marquat for another military job well done via baseball, not merely lauding O'Doul.

Throughout the Japanese reconstruction, Marquat played second base on intramural baseball teams and despite being more than twice as old as some of his teammates, he was a major contributor to his teams, leading one league in hitting at age 54.

"[Marquat] seemed different from other career officers," wrote one MacArthur historian. "He was crazy about baseball, and any talk about the game would cheer him up."[208]

All of which helps to explain why Marquat and MacArthur were willing, thanks to unlimited M-Fund financing, to use baseball to battle North Korean aggression in 1950. On June 25, 1950, the North Korean People's Army (NKPA) crossed the Thirty-Eighth Parallel with 135,000 soldiers, who overwhelmed the Republic of Korea's Army. Within weeks, the NKPA had taken Seoul and Inchon, forcing the American troops to maintain a defensive posture in Pusan (now named Busan). Something needed to be done quickly.

Prior to the NKPA's crossing of the Thirty-Eighth Parallel, MacArthur's oversight and responsibility did not include Korea, only Japan. However, after the June 25 invasion, MacArthur was made supreme commander of the American-led United Nations effort to defend South Korea.

With the world looking to MacArthur and Marquat to find an answer to the NKPA's aggression, the two baseball fans turned to the sport they loved most and saw the chance to create a massive diversion, using millions if not billions of fans as unwitting pawns. With the mountainous resources that The M-Fund provided, Marquat oversaw simultaneous baseball tournaments in Japan and America. While the NKPA sought to take control of South Korea in the summer of 1950, Japanese and American semipro baseball teams competed to play in the first Inter-Hemispheric Semipro World Series. Hundreds of teams across Japan played in tournaments for the right to represent their country in the tournament, with the All-Kanebo team earning the honor. In the United States, the Fort Wayne Capeharts won the thirty-two-team tournament held by the National Baseball Congress (NBC).

Within hours of winning the NBC tournament, Capeharts players and management were on a plane to Japan despite not having any immunizations or official paperwork prepared. Government requirements and restrictions were no longer a concern because the Capeharts were now part of a national military mission, Marquat privately revealed to NBC executive secretary Charles Cookson, a former military officer who was restored to active duty as a captain during the tournament.

"[The baseball tournament was of] vital importance to the interests of the United States," Marquat confided to Cookson, who was told to reveal nothing to anyone in baseball about the importance of their mission, especially the media.[209]

"The series not only preoccupied the Japanese," explained historian Robert Elias, "but was publicized so grandiosely in the region that the North Koreans didn't suspect a military operation against them was about to be launched." The actual baseball games were nothing more than a "militaristic red herring" intended to dupe the NKPA.[210]

While Marquat was arranging the baseball diversion, MacArthur's men were sizing up locations for an amphibious attack. Due to its strategic importance, Inchon was selected despite that fact that there were thirty-three-foot tidal fluctuations for the port. Based on high-tide predictions, September 15 was the ideal date for a water-based assault.

September 15 was also the date of Game 5 between the Capeharts and All-Kanebo squad in the vital baseball distraction. The Capeharts won that day, 6-1, winning the series in five games.

Hours after the game's conclusion, MacArthur launched the Inchon landing which was called "the most masterly and audacious stroke in all history" by Fleet Admiral William "Bull" Halsey.[211]

Seoul was liberated less than two weeks later.

This program cover from the 1952 St. Louis Cardinals is a vivid representation of the relationship between baseball and the military. Pictured here is Tom Poholsky, a right-handed pitcher who pitched for the Cardinals for two years before being sent to the Korean War. He returned after the war to play four more seasons, three with St. Louis and one with the Chicago Cubs.

(49)

••••- ----•

Era of Irony: Us vs. Them vs. Us vs. Them

During and after the Korean War, global politics became an Us vs. Them drama between communist/socialist regimes and democratic governments. It seemed no political topics could be trusted at face value and baseball, whose century-plus involvement in American politics (and global military actions as witnessed in the Inchon Landing deception), was every bit as twisted in the difference between its public proclamations and backroom dealings. The fate of former MLB commissioner Happy Chandler was perfect testimony to the topsy-turvy political times during the 1950s.

A former senator and governor of Kentucky, Chandler lasted just one six-year term as commissioner after taking over for Kenesaw Mountain Landis in 1945. But on July 15, 1951, Chandler was forced by the league's owners to resign as commissioner due in no small part to his patriotism, which was too vocal for most owners. As a supporter of Jackie Robinson and other minority players, Chandler had already rankled many racist owners who preferred the players remained the same color as the bleached hide of a baseball: white. But after the Inchon Landing, Chandler made public statements that questioned if

Happy Chandler

MLB games should continue to be played during the Korean War.

Owners who fought a decade earlier to keep the sport going during World War II were incensed that the topic of shutting down baseball due to a war would be broached publicly again. The fact that the topic was raised by the sport's own commissioner who, unprovoked, mentioned the repugnant idea was simply unacceptable. For baseball owners, national loyalty had its limits and Chandler had crossed the line.

"Happy Chandler championed baseball during World War II, but as commissioner, he said it might have to stop for the Korean conflict," explained one historian. "For many owners, this took baseball patriotism too far."[212]

To maintain its connections to the American military, baseball considered as its third commissioner General Douglas MacArthur, who was fired by President Harry Truman on April 11, 1951. Instead, Ford Frick, the National League president and a former sports reporter, was given the job.

Shot (Not) Heard Round The World

Growing mistrust and fears gave rise to increasing misinformation in all political arenas with baseball used as a common way for communist-leaning countries to softly attack American-supported governments everywhere. Even unsuspecting baseball stars became involved in the covert world of international politics and the mental manipulation of the masses without even knowing it.

One of the most famous home runs in baseball history occurred on October 3, 1951, when Bobby Thomson belted a three-run homer in the bottom of the ninth to give his New York Giants a 5-4 win against the Brooklyn Dodgers to claim the NL pennant. Thomson's home run wasn't just baseball history, it became part of nuclear weapon lore, too, aiding the Atomic Energy Commission (AEC) in a way no other person or event could.

Thomson's headline-grabbing heroics were the precise distraction that Gordon Dean, Chairman of the AEC, was desperately seeking.

Dean had held a big secret for more than a week and had no idea how to share the information with the world: Russia had become a nuclear power, too.

Since the dropping of the atomic bombs dubbed "Little Boy" (on Hiroshima, August 6, 1945) and "Fat Boy" (on Nagasaki, August 9, 1945), the United States enjoyed exclusive company as the only country with nuclear capabilities. But in 1949, Soviet Union scientists conducted the country's first

In a 2008 photo (above) craters and bore holes are still visible at the Semipalatinsk Test Site in what is today Kazakhstan. Officials with the Atomic Energy Commission were unsure when to reveal the news to the U.S. media that the Soviet Union had become a nuclear power, but Bobby Thomson's baseball heroics offered the ideal opportunity to disclose the atomic testing at the Soviet site that many people called "The Polygon."

nuclear bomb test at the Semipalatinsk Test Site (located in modern day Kazakhstan and dubbed "The Polygon"). On September 23, 1949, President Truman issued a statement about the nuclear test to the media in a brief that was purposefully low-key and relaxed, calmly stating that American scientists and military leaders always expected other countries to develop nuclear abilities.

Over the following two years, the Soviet test faded from public concern. That changed at 9:19 a.m. on September 24, 1951, however, when the Soviet Union detonated a second a plutonium device in Semipalatinsk. The Soviet's second nuclear detonation was clear and unequivocal confirmation that the American nuclear monopoly was over. No soft statement from the White House could hide that fact from the public. Fearing how Americans would react to the news, Dean kept the nuclear test a secret, hoping someone or something would help distract the masses from his revelation to the country and the world. Thomson's pennant-clinching home run was exactly what he needed.

The New York Times ran dueling headlines in the October 4, 1951, newspaper with *GIANTS CAPTURE PENNANT, BEATING DODGERS 5-4 IN 9TH ON THOMSON'S 3-RUN HOMER* on the left side of the page balancing the headline on the opposite side of the page: *SOVIET'S SECOND ATOM BLAST IN 2 YEARS REVEALED BY U.S.; DETAILS ARE KEPT A SECRET.*

Much like it had done with MacArthur in Korea just thirteen months earlier, baseball provided Dean and the AEC a global distraction from much more serious on-going military actions. Dean was forever grateful to Thomson for his attention-grabbing deeds.

"Did not receive as large a headline in the evening paper as the play-off for the world series game," Dean noted approvingly in his journal.[213]

What's In a Name?

Paranoid jousting between U.S. and Soviet institutions increased throughout the 1950s leading to an escalation in deadly weapons and lethal commentary. While their respective war departments were busy building bomb reserves that could destroy the world many times over, propaganda professionals were also working overtime to use baseball as a way to attack their enemies.

In September 1952, Russian newspaper *Smena* ("Change") ran an article claiming that baseball was not the American Pastime, but was, in fact, an old Russian game called *lapta.* It seemed odd that the Soviet Union would brag about creating a sport that it only recently had banned in Czechoslovakia (and would soon be banned in communist China), but competition, paranoia and fears can make organizations do some unusual things.

The season after the *Smena* story made baseball fans around the world giggle, the Cincinnati Reds changed their moniker to the Redlegs for fear of anyone thinking their team sided with the Soviets. The organization kept their new team name for six seasons (1954-59) before common sense and the Reds former nickname returned.

Don't Throw It Back!

At the end of World War II, Berlin was divided into four zones, one for each superpower: England, France, the United States, and the Soviet Union. Diplomacy between the four zones grew strained throughout 1946 over disagreements on reparation negotiations. In response, the three democratically controlled zones combined their regions into one. On June 23, 1948, the split between East and West Berlin was formalized with the introduction of new currency in West Berlin. One day later the Soviet Union countered by imposing the Berlin Blockade that sealed off Eastern Berlin. The Berlin Wall was erected on August 12, 1961, cementing the divide.

Before the Berlin Wall was erected, Western forces elevated the need to spy on Soviet communications in East Berlin to the highest priority. From 1952

CIA experts and their British counterparts in MI-6 used baseball as a way to conduct proper measurements while building the infamous Berlin Tunnel. A portion of the tunnel is preserved in the Allied Museum in Berlin (above). The tunnel was considered to be one of the most "valuable" assets to Allied information gathering, according to CIA Director Allen Dulles (right). Unknown to Dulles and other espionage experts at the time was that Soviet spies knew about the tunnel's existence from the beginning, rendering all information gathered useless.

to 1956, the Central Intelligence Agency ran a clandestine espionage project nicknamed PBJOINTLY that became commonly known as the Berlin Tunnel Project. Though former CIA Director Allen Dulles referred to the Berlin Tunnel as "one of the most valuable and daring projects ever undertaken" by his clandestine organization, details of the vital operation only emerged a half-century later when heavily-redacted documents were unclassified.[214]

In an era before satellite technology, when it was estimated that nearly one hundred percent of Soviet communications were delivered via military telephone wires that relayed vital information from deep within Berlin to Moscow and other Soviet locations across Europe, PBJOINTLY's mission was to tap the Soviet phone lines and extract intelligence. The CIA and British Secret Intelligence Service (MI-6) determined that a buried grouping of phone cables located twenty-seven inches below a major highway in East Berlin was the best target.[215]

As outlined in declassified CIA document 5166d4f999326091c6a6081c (prepared in 1967, declassified in 2007), the 1,476-foot tunnel had to be dug at angles to avoid local buildings and buried infrastructure. Built in a yawning V shape, the tunnel's center point was its lowest, sloping upward on both ends. Without a solid baseline for comparison to properly measure distance, engineers found it difficult to dig the tunnel. It was determined that a reference point of a known size on the eastern side would help. So the engineers devised a tactical plan to insert an object into East Berlin: a baseball game.

CIA and MI-6 operatives played a baseball game on the border of East Berlin so that they could purposefully hit the ball into the Soviet side and use it as a reference point. There was only one problem the spies hadn't counted on in their plan: kindness.

"This scheme was frustrated by the friendliness of the East German guards who kept returning the baseball," wrote the author of the CIA briefing from 1967.[216]

To further underscore the extent of misinformation omnipresent during this political era consider this: British and American networks transcribed approximately 443,000 conversations, recorded more than 40,000 hours of phone dialogue and produced 1,750 official intelligence reports that took more than two years to examine only to discover later that the Soviets knew about the tunnel the entire time thanks to a double agent embedded within MI-6. The KGB, Soviet Union's main security agency that oversaw the world's largest spy network, knew about the tunnel before digging began thanks to George Blake, a Soviet spy planted deep within British intelligence, who updated his Soviet superiors throughout its construction. In order to protect the identity of their valuable mole, the Soviets allowed the tunnel to be built and used until April 1956 when they "accidentally" discovered it while ostensibly repairing underground cables.[217]

To muddy the intelligence waters even more, Communist Party Chief Nikita Khrushchev was scheduled to visit with Queen Elizabeth at Windsor Castle the day following the Soviet's "discovery" of the Berlin Tunnel. To foster better relations between the two countries, Soviet and British leaders decided to diminish MI-6 involvement in the Berlin Tunnel, allowing the CIA to take extra (and undue) credit for the tunnel project.

"To this day British Intelligence Services are usually tight-lipped when it comes to discussions of the Berlin Tunnel," officials at the Cold War Museum in Virginia point out, "or any post-1945 intelligence operation for that matter, while the Americans have declassified the in-house history of the project."[218]

It's easy to get lost in the fascinating interplay of Cold War politics, but baseball is our vehicle to the topic and we need to return to the diamond. *Battle-*

ground Berlin by David E. Murphy and Sergei A. Kondrashev is a prime source for more information about this topic if you wish to learn more about the war of misinformation between the KGB and CIA.

One unlikely organization proved to be as big an ally to the CIA as MI-6 or any other intelligence network: the Dodgers. Thanks to big personalities (Branch Rickey and Walter O'Malley) and big decisions (relocating from New York to California), the Dodgers arguably altered American politics in the Cold War era more than any other professional sports team.

It wasn't all for patriotic reasons, however.

Anti-Communism and the Dodgers

One team helped change the 1950s and was changed by the 1950s more than any other franchise. Branch Rickey, general manager and part owner of the Brooklyn Dodgers from 1942 to 1950, was a well-known "major anticommunist ally" who used his power to make the Dodgers "into baseball's fiercest bastion of antiradicalism."[219] Though Brooklyn didn't change its name like Cincinnati had, Dodgers historian Carl Prince made clear that Rickey's patriotic zeal became an organizational dictum: "Anticommunism permeated the Dodgers locker room as well as the front office. … [Rickey] willingly delivered a lecture on Americanism to any who weakened."[220]

In 1949, Rickey used his influence over Jackie Robinson to convince his star player to speak against fellow African American celebrity Paul Robeson before the House Un-American Activity Committee (HUAC), which Robinson later regretted and lamented about in his autobiography. In 1950, Walter O'Malley bought out Rickey's Dodgers shares, became the team's majority owner and president, and made sure to continue the organization's avid jingoistic messages. O'Malley befriended political heavyweights such as anticommunist crusader Richard Nixon and international war hero General Douglas MacArthur, who witnessed O'Malley's Dodgers beat their heated rival, the New York Giants, 6-5, on August 9, 1951. The following year, O'Malley underscored the Dodgers' patriotism even further after the U.S. government announced a new educational campaign called "Alert America!" that comprised three convoys across the country, each with ten thirty-foot trailers to teach citizens what to do in case of an atomic attack. When the northeast convoy reached New York City, O'Malley made sure that Happy Felton, host of the Dodgers' *Knothole Gang* television show, led the parade of approximately 250,000 participants marching in front of one million attendees.

Meanwhile, the Dodgers' biggest impact on the country was beginning on the other side of the nation where anticommunist business leaders were starting a land war in Los Angeles. In 1949, residents of Chavez Ravine were informed that their community was going to be leveled and turned into public housing. The plan angered both the residents losing their homes and local business leaders who didn't welcome the lower-income customer base it would create. Knowing that anticommunism was the buzzword of the era, local leaders began accusing the project's leaders of being communists and organized the Citizens Against Socialist Housing (CASH). Though the accusations by CASH that assistant director of the Los Angeles City Housing Authority Frank Wilkinson, one of the main supporters of the project, was a communist were ludicrous (greedy, maybe, but not a socialist) CASH demonstrations hampered and eventually killed the housing project. Wilkinson was called before HUAC, where he refused to answer questions, asserting his Fifth Amendment rights. Found guilty of contempt, Wilkinson spent nine months in prison in 1958.

By the time Wilkinson got out of jail, he could have attended a game featuring the city's new major-league team: the Los Angeles Dodgers.

The protestations of CASH and other local leaders squelched the public housing project in Chavez Ravine and, in 1957, allowed a businessman from New York to buy the controversial land for pennies on the dollar. O'Malley decided Chavez Ravine was the ideal new home for his team, which began playing in Los Angeles the next season. After four seasons at Los Angeles Memorial Coliseum, the Dodgers moved into the brand new 56,000-seat Dodger Stadium in Chavez Ravine beginning with the 1962 season.

The Greatest Game Ever Played

Walter O'Malley's decision to buy Chavez Ravine and move the Dodgers west changed sports and cultural history on both coasts and came about because of anticommunist allegations by California leaders (CASH and its supporters) and the intervention of the insidious HUAC. The Dodgers were not the only team to benefit from the entire Chavez Ravine fiasco. Their National League and New York City sibling, the Giants, joined the Dodgers on the NL's expansion west, forever altering baseball's national footprint.

Football, the National Football League specifically, also benefitted immeasurably from the westward move of the Dodgers and Giants.

The 1958 NFL championship between the Baltimore Colts and New York Giants became known as the "Greatest Game Ever Played" and launched the future of professional football when Johnny Unitas led the Colts to a 23-17 win at Yankee Stadium. That one game was a benchmark in NFL history when the sport equaled (and likely surpassed) the MLB in popularity and one of the main reasons was that bitter New York baseball fans who saw their beloved Dodgers and/or Giants move away gave their emotional support to the city's only successful pro team not named the Yankees or Rangers: the New York Giants of the NFL.

"The move of the Giants to San Francisco and the Dodgers to Los Angeles also left scores of baseball beat writers on New York newspapers without a team to cover," journalist Jack O'Connell explained. "When the Colts and Giants hooked up in the overtime game for the NFL championship in 1958, the

Yankee Stadium press box was filled with former baseball writers who did not know a halfback from halftime. But with no NL baseball to cover, they were left with the NFL. The Giants became New York's glamour team … as they reached the NFL title game six times in eight years."[221]

(50)

●●●●● ▬▬▬▬▬

Vice President Attacked

Venezuelan protestors filled the road, their human blockade forcing the convoy of the American vice president to stop. The vice president's car was pelted with rocks, beaten with clubs and when the windows were smashed members of the Secret Service covered the second most important man in the world, using their bodies as a shield. Though the cars were able to soon push forward, the rest of the trip was cancelled and the vice president flew home the following day due to concerns about deteriorating safety. News of the attack reached the White House minutes after it occurred and the president of the United States rushed American troops into the Caribbean for support.[222]

When the vice president's plane touched down on American soil, President Dwight D. Eisenhower was there to greet it, making a rare personal appearance to welcome home the country's second-in-command: Richard Nixon.

The attack on Nixon's motorcade diminished the political relationship between Venezuela and America to one of its lowest moments to that point (but it would get worse, as we'll soon see). Nixon suggested a solution to the problem that happened to be a soft spot for his boss, Ike: baseball.

Eisenhower was a former professional baseball player and remained an avid fan his entire life. Evidence and accidental admissions by Eisenhower in interviews over the decades revealed that Ike actually played in both the Kansas Central League, the summer after graduating high school, and the Kansas State League, while attending West Point, where he played on the Army football team. Had his professional playing career been revealed to West Point officials, Eisenhower could have been expelled for violating the school's code of conduct. The revelations were serious enough to Ike's reputation that in 1961, while in the Oval Office, he gave orders to his staff to never answer any questions regarding his baseball past as it would "become too complicated."[223]

In the aftermath of the 1958 attack on his convoy, Nixon suggested that the State Department send major leaguers as diplomatic envoys to Venezuela. While using MLB players to build international rapport became an official diplomatic gesture after President Franklin D. Roosevelt created the Office of Inter-American Affairs in 1941 and enlisted Moe Berg as his first baseball ambassador, this was the first time that Nixon was directly involved. Over the next two decades, Nixon would use more sports (football, bowling, ping pong and baseball among them) to reach more international citizens (Venezuelan, Chinese and American) than any other American president.

MLB commissioner Ford Frick accommodated Nixon's request and in November 1958 Frick led a group of nine MLB personnel to Venezuela to offer baseball instruction to eager young players. The group included six players (Richie Ashburn, Philadelphia Phillies, the 1958 NL batting champion; Bob Friend and Dick Groat, Pittsburgh Pirates; Elston Howard, New York Yankees; Pete Runnels, Boston Red Sox; Gus Triandos, Baltimore Orioles), retired player-manager Frankie Frisch, umpire Cal Hubbard, and broadcaster Eloy "Buck" Canel.[224] The trip was so successful that one official described it as doing "more to clear the atmosphere than a dozen top-echelon conferences."[225]

In 1945, the OIAA and its MLB ambassadors were moved under the wing of the Department of State, and on August 31, 1946, the OIAA was officially abolished and its duties were transferred to the State Department.[226] The Mutual Educational and Cultural Exchange Act of 1961 created within the Department of State the new Bureau of Educational and Cultural Affairs (ECA), which continues to use MLB players today as international speakers to help "bridge the last three feet" of international goodwill.[227]

On January 12, 2015, the U.S. Department of State and MLB announced the continuation of the relationship with a new "diamond diplomacy" program that would focus on connecting with youth throughout the Western Hemisphere, just the way that FDR had envisioned and Berg pioneered nearly seventy-five years earlier.[228]

However, in the twenty-first century the Sports Envoys dispatched by the Department of State have focused more on African and Asian countries than such Central American neighbors as Venezuela and Colombia. In fact, the five Sports Envoys to visit Venezuela from 2005 to 2013 were either basketball or soccer players, not baseball; and no athletes were sent in 2014 or 2015. Concerns about violence and crime in Venezuela have led the Department of State's Sports Envoy program and MLB to avoid the country. In the 1990s, more than twenty MLB organizations maintained academies in Venezuela; in 2015 there were only four (Cubs, Phillies, Rays and Tigers). Between the everyday violence on the street, the increase in kidnappings and the strained political relations between the two countries, it would appear that the one bridge between the two nations—baseball—is crumbling. Even though sixty-five Venezuelan players were on MLB rosters in 2015 (second only to the Dominican Republic's eighty-three for foreign-born players), baseball insiders forecast a bleak future for baseball and Venezuela.

"If it's two comparable guys, I'll just go with the Dominican guy," one MLB scout told the *Wall Street Journal* about the difference between signing a Venezuelan player versus one of equal talent from any other country.[229]

On September 17, 2015, President Obama announced the start of a new U.S. diplomatic program called the "Stand Stronger" Citizen Awareness Campaign. Created to foster the integration of immigrants into American society, the campaign is modeled on decades of success that similar previous envoy and diplomatic programs had beginning with the OIAA generations ago. In his announcement, Obama identified four recent American citizens as ambassadors to the program: chef/restaurateur José Andrés, actress Diane Guerrero, singer/songwriter Dave Matthews and baseball star Fernando Valenzuela, who was born in Mexico but became a U.S. citizen earlier in the year.

The inclusion of one of the Dodgers' most famous players was clearly intended to help steady the increasingly turbulent rhetoric surrounding immigration issues with a neighboring country. However, the inclusion of baseball in international diplomacy doesn't always smooth out the wrinkles in global relationships, sometimes it makes them worse.

Hugo Chávez vs. MLB

Hugo Chávez loved the San Francisco Giants, but hated America. Elected as Venezuela's president in 1999, Chávez was openly socialist and antagonistic toward U.S. interests fueled, literally, by his country's massive, lucrative petroleum output distributed through CITGO, the nation's oil company since 1990. A failed U.S.-backed coup to topple the Venezuelan government in 2002 forced Chávez to cancel that year's winter baseball league in retaliation.[230]

Part of Chávez's 2004 reelection campaign included his promise to "hit a home run that would soar over Cuba and land on the White House." After his election victory, supporters gleefully chanted *"home run!"* to celebrate.[231]

In 2006, baseball contributed to making matters even worse between the two countries. Despite being warned repeatedly against doing so, U.S. Ambassador William Brownfield visited Chávez's home state of Barinas in June to cut the ribbon on a new ballpark and distribute baseball equipment to locals. Brownfield's "baseball diplomacy" backfired, as experts predicated, and Chávez threatened to deport him.[232]

Meanwhile back in the U.S., the National Baseball Hall of Fame Museum began a traveling exhibit named *Baseball! Beisbol!* that honored Latino players. The plan was to have the exhibit travel the country before having a permanent home in Cooperstown. Curiously, CITGO was announced as a five-year partner despite the company being controlled by Chávez. Months later, Chávez spoke to the United Nations General Assembly on September 20, where he gave one of the most infamous anti-American speeches in history, calling President George W. Bush the "devil" and claiming that the podium "smells of sulfur still today." Six months later, the Hall of Fame cancelled its agreement with CITGO and ended the traveling tour. In 2009, an interactive-only exhibit named *Viva Baseball!* began with no sponsor.

Though baseball has offered countless Venezuelan youth hope of a better future, the sport instead has become a contemporary weapon for a bloodless attack between the two countries for more than a quarter century. The old adage of baseball being a "moral equivalent of war" can aptly describe America's simmering relationship with Venezuela.

Unfortunately, baseball's ability to foster violence against Americans wasn't created solely on foreign ballfields. Some of the most violent criminals of the twentieth century learned how to create profitable and vicious street gangs thanks to the American Pastime.

(51)

●●●●● ●▬▬▬▬

Street Gangs, Vietnam, & Big Brother

In the 1960s and early 1970s, gang activity, civilian rioting and heightened security and new surveillance technology converged in the home town of William Hulbert, one of fathers of professional baseball: Chicago.

Some of the most notorious gangs in Chicago's history got their start as baseball teams including the Vice Lords, Gangster Two Six's (aka Two Sixers, GTS), the Bishops (aka Almighty Bishops) and Gaylords, according to researchers at the University of Illinois at Chicago.[233] The mutation of youthful baseball team into violent adult gang has been a part of Chicago history for generations going back to the late 1800s when neighborhood teams were hired to be the muscle for the local political machine. In the 1920s, prominent University of Chicago sociologist Frederic Thrasher studied 1,313 gangs in the city to learn about all aspects of their creation, continuation and evolution. He discovered baseball acted as a catalyst for the development of gang activity, helping the young men establish a hierarchy of leadership while learning teamwork.

"Frederic Thrasher's 1927 study of Chicago gangs revealed that delinquents loved baseball," explained historian Harold Seymour, "so much so that they not only had their own teams but played hooky from school to go to games."[234]

One of the gangs Thrasher studied was Ragen's Colts, one of the strongest, most politically-connected gangs in the city that began as a baseball team of Irish immigrants named the Morgan Athletic Club. Named for founder and sponsor Frank Ragen, a Cook County Commissioner and powerful Chicago politician, Ragen's Colts "not only took part in electoral violence but became notorious bootleggers."[235]

Like Ragen's Colts, the Hamburg Athletic Association was a street gang that began as a group of Irish youth who played baseball and other sports, but evolved into one of the most powerful street gangs in Chicago's history. Members of the Hamburgs "played sports, but they also terrorized and beat people senseless, and got out the vote."[236]

The power wielded by these street gangs that started as baseball teams was substantial. In 1919, the Hamburgs and Ragen's Colts were the two key groups that terrorized the city during race riots that left thirty-eight dead, more than 500 injured and 1,000 homeless. "Most of the victims were African-Americans, hunted down in the streets."[237] The gangs "hunted down" African Americans by innovating a new way to terrorize neighborhoods: the drive-by shooting.[238]

"Are people naïve enough to think that the gangs of Chicago are only about blacks and Hispanics?" Asked Benny Lee, a former leader in the Vice Lord gang who became a college lecturer after spending most of his life incarcerated. "The Hamburgs were definitely a gang. A gang of tough white guys. … They were a gang and he was a member."[239]

Who was the "he" Lee referred to?

None other than one of the most (in)famous politicians in Chicago history: "Hizzoner" Richard J. Daley. Mayor of Chicago for twenty-one years after serving for years as a state representative and senator, Daley was a proud member of the Hamburgs as a teenager. Daley, the gang member turned politician, was also the strong-willed Chicago mayor when baseball ushered in the era of Big Brother and forever changed public surveillance.

Vietnam Invades Baseball

Chicago became a hotbed for political protestors as America's military action in Vietnam continued throughout the 1960s and into the 1970s. Daley's heavy-handed retaliation on anti-war protestors during the 1968 Democratic Convention led to five days of confrontation between protesters and police, leading to a legal first when seven activists, known as the Chicago Seven, were arrested and charged with violating recently-enacted laws by crossing state lines and/or using interstate commerce to incite a riot. (Chicago Eight also refers to the group because an eighth conspirator was arrested, but Judge Julius Hoffman

On February 6, 1970, eight days before the Chicago Seven's guilty verdict was announced, Chicago Mayor Richard J. Daley greeted President Richard Nixon at O'Hare International Airport. Though unknown to either of them at the time, both men would have political careers associated with riots, surveillance and baseball before their careers ended.

separated Bobby Seal's trial from his colleague's, eventually sentencing him to forty-eight months in prison.)

The Chicago Seven were the first Americans arrested for these new anti-riot laws (known as the Rap Brown Law) that were passed to combat and contain public dissent in communities whipped into a fury by people who do not reside there. Ironically (and predictably), the trial of the Chicago Seven (Rennie Davis, David Dellinger, John Froines, Tom Hayden, Abbie Hoffman, Jerry Rubin and Lee Weiner) led to even more rioting nationwide after they were given a guilty verdict by a jury on February 14, 1970, and sentenced to five years in jail. Even their lawyer, William Kunstler, was found guilty of contempt.

Two months later to the day, the Chicago Cubs won their home opener against the Phillies, 5-4, but the real action of the day began when the game ended. Fans littered the field with objects before some of them began to leap onto the playing surface. Security responded aggressively, which only prompted a flood of fans to take the field. Players and coaches from both the Cubs and Phillies ran into the locker room for safety in what became known as the Home Opener Riot. (Chicago police officials later acknowledged that they were aware of visiting protestors who were planning demonstrations in the city and that there was a high likelihood that many of them would converge on the home opener at Wrigley Field.)[240]

Cubs officials knew they had to act immediately to prevent further such problems. An unlikely ally stepped forward to help the team determine the best next step. The St. Louis Cardinals had recently installed baskets along their outfield wall to prevent fans from dropping onto the field and team officials consulted about the baskets with their Chicago peers, who had even bigger plans in mind. In early May 1970, the Cubs not only installed the famous baskets that still ring the perimeter, but also installed security cameras throughout the park to monitor fans' behavior, which "was the first use of cameras at any park in baseball."[241]

Within years other stadiums (and even entire cities) copied the pioneering efforts in video surveillance begun at Wrigley Field. Today, closed circuit television monitoring is omnipresent at all major sporting events around the world and it all began on April 14, 1970, thanks to the Home Opener Riot at Wrigley Field.

The Twins Platoon

Chicago wasn't the first Midwest city to become involved directly with the Vietnam conflict. In fact, Minnesota's connection was to the military directly, not via riots or protesters. On June 28, 1967, after the national anthem was sung during pregame ceremonies, 150 local Minnesotans officially enlisted by taking the U.S. Marines oath. The recruits were allowed to remain at the game, seated along the first and third base lines, until the sixth inning. At the end of the sixth, the recruits were led outside where they boarded buses that ushered them to the airport.

Known as the Minnesota Twins Platoon, the recruits were actually broken into two platoons, both of which were flown for training to San Diego, California, before being shipped to Vietnam weeks later.

Official letters to the 150 recruits explained that "the Minnesota Twins Baseball Team is sponsoring this unit" by televising their swearing-in ceremony in pregame festivities. Aside from providing the Marines with an affective propaganda tool by televising their ceremony, there's no evidence that the Twins had any direct involvement with "their" platoons once the recruits boarded the buses for the airport.[242]

(52)

••••• ••---

The Kleptocrat & Clemente

Four decades prior to the horrific Indian Ocean tsunami that became a liquid land grader, destroying everything in its path on December 26, 2004, the December 23, 1972, earthquake in Managua, Nicaragua was a natural disaster of historic proportions that left more than a quarter of a million people dead or homeless during the holiday season. The smell of burning flesh wafted through Managua before sunrise revealed the extent of the damage: more than three-quarters of the city reduced to rubble or worse. Gaping maws in the earth turned neighborhoods into valleys so quickly that entire homes disappeared. Ruptured gas lines created fires across a city that sustained three significant earthquakes within minutes of each other. After the initial earthquake that registered 6.2 on the Richter scale, two after shocks with magnitudes of 5.0 and 5.2 struck one hour later.[243]

President Richard Nixon was briefed immediately because he was a personal friend of Nicaraguan president Anastasio Somoza Debayle. Somoza Debayle was the third, and last, member of the Somoza family to run Nicaragua like a family business, taking what it wanted for personal use along the way and changing laws to fit their whim. The U.S. Government supported Anastasio Somoza Debayle's father, Anastasio Somoza Garcia, in his 1936 coup of the nation's elected president, Juan Bautista Sacasa. Corruption became omnipresent under Somoza Garcia, leading to his assassination in 1956. His death didn't stop the family's unscrupulous practices, which continued under the dictatorial reigns of his elder son, Luis Somoza Debayle, and his younger brother, Anastasio.

Knowledge of Nicaragua's dishonest leaders and their close ties to America forced Nixon's staff to be extra careful when preparing the President's public comments about the tyrannical family, especially in the days and weeks after the horrific earthquake that had people around the world paying attention while they celebrated their holiday festivities at home.

Just eighty-four days before the earthquake, Pittsburgh right fielder Roberto Clemente knocked his 3,000th (and last) career hit on the final day of the season in what proved to be the last game of his Hall of Fame career. During his eighteen years in the big leagues (all with Pittsburgh), Clemente won the Gold Glove Award twelve times, was a twelve-time All-Star, won the 1966 MVP Award (was a top-five finalist three other times) and was the 1971 World Series MVP, but that was not why he was dubbed "The Great One." He earned that nickname as much for his lifetime of philanthropy and relief efforts as for his baseball excellence. Within three days of the earthquake, the Pittsburgh outfielder established, from his home in Puerto Rico, the Roberto Clemente Relief Committee for Nicaragua that accumulated more than $100,000 in cash donations and hundreds of tons of clothing and food. Contributions were so large that even though the ocean freighter *San Expedito* was stuffed with 210 tons of clothing and thirty-six tons of food there were still enough supplies to be delivered that four plane trips were needed.

The widespread corruption in Nicaragua was common knowledge throughout Latin America since Anastasio "Tacho" Somoza Garcia began his family's decades-long reign. With the support of the United States, the Somoza family was able to steal their way to wealth by taking control of companies in nearly every area of life from cattle farms and sugar plantations to car dealerships, hotels, airlines, newspapers, sugar mills, distilleries and immense real estate holdings. By the time leadership fell to Anastasio "Tachito" Somoza Debayle, who graduated at the bottom of his 1946 West Point class (752 out of 875), it was estimated that the Somoza family owned twenty-five percent of the country's entire gross national product through their systematic embezzlement and theft, leaving Henry Kissinger, chairman of a Central American committee investigating Nicaragua, and other politicians stunned. The extent of the Somoza family's larceny was historic, Kissinger's committee reported, claiming that the family's "achievements gave new meaning to the term kleptocracy, that is, government as theft."[244]

The despicable extent the Somoza family was willing to stoop to was revealed with the 1972 earthquake, which the First Family of Nicaragua regarded as a moneymaking moment. In May 1972, Tachito stepped down as the president of Nicaragua, agreeing to allow a three-member junta to take the presidency in exchange for allowing him to remain in charge of the National Guard. Seven months later the devastating earthquake hit and martial law was declared, putting the commander of the National Guard, Tachito, back in control of the country his family had been fleecing for years. Somoza Debayle wasted no time in routing financial aid donated from around the world sent to help the survivors directly into his family's accounts instead. While he was busy stealing millions in financial aid, Tachito also oversaw the sequestering and theft of clothing, food and water that arrived on humanitarian planes. Though starving and dying citizens clawed at the airport's fences, Tachito made sure that every palette of dry goods was thoroughly wrapped in barbed wire. Soldiers shot any of their starving, needy countrymen who attempted to acquire the donated goods. One doctor reported that he had more patients suffering from bullet wounds then earthquake injuries. Dying from thirst and starvation, his patients were shot by soldiers for trying to obtain the supplies air shipped for their survival.

Before a State Dinner on June 2, 1971, President Richard Nixon and Deputy Assistant to the President for National Security Alexander M. Haig, Jr. entertain Nicaragua President Anastasio "Tachito" Somoza Debayle (middle).

"It was sickening," said Dr. Frederick Zugibe, one of the doctors attempting to help. "I remember operating on young kids to remove bullets."[245]

In the midst of all this theft, violence, death and treachery, Clemente's first planeload of supplies arrived the afternoon of December 27. Raul Pelligrina, Clemente's trusted friend, flew with the shipment and was furious by what he encountered. Having heard rumors of the despicable acts being committed in Managua, Pelligrina planned to escort the donations directly to shelters in Masaya, a town outside of Managua where tens of thousands of evacuees had fled.

Upon landing, however, Tachito's soldiers attempted to take everything in the plane. Pelligrina fought off the soldiers, telling them that if they didn't leave everything as it was, he would board up the plane, fly back to Puerto Rico and personally tell Clemente why the shipment wasn't delivered.

Clemente's name made the Nicaraguan soldiers stop. Not only was the ballplayer a celebrity throughout Latin America, but he was also the headliner of a tournament held in Nicaragua just weeks earlier (ironically sponsored by the Somoza family). Clemente had enjoyed his time in Nicaragua so much that the countrymen had become more like long-distance relatives, not merely citizens of a neighboring nation. Remembering the affection that Nicaraguans heaped upon him so recently made Clemente adamant to help the country's earthquake victims: just weeks earlier these same dead and dying people were part of the huge crowds that welcomed him and his Puerto Rican baseball team.

Pelligrina's standoff on the tarmac with the soldiers paused. Frozen by the evocation of Clemente's name, the unscrupulous soldiers weren't sure what to do. Tachito was summoned; he would have to decide. Reluctantly, Tachito allowed Pelligrina to continue his delivery to Masaya. But there was no way to make sure the goods were not looted as soon as the plane departed, Pelligrina explained to Clemente in person later that night back in Puerto Rico. Nicaragua was lawless, except, of course, for the rule requiring everything to go through (and likely to) the Somoza family. Clemente decided he would personally make sure that all the contributions would arrive as intended.

A Miami-based air transport company handled the first three plane-loads of goods from San Juan to Managua, Nicaragua, but there were still nearly 50,000 pounds of goods remaining. For the fourth planeload, which Clemente was going to escort himself personally, a decrepit DC-7 was hired to make the round trip. Arthur Rivera had recently bought the plane that was in dire need of extensive engine and propeller repairs. Instead, Rivera focused on cosmetic improvements like replacing the tires and a new paint job.[246]

Needing one more plane to complete his shipments, Clemente looked at the bright, freshly-painted, orange plane and, knowing nothing about aviation, decided the DC-7 would suffice. Aviation officials in San Juan knew that Rivera was a crook and liar, they had tried to end his flying career multiple times already, but he managed to avoid their grasp every time. Those officials should have been suspicious when Rivera turned in a cargo weight of 39,288 pounds, conveniently under the 40,000-pound weight limit. Rivera's report was a lie, of course. Officials determined later that the cargo was at least two tons over the limit and visual inspections by witnesses claimed that little if any of the cargo was tied down or secured.[247]

At 9:30 p.m., after a delay of more than three hours to try and fix engine problems, the overloaded DC-7 taxied down the runway flown by a pilot with thirteen flight violations, whose copilot was Rivera, untrained for such a role and owner of sixty-six violations, and a flight engineer who, like Rivera, had no training, and Clemente. The plane barely made it over the trees at the end of the runway before crashing into the ocean seconds later. Clemente's body was never found. Hope for the ballplayer was abandoned after the pilot's body was discovered. The violence of the crash was revealed in the pilot's autopsy that identified at least six fatal injuries in addition to having his right leg completely ripped from the body.

Today, Clemente is regarded as something close to a saint in both Puerto Rico and Nicaragua where generations of baseball players, coaches and fans remember him more for his accomplishments off the field more than his feats on it.

Aftermath

Discussing global events and baseball in the early 1970s cannot be discussed without Clemente and his personal mission to thwart Somoza's kleptocratic family. However, the sad fact is that Anastasio Somoza Debayle remained in power until 1979. Clemente's death didn't lead to new aviation laws either, just strict enforcement of rules that were passed only three months before the superstar's death.

Yet, more than forty schools and 200 ballparks bear Clemente's name at institutions in Europe, Africa and, of course, throughout the Western Hemisphere. In Masaya, Nicaragua, the 6,000-seat Estadio Roberto Clemente (Roberto Clemente Stadium) is the city's main sporting venue. Additionally, since 2003 The Roberto Clemente Clinic has provided medical assistance to approximately 100,000 residents throughout Nicaragua, that, for decades, has been one of the poorest countries in the Americas.

Music is not the notes, according to an old saying, but the space between the notes. Sometimes what we don't hear is just as important as what we do. Which may help explain the weird relationship between Nixon and his use of sports. The obvious question everyone around the world asked upon hearing about Clemente's death in 1972 was simple: *Why was he on the plane?*

In his presidential comments about Clemente, Nixon answered the question with the following carefully-crafted words: "He was aboard the airplane because he had heard that a previous shipment had been diverted by profiteers and he wanted to make certain that the clothing and food reached the people in need."

Clemente biographer David Maraniss summed up the conflict-of-interest inherent in Nixon's friend, Somoza, being responsible for Clemente's death: "In citing "profiteers," the memo avoided saying that these were the sons and relatives of General Somoza, a great Nixon fan who had recently sent a letter supporting the President for the Nobel Peace Prize."[248]

It wasn't the only subterfuge Nixon would be known to share, but the Watergate investigation that forced him from the Oval Office would also reveal Tricky Dick's extensive use of sports figures to dupe the American public and government investigators.

(53)

●●●●● ●●●▬▬

FBI, The Boss, & Watergate

FBI agents in the Cleveland field office had just received orders from headquarters in the J. Edgar Hoover Building in Washington D.C. that forced the best agents in the office to change their schedules, giving priority to their new target of attention. There probably wasn't a person in the country, at least not a sports fan anyway, who didn't recognize the target's name considering that he had just purchased the New York Yankees nine months earlier.

George Steinbrenner's role in the Watergate scandal spanned nearly two decades and his involvement proved to be the catalyst that launched the investigation that eventually forced President Richard Nixon to become the only U.S. president to voluntarily leave office. Ironically, the legacy of the biggest presidential sports fan in history was undone in part by the owner of a baseball team, himself a lifelong Democrat whose clandestine bribes of the Republican POTUS backfired with historic consequences.

Owner of Ohio's American Ship Building Company (Amship), Steinbrenner enjoyed the political friendships of such Democratic Party leaders as

Ted Kennedy and Tip O'Neill while fundraising for the 1969 and 1970 Democratic Congressional Dinners. But being a rising name in Democratic Party circles didn't give Steinbrenner any friends in Nixon's Republican administration. In 1970, the National Oceanic and Atmosphere Administration took possession of Amship's most recent construction, the *OSS Researcher*, a multi-use survey vessel. But the ship was delivered late, causing $5.4 million in cost overruns that the government refused to pay. Steinbrenner determined that the best way to get reimbursed for the overruns (and to secure future contracts) was to increase his political standing with Nixon's administration.

In March 1972, Steinbrenner was directed to Herb Kalmbach, Nixon's personal lawyer and the fundraiser in charge of the Committee to Re-elect the President (CREEP), who quickly informed the shipbuilder that the minimum contribution needed to move forward was $100,000. It was a small amount to pay in hopes of recouping $5.4 million, so Steinbrenner agreed. Kalmbach then wrote a cryptic message down: "33 @ 3, 1 @ 1." Translation: thirty-three checks at $3,000 each and one check for $1,000. Due to regulations enforced at the time, $3,000 was the most an individual could contribute without disclosing the contributor's name, which, in Steinbrenner's situation, would alert officials and raise suspicion considering there were so many checks.[249]

On April 6, 1972, hours before a new law would become enacted that restricted campaign contributions, Steinbrenner instructed Amship officials to cut fake bonus checks to eight employees for a total of $42,325.17 (after taxes, the bonuses equaled $25,000). Six employees were instructed to write a personal check for $3,000 to one of the more than thirty fundraising companies run by CREEP, the other two employees were to write checks of $3,500. Steinbrenner then wrote a $3,000 check to each of twenty-five companies on the CREEP list provided by Kalmbach. The thirty-three checks totaled $100,000, but they were not for the exact amounts Kalmbach had instructed. The two checks for $3,500 were over the $3,000 threshold and would eventually provide investigators with evidence of the Amship cover-up.

As the 1972 baseball season began, Steinbrenner learned that his $100,000 bribe was wasted. Instead of earning better treatment from the Nixon administration, Amship was hit with three major blows in April: the Justice Department began an antitrust investigation, the Labor Department slapped Amship with safety code violations and the Secretary of Commerce not only confirmed that the U.S. Government would not pay the $5.4 million in overruns on the *OSS Researcher*, but also demanded $230,000 in late fees and fines.[250]

"They're holding the lumber over my head," Steinbrenner confided to his political friend and one of the most powerful Democrats in Washington D.C., Tip O'Neill, who was the majority leader of the Democratic Party at the time of their discussion. After hearing what Nixon, via Kalmbach, was doing to

Steinbrenner, O'Neill knew "the conclusion was inescapable: what we had here, plain and simple, was an old-fashioned shakedown. I thought I had seen it all, but never in my life had I seen outright blackmail."[251]

Thanks to Steinbrenner's tip, O'Neill noticed donors who traditionally aided him and his fellow Democrats were unexpectedly contributing to Nixon's CREEP fund instead. Initially, O'Neill had no reason to connect his suspicions about Nixon's unusual campaign financing with the infamous break-in on June 17, 1972, at Democratic Headquarters located in the Watergate (an office-hotel-apartment complex in Washington D.C.). But by the time that Steinbrenner bought the New York Yankees on January 3, 1973, the pieces of the puzzle were starting to fit into place for investigators.

April 7, 1969, was a day of firsts for both President Richard Nixon and Washington Senators manager Ted Williams (left). Having taken office only months earlier, it was Nixon's first chance to throw out the ceremonial first pitch of the season that marked the debut of Williams as a manager, not all-star player.

Within months of Steinbrenner taking control of the Yankees, six major corporations admitted to making illegal contributions to CREEP in the same manner Amship had. There was a significant difference, however, in the actions taken by the executives of the other guilty corporations and what the implacable Steinbrenner, known as The Boss, decided to do. The executives who admitted their wrongdoing and allowed investigators to study their finances were not charged with their crimes. The Boss, conversely, insisted that Amship had done nothing wrong, that the employee contributions were not coerced. On September 5, 1973, Amship's connection to the Watergate investigation became public after company employees were subpoenaed to appear before a grand jury. Their grand jury testimony prompted FBI officials in Washington

D.C. to alert their Cleveland colleagues that one of their local businessmen, Steinbrenner, was a priority target of surveillance.[252]

On November 13, 1973, Amship employees testified before the Watergate Committee in Washington that the $25,000 in 1972 political contributions were part of a fake bonus system that was used in 1970 and 1971 as well. On April 5, 1974, Opening Day of the MLB season, Steinbrenner became the first corporate executive brought up on felony charges related to illegal campaign contributions for Nixon, with fourteen counts adding up to a possible fifty-five years in prison and $100,000 in fines.

As the 1974 baseball season commenced, both Nixon and Steinbrenner were too busy proclaiming their innocence to enjoy any games. By August, there was nobody left to listen to all the false denials. On August 8, 1974, Nixon resigned and departed the White House the next day. Two weeks later, on August 23, Steinbrenner's lawyer negotiated a guilty plea to one felony and one misdemeanor, with no prison time and a $15,000 fine.

On November 27, Bowie Kuhn suspended Steinbrenner for two years from having anything to do with the Yankees (later reduced to fifteen months).

President Jimmy Carter refused Steinbrenner's request for a presidential pardon on January 15, 1981. As one of his last gestures before leaving the Oval Office, President Ronald Reagan gave Steinbrenner the pardon he desired on January 19, 1989. The only individual who had to wait longer for a presidential pardon regarding illegal contributions was Armand Hammer, who was pardoned seven months later by President George H. W. Bush.

Questions about Watergate irritated Steinbrenner until his death in 2010. His frustration was somewhat understandable: in the final months that Steinbrenner was alive, the U.S. Supreme Court issued two rulings (*Citizens United vs. Federal Election Commission,* January 21, 2010; and *SpeechNow vs. FEC,* March 26, 2010) that began the era of Super PACs (Political Action Committee), essentially legalizing the very thing that made the Yankees owner a felon.

In the end, forty-eight individuals and twenty corporations pleaded guilty to charges related to Watergate. Steinbrenner was the only baseball executive caught up in the scandal, involved in it longer than any non-elected individual with only Hammer waiting longer for a pardon. It's impossible to know if the Watergate investigation would have proceeded without Steinbrenner's involvement, but O'Neill credited his "lumber over my head" conversation with The Boss as the event that caused Nixon's eventual historic downfall.

(54)

••••• ••••-

Cocaine & the Korean Nixon's Massacre

Willie Stargell won the game single-handedly, going 4-for-4 with two home runs and accounting for all the runs in Pittsburgh's 5-4 win against the visiting Houston Astros, which was good news for the cocaine dealer busy selling drugs in the locker room of the defending World Series champions. Stargell was the cornerstone of the Pirates' "We Are Family" 1979 championship team, emotionally leading his freewheeling teammates while skillfully locking down first base, with utility player John Milner occasionally substituting for the aging future Hall of Famer. Their roles were reversed for the 1980 season, however, with Milner manning first while Stargell occasionally filled in for his younger teammate, whose affection for cocaine would help reveal the extent of illegal drugs in the MLB.

June 13, 1980, was a Friday night and after the long work week 31,854 fans packed Three Rivers Stadium to see their hero, Stargell, not Milner, his replacement. That was just fine with Milner, who used the night off to buy cocaine in the safety of the World Champions' locker room. Five years later, the extent of MLB's 1980s drug-filled era became undeniable public knowledge when Milner testified before a federal grand jury about the extent of ubiquitous drug use in the Pirates locker room and around the league. Milner testified that he bought $200 worth of cocaine from his dealer, Curtis Strong, that Friday night in the Pirates locker room while fans above them cheered on Stargell's heroics.

Milner's testimony, given on September 12, 1985, implicated generations of baseball icons, revealing that aging superstars such as Willie Mays regularly took amphetamines while the younger generation of stars, such as Dave Parker, preferred cocaine. Both drugs were a regular element of locker rooms across the nation, Milner said, as were many other illegal drugs. Players all across baseball were dragged into the scandal: Keith Hernandez, Tim Raines, Dale Berra (Yogi's son), Lonnie Smith and Stargell, too, in addition to Milner, of course.[253]

In the aftermath of the Vietnam Conflict protests, Watergate and heightened Cold War animosity, the 1980s was a bad time for baseball and government partnerships. MLB officials could hardly blame the U.S. government for prosecuting their own players as part of the government's declared war on drugs, even if it included All-Stars like Mays, Stargell and Parker. After all, on the other side of the world, South Korea had learned from other countries—including the U.S., Japan, Venezuela, Cuba and Dominican Republic—how to use baseball to distract from and disguise the government-sanctioned murder of anti-establishment factions.

Gwanju Massacre

The Korean Baseball Organization (KBO), South Korea's baseball league, began on March 27, 1982, when the founder of the league, Chun Doo-hwan, threw out the first pitch. Chun was able to turn the KBO from a simple idea back in December 1981 into a six-team league just fifteen months later because Chun wasn't only the creator and commissioner of the KBO, he was also South Korea's dictator, who needed baseball to distract his citizens from his bloody reign that left hundreds murdered and thousands brutalized, jailed or missing.

MLB commissioner Bowie Kuhn was seated near Chun for KBO's first game, as was Kuhn's Japanese counterpart, Takeso Shimoda.[254] Whether Kuhn and Takeso knew the real reason Chun launched the KBO is up to conjecture, but what isn't debatable to historians is that "since it's birth in December 1981, there was never any doubt that one of the primary objectives of the Korea Baseball Organization (KBO) was to provide an outlet for restless and increasingly rebellious elements of society, particularly young males."[255]

A key aspect of Chun's state-supported league became obvious at the inaugural game between electronics manufacturer Samsung and MBC, Korea's main television network. All six teams that first season were sponsored by

Evoking images of the United States' Arlington Cemetery, South Korea's May 18th National Cemetery (above) allows mourners to remember the hundreds of people slaughtered in the massacre created by Chun Doo-hwan's political coup.

Korean corporations with close ties to the government, which was controlled by Chun. To ensure cooperation and success, Chun approved tax breaks and financial considerations for the six companies and made sure that media outlets created fluff pieces promoting the national good each team (and company) contributed to South Korea's future. To encourage attendance, Chun lifted state-mandated curfews and other restrictions.[256]

"[Chun's] government actively began trying to put a kinder, gentler face on its authoritarian image," explained historian George Gmelch. "Baseball became an important part of those efforts. ... Baseball became a convenient and important instrument of cultural conciliation."[257]

Chun needed to foster better relations with South Koreans because he rose to power in a bloody coup on May 17, 1980, that left the country's former leader, Park Chung-hee, assassinated and the country under martial law. The following day, pro-democracy activists began protests across the country with a particularly strong movement in the southwestern city of Gwangju (also spelled

Kwangju). Paratroopers and soldiers descended on the city, killing hundreds of civilians and maiming countless others who opposed Chun's dictatorship and demanded democracy instead. After ten days of protests, approximately 300 people were murdered by the military. A sham election in 1981 made Chun (the only candidate) the president of South Korea until 1988.[258]

Every Napoleon has his Waterloo and, like Nixon years earlier, Chun's far-reaching corruption, bribery and extortions caught up to him. In 1996, Chun was sentenced to death for mutiny, bribery and insurrection, but a 1997 decision changed the punishment to life in prison. He was ordered to repay $229 million in restitution, but after paying roughly one-quarter of that amount, Chun claimed to be broke despite living in opulent luxury. Investigators claimed that Chun transferred the bulk of his illegal graft to his wife and family members to avoid payments, but were thwarted in efforts to find the missing fortune.

"Koreans regard him as a Nixonian schemer, one whose corruption was legendary," explained *Washington Post* reporter Chico Harlan, who noted that the 2012 revenge movie *26 Years* was one of the most popular movies in South Korean theaters that year. (The film's plot was a fictional story of soldiers assassinating Chun twenty-six years after the Gwangju Massacre.)[259]

Just like Nixon did a few years earlier, Chun used sports, baseball specifically, to distract furious citizens from the ugly truth about his illegal activity. The infamous "plumbers" break-in at the Watergate, one of the key moments in Nixon's scandal, occurred on June 17, 1972. Six days later, Nixon signed into law Title IX of the Education Amendments of 1972 to much media fanfare, and just nine days after that headline-grabbing sports moment, Nixon unveiled his all-time All-Star baseball rosters to the Associated Press. After the Gwangju massacre, Chun didn't have an All-Star roster to share with the public to soften his image because South Korea didn't have any professional baseball teams, which is why the South Korean dictator created the KBO.

"Chun used sport and media to quell opposition to his brutal military policies and distract from the illegitimate basis of his power," sociologist Rachael Miyung Joo explained. "The emotional energy of the public was diverted from anger about the conditions of inequality and corrupt military authority toward frenzy over televised sporting competitions, and the political consciousness of the Korean citizenry fell into a televised sport-induced torpor. … The excessive attention Chun placed on sport plunged Koreans into a … "Wasteland of Sport.""[260]

On November 10, 2015, Attorney General Loretta E. Lynch announced that the U.S. government would return to South Korea $1.1 million in funds seized from companies run by Chun's son, who admitted that the funds for his investments came from his father. The remainder of the illicit fortune Chun amassed is still missing.

(55)

●●●●● ●●●●●

The Baseball-ocracy of Cuba

The diminutive infielder was one of the smallest players on the field that day, but he must have had one of the biggest smiles: not only had he helped lead his team to a narrow victory, but there were thousands of people in paid attendance which meant he could buy many more guns and ammunition to arm his fellow rebel soldiers. His smile would have been difficult to see under his large mustache, a signature affectation that he would become known for to his countrymen generations later who would revere him as the daring visionary who helped start a new country by first founding a new baseball league to pay for it.

On December 29, 1878, Emilio Sabourín's Havana (Habana) club defeated the Almendares, 21-20, in the first Cuban League game. While any serious player who has ever taken the field wants to win, the final score wasn't *that* important on that particular day. There were many larger things going on than just a ballgame, especially for the rebel infielder with the big mustache whose love of baseball and country helped turn one of Spain's colonies into its own independent country.

Sabourín may well be the best and most complete embodiment of the multiple ways baseball can be used to change the world and help build a nation in his dedication to Cuban independence from Spanish rule. Born in Havana in 1853, Sabourín would become known to his fellow patriots and teammates for three passions: "baseball, his family and his homeland." By the time he was a teenager, Sabourín developed two very important skills: how to use his small size to great advantage on the baseball diamond and how to repair, and rebuild if necessary, old weapons discarded by the Spanish.[261] The two skills would become inextricably interwoven, leading to the creation of Cuba's identity and passion, but also to Sabourín's painful death.

Under Spanish control since Christopher Columbus claimed the island for Spain in 1492, native inhabitants of the island fought against Spanish imperial domination, culminating in The Ten Years' War (1868-1878) that unsuccessfully fought for Cuban independence. Sabourín was thirteen years old when baseball was introduced in 1866 to the island by children of wealthy families schooled in the United States who brought the game home and by American sailors whose ships were anchored in the harbors. With equal influence on both children and adults, baseball grabbed the interest of Cubans like nothing had before. Spanish authorities took notice and began the first of several government bans against the sport.

When The Ten Years' War ended without Cuban independence, Sabourín founded La Liga General de Base Ball de la Isla de Cuba in Havana (Cuban League). The Cuban League allowed Sabourín to do several things at the same time: it offered indigenous Cubans sporting entertainment alternatives to the Spanish bullfight spectacles reviled by most natives, provided a source of homegrown pride for local players and teams but mostly the league created a way to generate funds for the revolutionary efforts of anti-Spain rebels. In the early years of the Cuban League, players learned to use the game as a way to conduct revolutionary meetings out in the open, during games, where no government agents or spies from local fruit company manufacturers could eavesdrop. Banned from meeting in public outside of the ballpark, the players were able to make revolutionary plans while ostensibly discussing baseball strategy on the field.[262]

The Cuban League was so successful at raising funds that were channeled into revolutionary coffers, that Cuban baseball teams were created in Florida to raise additional money in the United States. Sabourín's love of baseball and country cost him his life. After thirteen seasons with his beloved Havana club (seven as player, six as manager), Sabourín was arrested on December 15, 1895, by Spanish authorities for conspiracy. Less than eighteen months later he died from pneumonia and malnutrition in a Spanish prison in Africa.

Sabourín was hardly the only person in baseball locker rooms to give their life for Cuban independence. Both outfielder Ricardo Cabaleiro and pitcher Juan Manuel Pastoriza are enshrined in the Cuban Baseball Hall of Fame and died in military action fighting for Cuban independence. In 1897, sports reporter Luis Someillan was sentenced to life in prison for rebellious actions. The difference between the strategy of winning a baseball game and winning a revolution was very little, according to some Cuban rebels. Aurelio Miranda, one of Sabourín's teammates who helped establish the Havana Base Ball Club, explained that the sport taught young Cubans how to prepare for war and fight for their political independence.

Though he played for parts of six unspectacular seasons with the Chicago Cubs, Bob Will stands out in the photo that he signed before his death in 2011. The former outfielder took with him to the grave the details of what transpired behind this stunning overlap in revolution and baseball history that occurred in 1959 after Fidel Castro's rebels took control of Cuba.

"The baseball player must learn to wait for his pitch, his play, his moment," Miranda explained. "An untimely move, a base taken prematurely, a ground ball fielded hastily leads to a game lost. The same impatience, the absence of the virtue of knowing how to wait, leads to a loss and often leads to the loss of the nation."[263]

Indeed, few countries have embraced baseball more than Cuba, which used the sport to foster independence from Spain in the nineteenth century and to fight the United States in the twentieth.

"Baseball and the idea of a proud Cuban nation have indeed been intimately linked from the outset of Cuban national history in the 1870s and 1880s; the island's professional league and its status as sovereign nation were born hand in hand during the same decade" explained Cuban historian Peter C. Bjarkman. "No other national institution so clearly reflects what most Cubans have long held sacred as constituting the very essence of what it means to be distinctly Cuban."[264]

CASTRO

It was technically a softball, not a baseball, that was going to kill the world leader during his stay in New York City. The CIA-trained explosives expert needed the larger ball in order to fully contain the artisan contact bomb inside; a baseball was just too small for the huge detonation that was desired. After all, the ball was going to be tossed into, or at least strike, Fidel Castro's vehicle, exploding on contact and destroying the car and the Cuban leader, if everything went according to the plan. Scheduled to give a speech at the United Nations, Fidel Castro's rare visit to American soil coincided with the 1979 World Series and provided assassins a prime opportunity. By the time Game 2 of the 1979 World Series between the Orioles and Pirates was over later that night, Castro would be dead, the killers hoped.

Ironically, American forces protected Castro and squelched the assassination attempt. The head of Castro's intelligence and security, Fabian Escalante, became aware of the exploding softball plot and alerted the Federal Bureau of Investigations, which ended the scheme. The following day Castro gave his speech to the United Nations as planned.

According to Escalante, it wasn't the first time that baseball, or, in this particular instance, a softball, was used to try and kill Castro. In the documentary *638 Ways To Kill Castro,* Escalante revealed that another assassination attempt on Castro was planned for his attendance at a baseball game. Anti-Castro assassins would pose as band members and when the marching band approached Castro's seats, they would throw hand grenades at the Cuban leader. All 638 assassination attempts during Castro's forty-nine-year Cuban reign failed, including the historically disastrous Bay of Pigs invasion, and through it all Castro became one of the most influential individuals in baseball history.

"No other ex-ballplayer has ever stepped more dramatically from the schoolboy diamond into a role that so radically affected the lives and fortunes of so many millions throughout the Western Hemisphere and beyond," explained Bjarkman, who has spent years studying Cuban baseball and its global influence. "Fidel may not have exercised much control over his fastball in long-lost schoolboy days. But he eventually proved a natural-born expert (a true "phenom") at controlling baseball (the institution) as a highly useful instrument for carefully building his revolutionary society and also for maintaining his propaganda leverage in worldwide Cold War politics."[265]

It was as if Castro was Sabourín reincarnated, the embodiment of baseball aiding Cuban politics and Cuban politics dictating baseball's future. The son of wealthy landowners, Castro learned to use baseball as a tool of manipulation and control as a youth, lessons he used later to launch his political career which vexed the United States for half a century. Though only a mediocre pitcher at best in his youth, Castro controlled all the action because his father paid for the equipment that was used. When his team was no longer winning or he was disappointed in any way, Castro literally took his ball and went home.[266]

Though he never played a competitive game beyond sandlot games as a child (the only team sport he played at his elite, private high school was basketball), Castro enjoyed a fictional reputation as being a fantastic pitcher, with a fastball that MLB teams were willing to pay top dollar to acquire.

Castro's wealthy family provided the means, money, education and connections Castro needed to succeed in politics, but his grassroots popularity was built upon the widespread stories of his pitching excellence in the baseball-crazy country. The Washington Senators, New York Yankees, Pittsburgh Pirates and New York Giants wanted to sign Castro, so the stories claimed, willing to pay as much as $5,000 for him to sign at a time when other pitchers signed for less than $200. Castro turned down the American offers to lead the Cuban people, his propaganda enthused, if you let him. Cubans and storytellers everywhere alike loved the story, except that it wasn't true. It was a perfect piece of propaganda that recalled Lucilla's comment to her father in the movie *Gladiator*: "This is a pleasant fiction, is it not?"

Castro was never scouted to play professionally, there were never any contracts offered, the stories were carefully created for Cubans to embrace Castro as their new leader. The mental manipulations worked, especially since Castro was eager to do everything to perpetuate the myths and rumors.[267]

On January 1, 1959, Cuban dictator Fulgencio Batista fled the country, leaving Cuba's leadership to Castro's July 26th Movement (named for Castro's failed rebel attack on a military base on July 26, 1953.) Six months later, in conjunction with July 26th celebrations, Castro solidified his role in the dual worlds of baseball and international politics.

The Rochester Red Wings were scheduled for a three-game stand at the Havana Sugar Kings for July 24-26, 1959. To elicit public support, Castro scheduled a special two-inning exhibition game before the Friday night game. Pitted against a team of military police were Los Barbudos (The Bearded Ones), a team of army soldiers that had Castro, Cuba's No. 1 Bearded One, as their pitcher. Wearing number nineteen, Castro pitched both innings for Los Barbudos, recorded two strikeouts and grounded out in his only at bat. Photos of him in carefully crafted nationalistic photo ops have often been mistakenly referred to as evidence of Castro's pitching prowess, when it was nothing more than a political outing disguised as a baseball performance.

The game on Saturday began late in order to have an audience for a planned midnight celebration of the July 26th rebellion, during which time many fans fired pistols to celebrate. After play resumed, however, Rochester third base coach Frank Verdi was grazed by gunfire, as was Sugar Kings shortstop Leo Cárdenas. The Red Wings retreated to the locker room and flew home the following day without playing the Sunday game.

After the holiday weekend, Castro resumed his political agenda of centralizing all corporate control with his communist regime. American businesses were forced to abandon Cuba, including Organized Baseball and mobsters who ran Havana casinos. In May 1960, Cuba established diplomatic relations with the Soviet Union and weeks later International League officials moved the Sugar Kings from Havana to Jersey City, New Jersey, ending professional baseball's existence in Cuba.

In January 1961, the United States cut diplomatic relations with Cuba and two months later, Castro's administration legislated National Decree Number 936, which banned all professional sports in Cuba. Just as when he was a child and would take his ball and glove and go home if his team was not winning, Castro decided that if professional baseball would not be welcoming to Cuba then Cuba would not welcome Organized Baseball of any kind, withholding his country's best players from playing for the enjoyment of foreign crowds.

Weeks after National Decree Number 936 became law, American and Cuban relations worsened with the April 17, 1961, Bay of Pigs invasion. On January 14, 1962, relationships between the two countries sunk further when Castro launched the Cuban National Series (widely referred to as the Cuban League) by hitting a ceremonial first pitch before the game. Photos of Castro making the ceremonial hit were reported as evidence of his prodigious baseball skills, even though it was yet, again, nothing more than a political photo op.

Castro's Cuban League would forever alter the balance of baseball power in world competition. While Castro had his mind on baseball games, his American counterparts were going to unthinkable extremes to remove Castro at all costs.

In early 1962, the Joint Chiefs of Staff reviewed a report prepared by the Department of Defense about The Cuba Project, the U.S. government's highly-classified secret plan to overthrow Castro and his communist regime. The Cuba Project had two separate but interrelated approaches dubbed Operation Northwoods and Operation Mongoose.

Operation Northwoods showed the violent (and morally questionable) lengths that the Department of Defense was willing to go to create public condemnation of Cuba. On March 13, 1962, Army General Lyman L. Lemnitzer, Chairman of the Joint Chiefs of Staff, prepared a Top Secret memorandum titled "Justification for U.S. Military Intervention in Cuba" that outlined the chilling options being considered at the time, including creating fake terrorist attacks that American forces would perpetrate against American citizens, planes, ships, businesses and buildings, followed by creating circumstantial "evidence" that clearly implicated Cuba. DoD officials outlined plans to crash commercial planes, explode military ships and to conduct terrorist attacks against communities of Cuban defectors, located primarily in Florida, in order to manufacture an excuse for overt U.S. military action against Cuba.[268]

Working in conjunction with Operation Northwoods was Operation Mongoose, managed by Brigadier General Edward Lansdale. On July 25, 1962, Lansdale prepared DoD document No. 620675 that detailed the mission to physically infiltrate Cuba with pro-American spies (both Cuban defectors who returned to their native nation for the mission and American-trained CIA agents), surveillance equipment, and communication devices, to create and train an anti-Castro resistance effort within the nation.[269]

Amid this tense atmosphere yet another Castro lie was told that only further enhanced the Cuban leader's baseball mythology and helped fuel suspicion of Cuban actions. In June 1964 writer Myron Cope and former big-leaguer Don Hoak penned an article for *Sport* magazine that claimed Castro and his rebels had infiltrated an on-going baseball game years earlier with Castro taking the mound and pitching to Hoak. Decades later, historians proved Hoak's story was a hoax, but by then Castro's status as leader of the amateur baseball world was solidified.[270]

On February 19, 2008, Castro announced he would step down as Cuban leader, giving power to his brother, Raúl. During his forty-nine-year reign, Castro turned Cuba into one of the world's strongest baseball powerhouses by publicly rejecting the American pro system. After turning the Cuban League into a de facto state-run baseball organization, the Cuban national team had a 159-game win streak from 1987 to 1997 and won an unprecedented forty-four international tournament titles in forty-nine years, including Olympic Gold-medal teams (1992, 1996, 2004), Olympic silver-medal teams (2000, 2008), and the 2006 World Baseball Classic runner-up.

More importantly, Castro used baseball as a political weapon to battle America where nuclear weapons and economic sanction had failed. Home-and-home exhibition games against the Baltimore Orioles in 1999 were highly controversial, prompting many protests in the U.S., but the games helped thaw the frosty Cold War relationships between the two countries. When MLB officials announced the creation of the World Baseball Classic, the U.S. boycott of Cuba initially forced MLB organizers to exclude the island nation from what was billed as the World Cup of baseball. International pressure made American policymakers relent and allow the inclusion of the Cuban national team, which went on to take second place in the inaugural global event won by Japan.

Already firmly entrenched as the Cuban Pastime, baseball became more than merely the most popular national sport; it had become an affective and effective way to fight the United States without bloodshed. In the twenty-first century, baseball's role in Cuban politics escalated even further, becoming a major source of economic income unlike anything else in the world.

CUBA TODAY

In 2015, there were eighteen Cuban-born players on MLB rosters, who earned a combined $83,626,717 in salary. That total would make baseball Cuba's sixth-grossing export, falling equidistant between No. 5 on the list (exports of liquor, $117 million) and No. 6 (glands/organs, $68 million).[271]

On December 17, 2014, President Barack Obama and Cuban President Raúl Castro announced that, after eighteen months of negotiations to free convicted and political prisoners, the two countries would resume official diplomatic relations for the first time since 1961. On July 20, 2015, the U.S. Interests Section in Havana officially became the U.S. Embassy, just days after the 2015 All-Star Game that featured three of Cuba's finest exports: Yoenis Céspedes (Tigers, who was traded in mid-season to the New York Mets and led his new team to the 2015 World Series), Aroldis Chapman (Reds) and Yasmani Grandal (Dodgers).

Rewriting of new U.S. legislation and laws regarding Cuba will take time, but every Cuban economist and baseball scout, coach and player will be focused on section 515.505 of Subpart E of the Federal Code of Regulations that outlines how baseball officials are allowed to legally deal with the unblocking of certain Cuban nationals.[272]

Big money is at stake, enough to alter both Cuba's economy and the future success of many MLB teams. New U.S. embargo laws, trade regulations and MLB international player acquisitions rules have not been rewritten yet as of the writing of this book, but Cuba tipped its hand to how it will likely handle future legislation immediately after the joint announcement in December 2014. Within weeks of the announcement, Cuban officials increased the minimum number of years players were required to play in Cuba before being allowed to play elsewhere from three to five years, keeping the talent home longer to both entertain the public and mature individuals into better players, which will likely increase their value.

In September 2013, Cuban officials changed regulations for baseball players, instituting a system where the government would negotiate the leasing of the players to foreign baseball leagues in Mexico, Japan, Korea or Taiwan, with the Cuban government collecting approximately ten percent of the contract. Complications with MLB's rules with the Mexican League created problems for the new Cuban rules, but preliminary deals with Japanese teams have been successful.

"Cuba will assuredly orchestrate an arrangement that will approximate if not exactly mirror the Japanese League posting system—a system also used by the professional leagues in Korea, Taiwan and Mexico," Bjarkman explained. "Cuba alone will stand as the largest winner under the likely scenario."[273]

Current MLB rules cap the price tag for international posting fees that Japanese teams can set for an individual player at $20 million. As the governing body for all of Cuban baseball, the Cuban government would receive the posting fees for players signed to MLB contracts. Given the high-caliber of Cuban talent signed by MLB teams in recent years, Cuban baseball officials could negotiate a higher cap for Cuban players.

The numbers could become staggering. In 2014 and 2015, it was estimated that 350 Cuban-born players played in foreign leagues.[274] If each player earned a million-dollar posting fee, the $350 million Cuba would receive would make baseball players the country's second-grossing export, trailing only raw sugar ($447 million per year). Baseball talent is inconsistent, of course, with many low-end players not worthy of a seven-figure posting fee. But the top-shelf talent at the other end has produced jaw-dropping contracts for Cuban prospects signed around the time that Obama and Castro made their initial announcement. After Yasiel Puig's harrowing experience to get to American soil, the Los Angeles Dodgers rewarded him with a seven-year, $42-million deal in 2012. The Dodgers' got a steal of a deal for the five-tool player considering that the average salary for Cuban talent quickly rose to $10 million per year. In 2013, Cuban first baseman José Abreu signed with the White Sox for $68 million over six years; in 2014, outfielders Rusney Castillo ($72.5 million, seven years) and Yasmany Tomás ($68.5 million, six years) signed with the Red Sox and Diamondbacks, respectively; and in 2015, Cuban second baseman Yoan Moncada shattered the MLB signing bonus record with a $31.5 million bonus, quadrupling the previous high of $8.27 million.

The next chapter in baseball's ongoing story of how it is intimately involved in international politics and policy has yet to be finalized.

Will the new influx of baseball money improve baseball conditions for Cuban fans, players and coaches, or will the rich posting fees merely pad the pockets of a few elite government figures?

Will the river of Cuban talent become siphoned off so quickly that it becomes merely a trickle in coming years?

Will the dreams of MLB academies erected throughout the island happen, or would they merely become the abandoned white elephants that dot Venezuela in the wake of fleeing MLB teams?

We don't know yet, unfortunately.

History is happening around the world as you read these words, not just in the ever-evolving Cuban-American relationship, but in all corners of the world. Future stories about historic actions are tales told about moments that have yet to happen. Regardless of what the future holds for geopolitical negotiations, international military actions and the need for events that foster peace between previously hostile neighbors, baseball will be there, no matter what language the players speak or where they call home, maintaining its special role as the world's preeminent "moral equivalent of war."

ACKNOWLEDGMENTS

.- -.-. -.- -. --- .-- .-.. . -.. --. -- . -. - ...

Though the detailed research for this book, the hours spent poring over hundreds of books in libraries and private collections, took a little more than a year to complete, the reality is that this book was a lifetime in the making. Raised in a family with strong military and governmental connections, I eschewed the life of a soldier in favor of publishing, but I have always been proud of the accomplishments and responsibilities of my family. Military intelligence was a part of my family life from the day I was born and goes all the way back to our Founding Fathers. Many things I grew up knowing and experiencing first-hand could never be discussed with colleagues, friends or classmates.

One of the thrills being a journalist is knowing tomorrow's headlines today, and so it is in military intelligence as well. The consequences and outcomes are much more severe in the military, so I want to extend special acknowledgement and thanks to military personnel everywhere, regardless of rank, military branch or theater of deployment. Many revelations in this book could be the things taught on the first day of any military training, but what is remedial for military people and their families is a revelation to anyone unfamiliar with that lifestyle.

I grew up knowing spooks (intelligence officers) both terrifying and kind. Surveillance, deception and the ability to detect both were part of everyday life growing up and it was only when I grew older that I realized the unusualness of knowing select state secrets or how to detect when phone conversations were being recorded and how to tell the difference from typical business buildings from "spook" ones.

Ignorance is bliss, as the old aphorism goes, but it can also be dangerous. My goal with this book was to help sports fans and the general public get a peek behind the curtain of many aspects of life that they take for granted, never knew about or felt was imagined or unreal such as the extent governments and various agents will go to in an effort to keep the peace or to camouflage their future intentions or past actions. Having worked with comedians, I believe the old adage is true that there is an ounce of honesty in every pound of humor. I also believe the same can be said for many conspiracy theories and alleged journalism: never believe everything you read, less of what you hear and always question what and why you are doing something important.

As a veteran journalist who was raised by military veterans, I find both fields use the same tactics of manipulating facts, figures and biased reporting to subtly convince the public to act, think and/or support a storyline that they are pushing. I simply want to help reveal these machinations to those who haven't thought about them, hopefully shining a light on something that tries so desperately to remain hidden: the mental manipulations inherent in contemporary life that go unnoticed. I chose baseball as the vehicle to get us there, but the ideas shared within this book are surfeit and ubiquitous in a world of ever-growing military operations (at home and abroad), in the marketing and advertising that engulfs every aspect of our lives and, most importantly, in media stories often created to support and/or sell both of them.

Just because you never heard a historical fact before doesn't mean it didn't really happen.

I have two groups of people I wish to thank. First, I want to thank the military personnel in my family who served in battle and whose conversations helped me understand many things I never had to experience:

Former Lieutenant Donald J. Rowan, U.S. Navy, Naval Intelligence, the Central Intelligence Agency, and my father. We didn't always agree, but this book would not have happened without the lessons I learned from you that will never be taught in any public school.

Retired Colonel Roger McCausland, U.S. Air Force, and my uncle. Our discussions about your missions helped me understand many difficulties of wartime better than any book.

Retired Lieutenant Colonel Charles Taylor, U.S. Air Force, and my cousin. Keep fighting the good fight, I'm proud to be related to you.

James Rowan, a member of the old Irish Republican Army, and my grandfather. Though your name is spelled Ruane not Rowan on the IRA monument in Menlough, Ireland, nothing changes my pride knowing you were one of the original freedom fighters who helped launch the battle for Ireland's independence.

Vice President and Governor George Clinton, my great-great grandfather (I'm not sure how my greats ago). One of our country's Founding Fathers, Grandpa

Clinton served this country as vice president twice (Thomas Jefferson, James Madison) and was the first governor of New York. Obviously I never knew him, but a dream I had once of him asking me *"What have you done to improve the world?"* haunted me enough to write this book.

The following people are those who helped me in various ways while working on this book.

Dr. Gary Skaletsky, thank you for your invaluable assistance. Your input was fascinating and I'm honored you allowed me into your sanctuary.

Harvey, Sean and Patrice - no matter how many miles apart, we'll always be together. I've never had any friends support and help me as much as you have. *Laissez les bon temps roulez!*

Holly Wilton, your support has always been superlative and though it's dangerous singling out family members there is no way I could acknowledge and thank anyone for their support without mentioning you and all you have done.

Katia and Kyriakos, your friendship and assistance will always be cherished. Merci. Efcharisto. Thank you.

Chicago Public Library, I spent so much time in the library stacks I felt like an employee. The CPL is simply the best, most extensive resource any researcher could hope to use.

Tony Kornheiser. No Mister Tony is not my personal friend, but I've been a Loyal Little from Day 1 and your radio show played in my ears while I spent countless hours doing research. Thank you. And thanks also to Nigel, Gary, Jeanne, David, and all the rest for the entertainment, especially Reginald, who will surely be our overlord after the animal apocalypse. Left out the bedroom, left at the kitchen and into my home office. Peanut butter and jelly sandwich with potato chips and milk. Please tell Michael: it's raining somewhere in the world, I'm just not sure where.

Bob Costas, your support for *The Cubs Quotient* will forever be evidence that Cardinals fans are a respectable class apart from others. Thank you.

END NOTES

Sources

●●● ▬▬▬ ●●▬ ▬●▬ ▬●▬● ● ●●●

SECTION I - PREGAME

1. Sofie Remijse, *The End of Greek Athletics in Late Antiquity* (Cambridge, U.K.: Cambridge University Press, 2004), 49.
2. David G. McComb, *Sports in World History* (New York: Taylor & Francis, Inc., 2004), 45-46.
3. Robert Elias, *The Empire Strikes Out* (New York: The New Press, 2010), 5-6.
4. "Reason Behind the Rhyme, 'Yankee Doodle,'" npr.org, http://www.npr.org/templates/story/story.php?storyId=4970266, accessed November 5, 2015.
5. "Battle of Bunker Hill," History.com, http://www.history.com/topics/american-revolution/battle-of-bunker-hill, accessed November 5, 2015.
6. Albert G. Spalding, *America's National Game* (New York: American Sports Publishing Company, 1911), 18-19.
7. George Ewing, *The Military Journal of George Ewing* (1754-1824) (Yonkers, New York: private printing, 1928), 34-35.
8. David Block, *Baseball Before We Knew It* (Lincoln, Nebraska: University of Nebraska Press, 2005) 237.
9. "Social Identity Theory," simplypsychology.org, http://www.simplypsychology.org/social-identity-theory.html, accessed November 5, 2015.
10. John Thorn, *Baseball in the Garden of Eden* (New York: Simon and Schuster, 2011), xii – xii.
11. Joseph Campbell, *The Power of Myth* (New York: Doubleday, 1988), 92.
12. Joel Zoss & John Bowman, *Diamonds in the Rough* (New York: Macmillan Publishing Company, 1989) 51-56, 385.
13. Block, *Baseball*, 250.
14. Zev Chafets, *Cooperstown Confidential* (Doubleday: New York, 2009) 34.
15. James Fenimore Cooper, *Home as Found* (New York: D. Appleton & Company, 1901) 181–185.

SECTION II - REACHING FIRST

16. Michael S. Green, *Lincoln and the Election of 1860* (Carbondale, Illinois: Southern Illinois University Press, 2011) 61-62.
17. George B. Kirsch, *Baseball in Blue and Gray* (Princeton, New Jersey: Princeton University Press, 2003) 134.
18. Alexander Kelly McClure, *"Abe" Lincoln's Yarns and Stories* (New York: Western W. Wilson, 1901) 271.
19. Kirsch, *Blue and Gray*, 90.
20. Zoss & Bowman, *Diamonds*, 234.

21. Abner Doubleday, *Reminiscences of Forts Sumter and Moultrie, 1860-1861* (New York: Harper & Brothers, 1876) 143-146.
22. "Manassass, First," NPS.gov, http://www.nps.gov/abpp/battles/va005.htm, accessed November 7, 2015.
23. "Ball's Bluff," NPS.gov, http://www.nps.gov/abpp/battles/va006.htm, accessed November 7, 2015.
24. J. David Hacker, "Recounting the Dead," The New York Times, September 20, 2011, http://opinionator.blogs.nytimes.com/2011/09/20/recounting-the-dead/#more-105317, accessed November 7, 2015.
25. William Ryczek, *When Johnny Came Sliding Home* (Jefferson, N.C.: McFarland & Company, 1998) 29.
26. William Ryczek, *Baseball's First Inning* (Jefferson, N.C.: McFarland & Company, 2009) 190.
27. Ibid., 213-214.
28. Thorn, *Eden*, 121-123.
29. Thorn, *Eden*, 123.
30. Thorn, *Eden*, 124.
31. "October 14, 1862: The Martyrdom of Jim Creighton," SABR.org, http://sabr.org/gamesproj/game/october-14-1862-martyrdom-jim-creighton, accessed July 17, 2015.
32. Thorn, *Eden*, 126.
33. Ryczek, *First*, 38.
34. Laura Nahmias, "Hilton Head swung for the fences with 1862 baseball game," The Island Packet, May 21, 2010, http://www.islandpacket.com/2010/05/21/1248288_hilton-head-swung-for-the-fences.html?rh=1, accessed November 5, 2015.
35. John Hanc, "That Time 150 Years Ago When Thousands of People Watched Baseball on Christmas Day," Smithsonian Magazine, December 21, 2012, http://www.smithsonianmag.com/history/that-time-150-years-ago-when-thousands-of-people-watched-baseball-on-christmas-day-170368208/?no-ist, accessed November 5, 2015.
36. "The Blockade of Confederate Ports, 1861-1865," history.state.gov, https://history.state.gov/milestones/1861-1865/blockade, accessed November 5, 2015.
37. "Blockade! The Blockading of Southern Seaports During the Civil War, CivilWar.org, http://www.civilwar.org/education/history/navy-hub/navy-history/blockade.html, accessed, November 5, 2015.
38. Kirsch, *Blue and Gray*, 32-33.
39. Ibid., 41.
40. Ibid., 31-32.
41. Ibid., 37.
42. Ibid., 36-37.
43. Ibid., 31-32.
44. Ibid., 40.
45. Ibid., 42.
46. Ibid., 39-40.
47. "July 4, 1862: The Civil War POW Game," SABR.org, http://sabr.org/gamesproj/game/july-4-1862-civil-war-pow-game#sdendnote8anc, accessed July 17, 2015.
48. George Kirsch, "Blacks, Baseball and the Civil War," New York Times, September 23, 2014, http://opinionator.blogs.nytimes.com/2014/09/23/blacks-baseball-and-the-civil-war/?_r=0, accessed November 5, 2015.
49. George Kirsch, "Blacks, Baseball and the Civil War," New York Times, September 23, 2014, http://opinionator.blogs.nytimes.com/2014/09/23/blacks-baseball-and-the-civil-war/?_r=0, accessed November 5, 2015.
50. Thorn, *Eden*, 130.
51. Ibid., 129-131.
52. Ibid., *Eden*, 153.

53. "Who Was Jim Crow?," Jim Crow Museum of Racist Memorabilia, Ferris.edu, http://www.ferris.edu/HTMLS/news/jimcrow/index.htm, accessed November 7, 2015.
54. "Researching African Americans In the U.S. Army, 1866-1890," Archives.gov, http://www.archives.gov/publications/prologue/2001/spring/buffalo-soldiers.html, accessed November 7, 2015.
55. Patrick Mendoza, *From Bunker Hill to Baghdad: True Stories of America's Veterans* (Santa Barbara, California: ABC-CLIO, LLC, 2014) 35.
56. John H. Nankivell, *Buffalo Soldier Regiment* (Lincoln, Nebraska: University of Nebraska Press, 2001) 165.
57. "Council's Decision May Bring on Baseball War,"Hawaiian Commercial Appeal, http://agatetype.typepad.com/agate_type/2009/09/25th_infantry_wreckers.html, accessed November 7, 2015.
58. "Council's Decision May Bring on Baseball War,"Hawaiian Commercial Appeal, http://agatetype.typepad.com/agate_type/2009/09/25th_infantry_wreckers.html, accessed November 7, 2015.
59. Tom Hayes, "Buffalo Soldiers Got Last Laugh on Custer," Desert News, June 16, 1996, http://www.deseretnews.com/article/496071/BUFFALO-SOLDIERS-GOT-THE-LAST-LAUGH-ON-CUSTER.html?pg=all, accessed November 7, 2015.
60. Frederick Whittaker, *A Complete Life of Gen. George Custer* (New York: Sheldon & Co, 1876) 1.
61. Michael Rutter, *Myths and Mysteries of the Old West* (Guilford, CT: The Globe Pequot Press, 2005) 59-60.
62. "Battle of Little Bighorn," historynet.com, http://www.historynet.com/battle-of-little-bighorn, accessed November 7, 2015.
63. "White Man Runs Him and Curley's Battlefield Interview with General H.L. Scott," astonisher.com, http://www.astonisher.com/archives/museum/white_man_runs_him_curley_little_big_horn.html#benteen_save, accessed November 7, 2015.
64. "Custer massacres Cheyenne on Washita River," History.com, http://www.history.com/this-day-in-history/custer-massacres-cheyenne-on-washita-river, accessed November 7, 2015.
65. "The Washita Letter That Enraged Custer," Astonisher.com, http://www.astonisher.com/archives/museum/frederick_benteen_washita.html, accessed November 7, 2015.
66. Harold Schindler, *Frederick Benteen and Fort Damn Shame* (Salt Lake City, Utah: Utah Historical Quarterly, 1998) 264-270.
67. Elias, *Empire*, 15.
68. "Frederick Benteen: Baseball & Custer's 7th Calvary," infinitecardset.blogspot.com, http://infinitecardset.blogspot.com/2011_06_01_archive.html, accessed November 7, 2015.
69. John Thorn, "Woodrow Wilson: The First Fantasy Baseball Player," OurGame.MLBlogs.com, http://ourgame.mlblogs.com/2014/02/24/woodrow-wilson-the-first-fantasy-baseball-player/, accessed November 7, 2015.
70. Ibid.
71. Thorn, *Eden*, 153.
72. "History of Firsts," Spalding.com, http://shop.spalding.com/info/Heritage, accessed November 7, 2015.
73. Thorn, *Eden*, 152-154.

Section III - Rounding the Bases

74. "Teddy Roosevelt and Conservation," nps.gov, http://www.nps.gov/thro/learn/historyculture/theodore-roosevelt-and-conservation.htm, accessed November 7, 2015.
75. "The Soldier," theodoreroosevelt.org, http://www.theodoreroosevelt.org/site/c.elKSIdOWIiJ8H/b.8344381/k.93E5/The_SOLDIER.htm, accessed November 7, 2015.
76. Louis A. Perez, Jr., *On Becoming Cuban* (Chapel Hill, N.C.: University of North Carolina

Press, 1999) 75-77.
77. Thorn, *Eden*, 188-190.
78. "USS Maine," Navy.mil, http://www.navy.mil/navydata/nav_legacy.asp?id=74, accessed November 7, 2015.
79. "The Spanish-American War – 1898," History.State.Gov, https://history.state.gov/milestones/1866-1898/spanish-american-war, accessed November 7, 2015.
80. Perez, *Becoming*, 78.
81. Elias, *Empire*, 40.
82. Joseph A. Reaves, *Taking In a Game* (Lincoln, Nebraska: Bison Books, 2004) 38.
83. Sayuri Guthrie-Shimizu, *Transpacific Field of Dreams* (Chapel Hill: University of North Carolina Press, 2012) 45.
84. Ibid., 45.
85. Gerald R. Gems, The Athletic Crusade: Sport and American Cultural Imperialsim (Lincoln, Nebraska: The University of Nebraska Press, 2006) 22.
86. "The Catcher Who Stopped a Revolution," Our Game blog, http://ourgame.mlblogs.com/2014/03/24/the-catcher-who-stopped-a-revolution/, accessed November 7, 2015.
87. Elias, *Empire*, 44.
88. Reaves, *Taking*, 89.
89. Ibid.
90. Elias, *Empire*, 44.
91. Charles Einstein, *The Second Fireside Book of Baseball* (New York: Simon & Schuster, 1958) 188.
92. *Public Laws Passed by Philippine Commission Vol. II* (Manila, Philippines: Bureau of Public Printing, 1904) 182.
93. Reaves, *Taking*, 42.
94. Ibid., 37.
95. Ibid., 75.
96. Ibid., 38.
97. Zhouxiang Lu and Fan Hong, *Sport and Nationalism in China* (New York: Routledge, 2014) 21.
98. Reaves, *Taking*, 38.
99. Lu and Hong, *Sport*, 21.
100. Ibid., 59.
101. Uli Schmetzer, "Chinese Baseball Hanging in There," Chicago Tribune, May 3, 1991, http://articles.chicagotribune.com/1991-05-03/sports/9102090387_1_baseball-gear-chinese-baseball-bats, accessed November 7, 2015.
102. Ibid.
103. Lee Khoon Choy, *Pioneers of Modern China* (Singapore: World Scientific Publishing Co., 2005) 152.
104. Neil Steinberg, "Ugly Presidential Campaigns Hit Their 100-Year Mark," Wilmette Life, December 6, 2012, http://wilmette.suntimes.com/news/elections/16155258-505/ugly-presidential-campaigns-reach-their-100-year-mark.html, accessed November 7, 2015.
105. Richard D. White Jr., *Roosevelt the Reformer* (Tuscaloosa, Ala.: University of Alabama Press, 2003) 91.
106. "President William Taft Baseball Game Attendance Log," Baseball Almanac, http://www.baseball-almanac.com/prz_cwt.shtml, accessed November 7, 2015.
107. Herbert S. Duffy, *William Howard Taft: A Biography* (New York: Minton, Balch & Co., 1930), 219.
108. Ibid., 275-276.
109. "Supreme Court rules in favor of Major League Baseball," History.com, http://www.history.com/this-day-in-history/supreme-court-rules-in-favor-of-major-league-baseball, accessed November 6, 2015.
110. "Portofino Diaz," PBS.org, http://www.pbs.org/itvs/storm-that-swept-mexico/the-revolution/faces-revolution/porfirio-diaz/, accessed November 7, 2015.

111. William Beezley, *Judas at the Jockey Club and Other Episodes of Porfirian Mexico, Second Edition* (Lincoln, Nebraska: University of Nebraska Press, 2004) 22-24.
112. Ilan Stavans, *Beisbol* (Santa Barbara, California:ABC-CLIO, LLC, 2012) 48.
113. James E. Elfers, *The Tour to End All Tours* (Lincoln, Nebraska: University of Nebraska Press, 2003) 70.
114. Elias, *Empire*, 67-68.
115. Eugene Converse Murdock, *Ban Johnson: Czar of Baseball* (Westport, Connecticut: Greenwood Press, 1982) 270-271.
116. "The United States Armed Forces and the Mexican Punitive Expedition: Part 1," Archives.gov, http://www.archives.gov/publications/prologue/1997/fall/mexican-punitive-expedition-1.html, accessed November 7, 2015.
117. "Pursuing Pancho Villa," NPS.gov, http://www.nps.gov/prsf/learn/historyculture/pursuing-pancho-villa.htm, accessed November 7, 2015.
118. Elias, *Empire*, 68.
119. Clarence Henley Cramer, *Newton D. Baker: A Biography* (New York: Garland Publishing, 1979) 99.
120. Zoss and Bowman, *Diamonds*, 88-92.
121. S.W. Pope, *Patriotic Games* (New York: Oxford University Press, 1997) 145 – 149.
122. Walter Camp, "Keeping the Nation Fit," The Independent, Dec 21, 1918, https://books.google.com/books?id=w3AeAQAAMAAJ&pg=PA381&lpg=PA381&dq=Keeping+the+Nation+Fit+1918+The+Independent+96&source=bl&ots=UFYx9HAgS2&sig=jKpEN0v-NLk5jk4JHI-Rs5k73Rs&hl=en&sa=X&ei=brgmVbitMMulsAXZoYHYDw&ved=0CCsQ6AEwAw#v=onepage&q=walter%20camp&f=false, accessed November 7, 2015.
123. Pope, *Patriotic*, 145 – 149.
124. "WWI Casualty and Death Tables," PBS.org, http://www.pbs.org/greatwar/resources/casdeath_pop.html, accessed November 7, 2015.
125. Zoss and Bowman, *Diamonds*, 88-92.
126. Billy Sunday, "A Defense of the Grand Old Game," Baseball Magazine, July 1917, 361.
127. Zoss and Bowman, *Diamonds*, 88-92.
128. "Bat and Ball Fund For the Boys in France," The Illustrated Milliner, Vol. 19, https://books.google.com/books?id=sNlOAAAAYAAJ&pg=RA1-PA155&lpg=RA1-PA155&dq=clark+griffith+ball+and+bat+fund&source=bl&ots=X1Hb_sUUFp&sig=tjp6B4ctDmKZd78fQR8SlFOpbf4&hl=en&sa=X&ei=PxUnVcHcLImFsAXGpIH4DQ&ved=0CD8Q6AEwCQ#v=onepage&q=clark%20griffith%20ball%20and%20bat%20fund&f=false, accessed November 7, 2015.
129. *The Chicago Daily News Almanac and Year-Book for 1918*, https://books.google.com/books?id=ZHIaAQAAIAAJ&pg=PA347&lpg=PA347&dq=1917+drill+competition+won+by+St+Louis+browns&source=bl&ots=aGvS3FAt8O&sig=73zPttareugYt4STmlG9CeIO6YY&hl=en&sa=X&ei=AJEmVdeQC4musAXq2IDwAQ&ved=0CDkQ6AEwBQ#v=onepage&q=1917%20drill%20competition%20won%20by%20St%20Louis%20browns&f=false, accessed November 7, 2015.
130. Pope, *Patriotic*, 146.
131. Zoss and Bowman, *Diamonds*, 88-92.
132. Ibid.
133. Steven R. Bullock, *Playing for their Nation* (Lincoln, Nebraska: University of Nebraska Press, 2004) 9.
134. Elias, *Empire*, 91.
135. "Work or Fight Order," in *The Chicago Daily News Almanac and Year-Book, 1919*, ed. James Langland, (Chicago: The Chicago Daily News, 1919) 680-681.
136. Zoss and Bowman, *Diamonds*, 88-92.
137. Elias, *Empire*, 92.
138. Albert R. Mann, *The Inter-Allied Games, 1919* (Paris, France: The Games Committee, 1919), http://archive.org/stream/cu31924014114353/cu31924014114353_djvu.txt., accessed November 7, 2015,

139. Lee Allen, *The Cincinnati Reds* (Kent, Ohio: Kent State University Press, 2006) 223.
140. Elias, *Empire*, 103.
141. Zoss and Bowman, *Diamonds*, 120.
142. David Fitzpatrick, *Harry Boland's Irish Revolution* (Cork, Ireland: University Press, 2003) 203.
143. Lyle Spatz and Steve Steinberg, *1921: The Yankees, the Giants, and the Battle for Baseball Supremacy in New York* (Lincoln, Nebraska: University of Lincoln Press, 2010) 121.
144. Elias, *Empire*, 104.
145. Tim Wyngaard, "Teapot Dome Rated Worst U.S. Scandal," Scripps-Howard News Service, November 12, 1973, https://news.google.com/newspapers?nid=1144&dat=19731112&id=u_IjAAAAIBAJ&sjid=hFQEAAAAIBAJ&pg=7289,5420839&hl=en, accessed November 7, 2015.
146. Ibid.
147. Ron Chernow, *Titan: The Life of John D. Rockefeller, Sr., 2nd Edition* (New York and London: Vintage Books, 2004) 388.
148. "Two Theories As To Fire's Origin," *Chicago Daily Tribune*, August 6, 1894.
149. Laton McCartney, *The Teapot Dome Scandal: How Big Oil Bought the Harding White House and Tried to Steal the Country* (New York: Random House, 2008) 239.
150. Ibid., 159.
151. Ibid., 311.
152. Ibid., 300-301.
153. "The Immigration Act of 1924," History.State.gov, https://history.state.gov/milestones/1921-1936/immigration-act, accessed November 7, 2015.
154. Reaves, *Taking*, 55.
155. Ibid., 66.
156. Ibid., 68.
157. Ibid., 31, 152.
158. Nicholas Dawidoff, *The Catcher Was a Spy* (New York: Vintage Books, 1995) 80.
159. Dawidoff, *Catcher*, 95-96.
160. Elias, *Empire*, 152.
161. Dawidoff, *Catcher*, 148-149.
162. Ibid., 203-204.
163. ""Moe" Berg: Sportsman, Scholar, Spy," CIA.gov, https://www.cia.gov/news-information/featured-story-archive/2013-featured-story-archive/moe-berg.html, accessed November 7, 2015.
164. Dawidoff, *Catcher*, 91.
165. Robert K. Fitts, *Banzai Babe Ruth* (Lincoln, Nebraska: University of Nebraska Press, 2012) 120.
166. Reaves, *Taking*, 69.
167. Elias, *Empire*, 159.
168. Reaves, *Taking*, 70.
169. Alan M. Klein, *Growing the Game* (New Haven, Connecticut: Yale University Press, 2006) 170.
170. Charles Kupfer, "Il Duce and the Father of Physical Culture," Iron City History, Volume 6, Number 2, January 2000, http://library.la84.org/SportsLibrary/IGH/IGH0602/IGH0602d.pdf, accessed November 7, 2015.
171. "The Fascist Saturday," archivio.siciliainformazioni.com, http://archivio.siciliainformazioni.com/now-italy/the-fascist-saturday/, accessed November 7, 2015.
172. David Clay Large, *Nazi Games: The Olympics of 1936* (New York: W.W. Norton & Company, Inc., 2007) 162-164.
173. Josh Chetwynd, *Baseball in Europe* (Jefferson, N.C.: McFarland & Company, Inc., 2008) 113-114.
174. Elias, *Empire*, 109.
175. Larry Tye, *Satchel: The Life and Times of an American Legend* (New York: Random House

Trade Paperback, 2010) 109.
176. Ibid.
177. Ibid., 120.
178. Ibid.
179. "I shot the cruelest dictator in the Americas," BBC.com, http://www.bbc.com/news/world-latin-america-13560512, accessed November 7, 2015.
180. John Virtue, *South of the Color Barrier* (Jefferson, N.C.: McFarland & Company, Inc., 2008) 112.
181. Armando Navarro, *Mexicano Political Experience in Occupied Aztlan* (Walnut Creek, California: Alta Mira Press, 2005) 236.
182. Andrew Zimbalist, *May the Best Team Win* (Washington, D.C.: Brookings Institute Press, 2003) 18.
183. Elias, *Empire*, 166-167.
184. Donald Honig, *Baseball When the Grass Was Real* (Lincoln, Nebraska: Bison Books, 1993) 219.
185. Steven R. Bullock, *Playing For Their Nation* (Lincoln, Nebraska: University of Nebraska Press, 2004) 2-3.
186. Bullock, *Playing*, 13-14.
187. John Klima, *The Game Must Go On* (New York: Thomas Dunne Books, 2015) 153-154.
188. Elias, *Empire*, 154.
189. Lawrence Baldassaro, *Beyond DiMaggio: Italian Americans in Baseball* (Lincoln, Nebraska: University of Nebraska Press, 2011) 110.
190. Lloyd R. Shoemaker, *The Escape Factory* (New York: St. Martin's Press, 1990) 57, 94, 104-113.
191. "Tools of the Trade," NationalMuseum.AF.mil, http://www.nationalmuseum.af.mil/Visit/MuseumExhibits/FactSheets/Display/tabid/509/Article/197473/tools-of-the-trade.aspx, accessed November 6, 2015.
192. "638 Ways to Kill Castro," documentary film, Silver River Productions, 2006, https://www.youtube.com/watch?v=VFQz8racYNk, accessed November 7, 2015.
193. "Exploding Baseball Bat in Chile Kills 1, Hurts American," UPI, http://articles.latimes.com/1990-11-18/news/mn-6936_1_baseball-bat, accessed July 23, 2015; Jo Beck and Scott Shane, "Secret 'Kill List' Proves a Test of Obama's Principles and Will," The New York Times, May 29, 2012, http://www.nytimes.com/2012/05/29/world/obamas-leadership-in-war-on-al-qaeda.html, accessed November 7, 2015.
194. Michael Beschloss, "For Incarcerated Japanese-Americans, Baseball Was 'Wearing the American Flag,'" The New York Times, June 20, 2014, http://www.nytimes.com/2014/06/21/upshot/for-incarcerated-japanese-americans-baseball-was-wearing-the-american-flag.html, accessed November 7, 2015.
195. Ibid.
196. Ibid.
197. Tracey Seipel, "Japanese-Americans recall baseball glory during internment camp years," Mercury News, October 27, 2014, http://www.mercurynews.com/bay-area-news/ci_26804023/japanese-americans-recall-their-baseball-glory-during-internment, accessed November 7, 2015.
198. Roger A. Bruns, *Negro Leagues Baseball* (Santa Barbara, California: ABC-CLIO, LLC, 2012) ix.
199. "Sports – Baseball, 1982 – Present," http://www.boxofficemojo.com/genres/chart/?id=baseball.htm, accessed November 6, 2015.

Section IV - Bringing it Home

200. Reaves, *Taking*, 94.
201. Roger Highfield, "Scientist calculate the exact date of Trojan Horse using eclipse in Homer,"

The Telegraph, June 24, 2008, http://www.telegraph.co.uk/news/science/science-news/3345362/Scientists-calculate-the-exact-date-of-the-Trojan-horse-using-eclipse-in-Homer.html, accessed October 28, 2015.
202. Guthrie-Shimizu, *Transpacific*, 206.
203. "Japan Policy Research Institute: Japan's M-Fund Memorandum," Januray 7, 1991, http://www.jpri.org/publications/workingpapers/wp11.html, accessed November 7, 2015.
204. Guthrie-Shimizu, *Transpacific*, 201-203.
205. Reaves, *Taking*, 82.
206. Ibid.
207. Ibid., 84.
208. Hiroshi Masuda, *MacArthur in Asia: The General and His Staff in the Philippines, Japan and Korea* (Ithaca, N.Y.: Cornell University Press, 2012) 16.
209. Ron Briley, editor, *The Politics of Baseball* (Jefferson, N.C.: McFarland & Company, Inc., 2010) 152.
210. Elias, *Empire*, 195.
211. Robert Leckie, *Conflict: The History of the Korean War, 1950-53* (New York: Da Capo Press, 1996) 142.
212. Elias, *Empire*, 177.
213. Joshua Prager, *The Echoing Green* (New York: Vintage Books, 2006) 252.
214. "The Berlin Tunnel Operation Gold (U.S.) Operation Stopwatch (U.K.)," coldwar.org, http://www.coldwar.org/articles/50s/berlin_tunnel.asp, accessed November 7, 2015.
215. "The Berlin Tunnel," CIA.gov, https://www.cia.gov/about-cia/cia-museum/experience-the-collection/text-version/stories/the-berlin-tunnel.html, accessed November 7, 2015.
216. "Clandestine Services History, The Berlin Tunnel Operation 1952-1956," foia.cia.gov, http://www.foia.cia.gov/document/5166d4f999326091c6a6081c, accessed November 7, 2015.
217. "The Berlin Tunnel," CIA.gov, https://www.cia.gov/about-cia/cia-museum/experience-the-collection/text-version/stories/the-berlin-tunnel.html, accessed November 7, 2015.
218. Ibid.
219. Elias, *Empire*, 190.
220. Carl Prince, *Brooklyn Dodgers* (New York: Oxford University Press, 1996) 24.
221. Jack O'Connell, "When Football Giants Picked Up the Beat," The Hartford Courant, January 28, 2001, http://articles.courant.com/2001-01-28/sports/0101294142_1_andy-robustelli-minor-league-deal-yankee-stadium, accessed November 7, 2015.
222. "Vice President Nixon is Attacked," history.com, http://www.history.com/this-day-in-history/vice-president-nixon-is-attacked, accessed November 7, 2015.
223. William B. Mead and Paul Dickson, *Baseball: The President's Game* (New York: Walker and Company, 1997) 99-101.
224. "Frick Plans Tour With Ball Players," Associated Press, October, 31, 1958, http://fultonhistory.com/Newspapers%2023/Rome%20NY%20Daily%20Sentinel/Rome%20NY%20Daily%20Sentinel%201958/Rome%20NY%20Daily%20Sentinel%201958%20-%204788.pdf, accessed November 7, 2015.
225. William B. Mead and Paul Dickson, *Baseball: The President's Game* (New York: Walker and Company, 1997) 133.
226. "Records of the Office of Inter-American Affairs (RG 229)," archives.gov, http://www.archives.gov/research/holocaust/finding-aid/civilian/rg-229.html, accessed November 7, 2015.
227. "About the Bureau of Educational and Cultural Affairs," eca.state.gov, http://eca.state.gov/about-bureau, accessed November 7, 2015.
228. "U.S. Department of State and Major League Baseball Announced Baseball and Softball 'Diamond Diplomacy,'" state.gov, http://www.state.gov/r/pa/prs/ps/2015/01/235835.htm, accessed November 7, 2015.
229. Brian Costa, "Why MLB Teams are Fleeing Venezuela," Wall Street Journal, May 4, 2015, http://www.wsj.com/articles/why-mlb-teams-are-fleeing-venezuela-1430751423, accessed

November 7, 2015.
230. Ed Vulliamy, "Venezuela coup linked to Bush team," The Guardian, April 21, 2002, http://www.theguardian.com/world/2002/apr/21/usa.venezuela, accessed November 7, 2015.
231. Elias, *Empire*, 265.
232. Danna Harman, "U.S. baseball strikes out with Chavez," USA Today, June 7, 2006, http://usatoday30.usatoday.com/news/world/2006-06-07-venezuela_x.htm, accessed November 7, 2015.
233. "Gangs in the Urban Crisis Era," uic.edu, https://www.uic.edu/orgs/kbc/ganghistory/Chi70pov.html, accessed November 7, 2015.
234. Harold Seymour, *Baseball: The People's Game* (New York: Oxford University Press, 1990,) 125.
235. John Hagerdorn, "The Gangs of ..." *Chicago Tribune*, http://articles.chicagotribune.com/2003-01-19/news/0301190019_1_gangs-race-riots-draft-riots January 19, 2003, accessed November 7, 2015.
236. John Kass, "Gangs that came to rule in seats of power," *Chicago Tribune*, June 22, 2012, http://articles.chicagotribune.com/2012-06-22/news/ct-met-kass-0622-20120622_1_gangs-conservative-vice-lords-museum-exhibit, accessed November 7, 2015.
237. Ibid.
238. John Hagerdorn, "The Gangs of ..." *Chicago Tribune*, http://articles.chicagotribune.com/2003-01-19/news/0301190019_1_gangs-race-riots-draft-riots January 19, 2003. Accessed October 26, 2015.
239. Kass, *Chicago Tribune.*
240. Stuart Shea, *Wrigley Field: The Unauthorized Biography* (Herndon, VA: Potomac Books, 2004) 269-270.
241. John Snyder, *Cubs Journal* (Cincinnati: Ennis Books, 2005) 465.
242. Christy W. Sauro, *The Twins Platoon* (St. Paul, MN: MBI Publishing Company, 2006) 16-25.
243. "Historic Earthquakes: Nicaragua, 1972 December 23 06:29:42 UTC Magnitude 6.2," usgs.gov, http://earthquake.usgs.gov/earthquakes/world/events/1972_12_23.php , accessed November 7, 2015.
244. David Maraniss, *Clemente* (New York: Simon & Schuster, 2006) 301.
245. Ibid., 303-304.
246. Ibid., 309-316.
247. Ibid., 324.
248. Ibid., 346.
249. Dick Schaap, *Steinbrenner!* (New York: G.P. Putnam's Sons, 1982) 122.
250. Ibid., 125-126.
251. Tip O'Neill and William Novak, "Nixon Played Harball O'Neill Believes Greed Kept Embattled President From Destroying Watergate Tapes," *Sun Sentinel*, September 14, 1987, http://articles.sun-sentinel.com/1987-09-14/news/8703130702_1_political-hardball-finance-chairman-richard-nixon-s, accessed November 7, 2015.
252. "Watergate Special Prosecutor Wanted Steinbrenner Investigated," *Associated Press*, December 23, 2010, http://www.nytimes.com/2010/12/24/sports/baseball/24steinbrenner.html?_r=2, accessed November 7, 2015.
253. Sam Smith, "Cocaine Bought During Game," *Chicago Tribune*, September 13, 1985, http://articles.chicagotribune.com/1985-09-13/sports/8503020248_1_adam-renfroe-cocaine-dock-ellis, accessed November 7, 2015.
254. Reaves, *Taking*, 128.
255. George Gmelch, *Baseball Without Borders* (Lincoln, Nebraska: University of Nebraska Press, 2006) 100.
256. Ibid., 100-101.
257. Ibid., 99.
258. Sheryl WuDunn, "The People of Kwangju Recall 1980 Massacre," *Washington Post*, August

29, 1996, http://www.nytimes.com/1996/08/29/world/the-people-of-kwangju-recall-1980-massacre.html, accessed November 7, 2015.
259. Chico Harlan, "South Korea goes after the fortune of Chun-Doo-hwan, its last military strongman," *Washington Post*, August 14, 2013, https://www.washingtonpost.com/world/south-korea-goes-after-the-fortune-of-chun-doo-hwan-its-last-military-strongman/2013/08/13/a3e2b35e-00be-11e3-9711-3708310f6f4d_story.html, accessed November 7, 2015.
260. Rachael Miyung Joo, *Transnational Sport: Gender, Media, and Global Korea* (Durham, NC: Duke University Press, 2012) 46.
261. David Wood and P. Louis Johnson, *Sporting Cultures: Hispanic Perspectives on Sport, Text and the Body* (New York: Routledge Publishing, 2008) 116.
262. Perez, *Becoming*, 259.
263. Ibid., 81.
264. Peter C. Bjarkman, *Diamonds Around the Globe* (Westport, CT: Greenwood Press, 2005) 5.
265. Peter C. Bjarkman, "Fidel Castro and Baseball," SABR.org, http://sabr.org/bioproj/topic/fidel-castro-and-baseball, accessed November 7, 2015.
266. Ibid.
267. Ibid.
268. "Pentagon Proposed Pretexts for Cuba Invasion in 1962," The National Security Archives, George Washington University, http://nsarchive.gwu.edu/news/20010430/, accessed November 7, 2015.
269. "Review of Operation Mongoose," The National Security Archives, George Washington University, http://nsarchive.gwu.edu/nsa/cuba_mis_cri/620725%20Review%20of%20Op.%20Mongoose.pdf, accessed November 7, 2015.
270. Peter C. Bjarkman, "Fidel Castro and Baseball," SABR.org, http://sabr.org/bioproj/topic/fidel-castro-and-baseball, accessed November 7, 2015.
271. "Learn More About Trade in Cuba," Observatory of Economic Complexity, https://atlas.media.mit.edu/en/profile/country/cub/, accessed July 25, 2015.
272. "Certain Cuban Nationals Unblocked," Electronic Code of Federal Regulations, http://www.ecfr.gov/cgi-bin/text-idx?SID=ed80887e80045395efd59f26720d986b&mc=true&node=pt31.3.515&rgn=div5#se31.3.515_1505, accessed July 25, 2015.
273. U.S.-Cuba Thaw Is Not So Hot For MLB," Peter C. Bjarkman, The Daily Beast, http://www.thedailybeast.com/articles/2015/02/19/u-s-cuba-thaw-is-not-so-hot-for-mlb.html, accessed November 7, 2015.
274. Ibid.

•• ▬▬ •▬ ▬▬• •

Image credits

▬•▬• •▬• • ▬•• •• ▬ •••

Images listed by page number.

16. Bunker Hill: Library of Congress. Painted by John Trumbull.
27. Albert Spalding: Library of Congress.
31. Elysian Fields: Library of Congress.
38. Abraham Lincoln portrait: Library of Congress.
40. Abraham Lincoln cartoon: Library of Congress.
42. Abner Doubleday: Library of Congress. No photographer credit provided.
59. Union Soldier in Salisbury, N.C.: Library of Congress.
64. Octavius V. Catto: Wikimedia Commons. This media file is in the public domain in the United States. This applies to U.S. works where the copyright has expired, often because its first publication occurred prior to January 1, 1923. No photo credit provided.
69. Buffalo Soldiers, Jim Crow cartoon: Library of Congress. No artist credit provided.
73. Frederick Benteen and George Custer: Library of Congress. No photo credit provided. White Man Runs Him: Library of Congress. Photo by Edward S. Curtis.
76. Woodrow Wilson: Library of Congress. No photo credit provided.
83. Lou Bierbauer: Library of Congress.
78. William Hulbert gravestone: Private collection.
88. Mount Rushmore: Library of Congress.
95. Robert Wilcox: Wikimedia Commons. This work is in the public domain in its country of origin and other countries and areas where the copyright term is the author's life plus 100 years or less. No photo credit provided.
98. Frederick Funston: Library of Congress.
99. Ifugao headhunter: Wikimedia Commons. This media file is in the public domain in the United States. This applies to U.S. works where the copyright has expired, often because its first publication occurred prior to January 1, 1923. Photo credit: Dean C. Worcester (1912).
103. Waseda University team: Library of Congress.
105. Sun Yat-sen: National Archives and Records Administration. No photo credit given.
101. He Long: Wikimedia Commons. This image is now in the public domain in China because its term of copyright has expired. According to copyright laws of the People's Republic of China (with legal jurisdiction in the mainland only, excluding Hong Kong and Macao) and the Republic of China (currently with jurisdiction in Taiwan, the Penghu, Kinmen, Matsu, etc.), all photographs and cinematographic works, and all works whose copyright holder is a juristic person, enter the public domain 50 years after they were first published, or if published 50 years from creation, and all other applicable works enter the public domain 50 years after the death of the creator. Photo credit: Sha Fei.
108. Theodore Roosevelt political cartoon "Lonesome": National Archives and Records Administration.

National Archives Identifier No. 6011130. Unrestricted access. Unrestricted use. Date of image: August 2, 1915.

110. Theodore Roosevelt: Library of Congress. No photo credit provided.

111. Charles and William Taft: Wikimedia Commons. This media file is in the pubic domain in the United States. This applies to U.S. works where the copyright has expired, often because its first publication occurred prior to January 1, 1923. Original photo credit: L.B. Benjamin (1907).

118. Pancho Villa: Library of Congress.

119. Newton Baker, Raymond Fosdick and John Pershing: all from Library of Congress.

116. Grover Cleveland Alexander: Wikimedia Commons. This media file is in the pubic domain in the United States. This applies to U.S. works where the copyright has expired, often because its first publication occurred prior to January 1, 1923. Original photo credit: Charles M. Conlon (1915). Eddie Grant: Library of Congress. Christy Mathewson: Wikimedia Commons. This media file is in the pubic domain in the United States. This applies to U.S. works where the copyright has expired, often because its first publication occurred prior to January 1, 1923. Original photo credit: Charles M. Conlon (1912).

117. Walter Camp: Library of Congress.

121. Arlie Latham: Library of Congress.

124. General Pershing and Babe Ruth: Library of Congress.

132. King George presenting game ball: National Archives and Records Administration. National Archives Identifier No. 20809564. Unrestricted access. Unrestricted use. Date of photo: July 4, 1918. Photo credit: War Department. Crowd reaction: National Archives and Records Administration. National Archives Identifier No. 20809576. Unrestricted access. Unrestricted use. Photo credit: War Department. Date of photo: July 4, 1918.

141. Harry Sinclair: Library of Congress.

143. Cox-Harding cartoon "Ambitious Home Run Hitters": National Archives and Records Administration. National Archives Identifier No. 1691372. Unrestricted access. Unrestricted use. Date of image: August 3, 1920.

151. Baseball Program photos from 1934: Private collection.

153. Morris Berg International Military Tribunal: Private collection.

156. Eiji Sawamura: Wikimedia Commons. This photographic image was published before December 31, 1956, or photographed before 1946, under the jurisdiction of the Government of Japan. Thus this photographic image is considered to be public domain according to article 23 of old copyright law of Japan and article 2 of supplemental provision of copyright law of Japan. No photo credit given.

158. Benito Mussolini and Adolf Hitler: National Archives and Records Administration. National Archives Identifier No. 540153. Unrestricted access. Unrestricted use. Date of image: circa 1940.

160. Bernarr Macfadden: Library of Congress.

162. Eva Braun and Adolf Hitler: Wikimedia Commons. This image was provided to Wikimedia Commons by the German Federal Archive (Deutsches Bundesarchiv) as part of a cooperation project. This file is licensed under the Creative Commons Attribution-Share Alike 3.0 Germany license. Attribution: Bundesarchiv, B 145 Bild-F051673-0059 / CC-BY-SA. Date of photo: June 14, 1942.

164. Eleanor Roosevelt with Rafael Trujillo: National Archives and Records Administration. National Archives Identifier No. 195944. Unrestricted access. Unrestricted use. Date of image: March 7, 1934.

168. Braceros being processed: National Archives and Records Administration. National Archives Identifier No. 7452192. Unrestricted access. Unrestricted use. No date of photo given.

172. President Roosevelt, Ford Frick and Clark Griffith: Library of Congress. Robert Hannegan: National Archives and Records Administration. Office of Presidential Libraries. Harry S. Truman Library. National Archives Identifier No. 199143. Unrestricted access. Unrestricted use. Date of photo: August 10, 1945.

173. Cubs program: Private collection.

175. X-ray of cribbage board: U.S. Air Force. National Museum of the U.S. Air Force.

177. I am an American: Library of Congress.

179. Martin Luther King: Library of Congress. Rosie the Riveter: National Archives and Records Administration. No. 535413. Unrestricted access. Unrestricted use. Photo credit: Office of Emergency Management. Evacuee boy at internment camp: National Archives and Records Administration. No. 538074. Unrestricted access. Unrestricted use. Photo credit: Dorothea Lange/War Department. Date of photo: July 1, 1942.

184. Inchon landing stranded crafts: Wikimedia Commons. This file is licensed under the Creative Commons Attribution 2.0 Generic license. Photo credit: U.S. Marine Corps Archives & Special Collections, 1950.

185. Douglas MacArthur: Library of Congress. William Marquat: Wikimedia Commons. From U.S. War Department archives. This work is in the public domain in the United States because it is a work prepared by an officer or employee of the United States Government as part of that person's official duties under the terms

of Title 17, Chapter 1, Section 105 of the US Code.
188. Cardinals program: Private collection.
190. Happy Chandler: Library of Congress.
191. Semipalatinsk: Wikimedia Commons. This file is licensed under the Creative Commons Attribution 2.0 Generic license. Photo credit: The CTBTO Commission (Comprehensive Nuclear Test Ban Treaty Organization). Photo taken on September 7, 2008. Atomic Energy Commission logo: Wikimedia Commons. This file is licensed under the Creative Commons Attribution 2.0 Generic license. Photo credit: Idaho National Laboratory.
193. Berlin Tunnel: Wikimedia Commons. This file is licensed under the Creative Commons Attribution 3.0 Unported license. Photo was resized from original. Photo credit: Anagoria. Date of photo: July 29, 2012. Allen Dulles: Wikimedia Commons. This work is in the public domain in the United States because it is a work prepared by an officer or employee of the United States Government as part of that person's official duties under the terms of Title 17, Chapter 1, Section 105 of the US Code.
205. Richard Daley and Richard Nixon: National Archives and Records Administration. National Archives Identifier No. 194669. Unrestricted access. Unrestricted use. Photo date: February 6, 1970.
209. Richard Nixon and Antonio Debayle: National Archives and Records Administration. National Archives Identifier No. 194723. Unrestricted access. Unrestricted use. Photo credit: Jack Kightlinger, White House Photo Office. Date of photo: June 2, 1971.
215. Richard Nixon and Ted Williams: Library of Congress.
219. Cemetery: Wikimedia Commons. This file is licensed under the Creative Commons Attribution-Share Alike 3.0 Unported license. Photo credit: Ulrich Lange, Bochum, Germany. Photo taken: April 23, 2011. Chun Doo-hwan: Wikimedia Commons. This image is a work of a U.S. military or Department of Defense employee, taken or made as part of that person's official duties. As a work of the U.S. federal government, the image is in the public domain.
223. Bob Will with Cuban rebels: Private collection.

Back cover images:
Bob Will with Cuban rebels: Private collection.
Adolf Hitler: National Archives and Records Administration.
George Custer: Library of Congress.
Douglas MacArthur: Library of Congress.
Richard Nixon: Library of Congress.
Sun Yat-sen: National Archives and Records Administration.
Benito Mussolini: National Archives and Records Administration.
Abraham Lincoln: Library of Congress.

INDEX

•• -• -•• • -••-

CODE BREAKING

-.-. --- -.. .   -... .-. . .- -.- .. -. --.

Throughout this book, you've been introduced to Morse Code (the dots and dashes at the start of each chapter and section). One of the themes in *Weaponized Baseball* has been deciphering the real intent behind actions and messages created by influential organizations and/or people. When it comes to deciphering the world, most people think about coded messages. I've created three coded messages to test your deciphering skills. Each of these codes uses basic encryption so you won't need a computer. Just use a logical approach and you'll figure them out.

Sherpa Multimedia is running a contest using these coded messages. Even when the contest is over, these codes can be a test of your skills. Feel free to consult the publisher's website (SherpaMultimedia.com) and its Facebook page (FB/SherpaMultimedia) to learn more. Here are the basics:

1. In one email, send your three answers to: WeaponizedBaseball@gmail.com.

2. Everyone who cracks all three messages correctly will be entered into a giveaway of free merchandise. You must answer all three codes correctly in order to be eligible for the giveaway. Answering one or two codes will only get you a hearty "good job!" but nothing more. (Sherpa editors will reply to your email letting you know if you've cracked the codes correctly.)

3. Every person who cracks all three codes correctly will be emailed a digital C.I.A. award (Certificate of Intelligent Achievement) that will also be posted on Sherpa's Facebook page to help you brag about your achievement.

3. During the first inning of the 2016 MLB All-Star Game, Sherpa Multimedia will randomly pick one of the code crackers who successfully solved all three codes. The winner will receive a special shirt along with an autographed copy of *The Cubs Quotient: How the Chicago Cubs Changed the World.*

4. It's that simple. Crack the codes. Win free stuff. Brag about how clever you are with proof to show off to everyone – your digital C.I.A. award!

After the 2016 MLB All-Star Game, the answer to all three coded messages will be posted on SherpaMultimedia.com. Good luck and get cracking!

- Scott

1. HINT: It's OK to sing in the shower, we all do at some time.

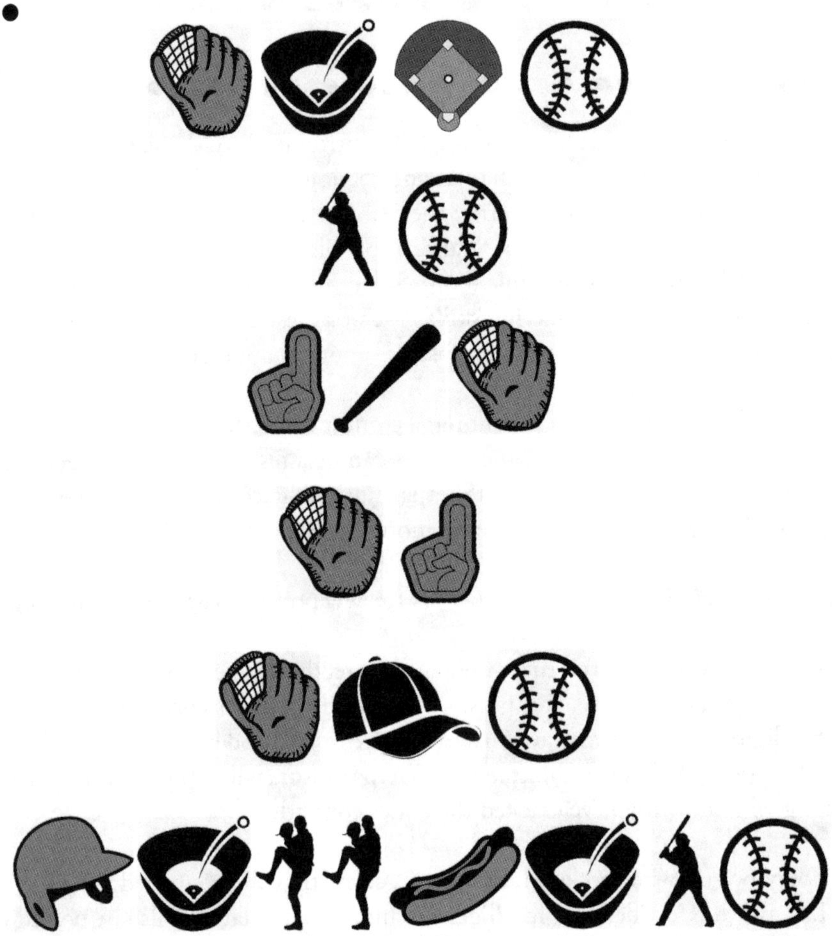

2. HINT: A fib is just the inverse of the truth.
(NOTE: I used a period between the numbers to indicate different letters in the same word.)

2.1.6765.8.2.1.233.233
55.6765
1
377.987.4181.1.233
8.2584.17711.55.28657.1.233.8.610.10946
987.13
46368.1.4181

3. HINT: This was created to be the kind of code you can work on either at day or at night, anytime around the clock.
(NOTE: The / indicates space between words.)

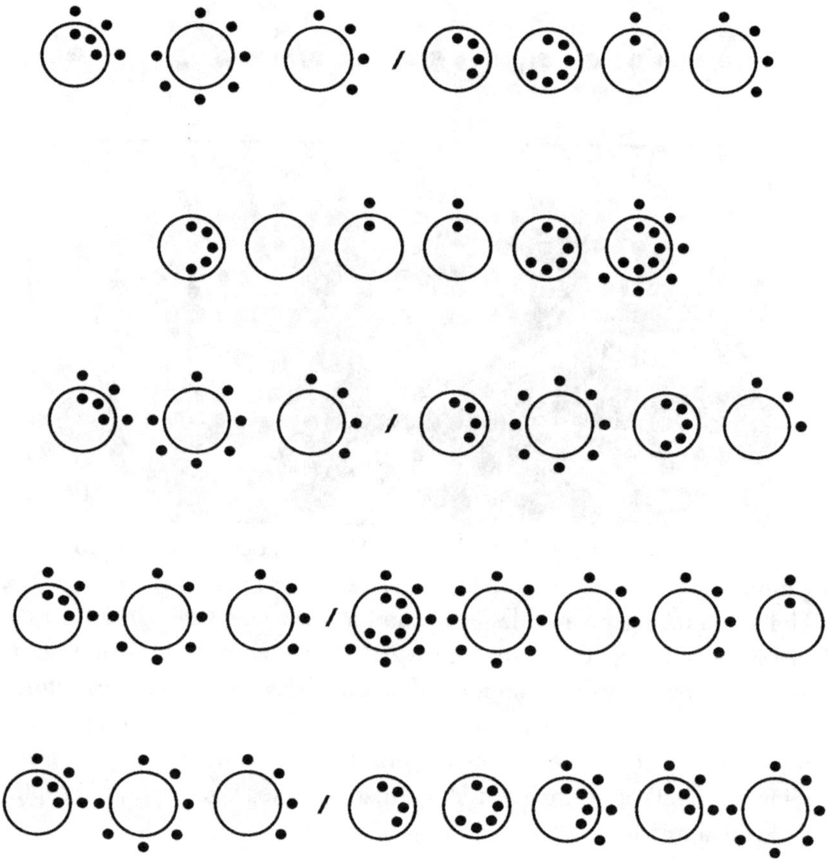

.- -... --- ..- -

ABOUT THE AUTHOR

- .... . .- ..- - .... --- .-.

A Maryland native raised in Richmond, Virginia, Scott and is a proud alumnus of Virginia Tech and lives in Chicago. He never misses a televised Hokies football game nor dessert. Scott's media career began in 1995 as a newspaper editor and reporter. Since 2002, he has been a book publishing executive and has worked on more than one thousand sports titles before turning his focus onto creating products that don't just entertain, but aim to educate at the same time. In addition to sports and history, Scott's edutainment publications focus on dogs, marine biology, geology, philosophy and global myths.